Microsoft®
Visual Basic® .NET: RELOADED Lab Manual

Diane Zak

THOMSON

COURSE TECHNOLOGY

Australia • Canada • Mexico • Singapore • Spain • United Kingdom • United States

THOMSON

™

COURSE TECHNOLOGY

**Microsoft Visual Basic .NET: RELOADED –
Lab Manual**

by Diane Zak

Executive Editor:
Mac Mendelsohn

Senior Product Manager:
Tricia Boyle

Marketing Manager:
Brian Berkeley

Associate Product Manager:
Mirella Misiasek

Editorial Assistant:
Amanda Piantedosi

Production Editor:
Melissa Panagos

Cover Designer:
Steve Deschene

Compositor:
GEX Publishing Services

Manufacturing Coordinator:
Laura Burns

Disclaimer
Course Technology reserves the right to revise this publication and make changes from time to time in its content without notice.

ISBN 0-619-21362-0

Contents

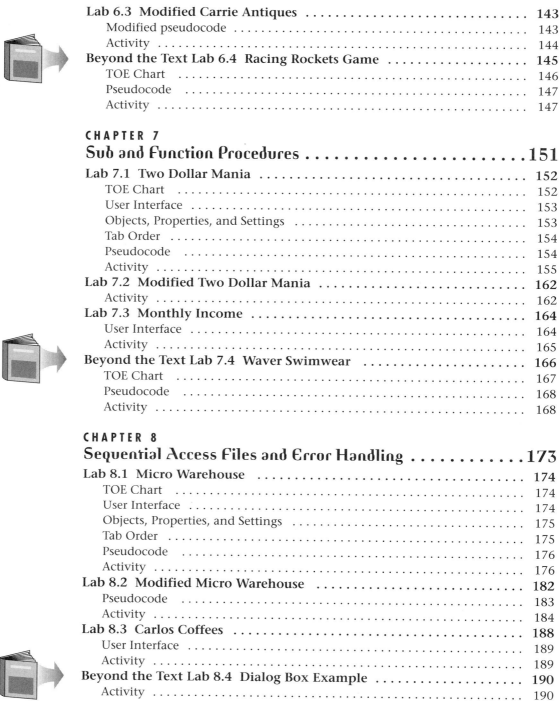

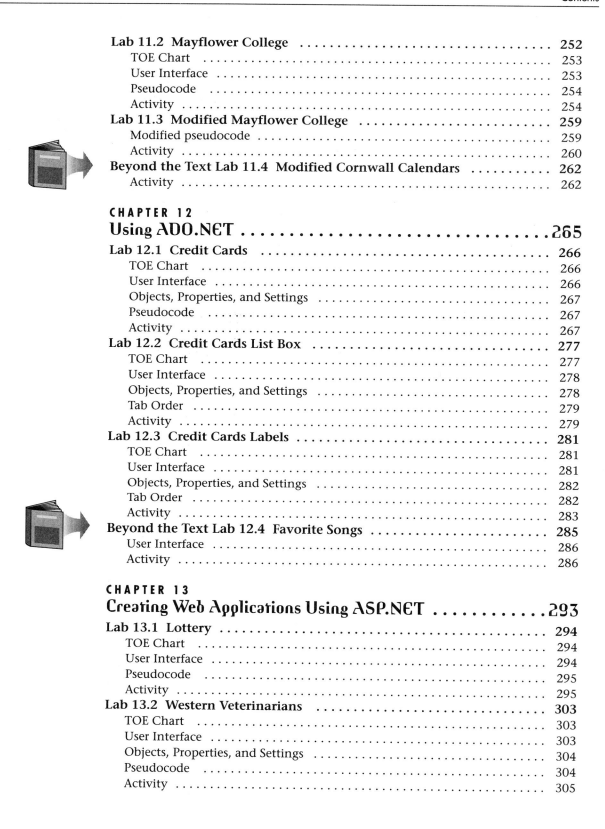

Preface

Microsoft Visual Basic .NET: RELOADED – Lab Manual is designed to be used with the textbook, *Microsoft Visual Basic .NET: RELOADED*.

ORGANIZATION AND COVERAGE

Microsoft Visual Basic .NET: RELOADED – Lab Manual contains 13 chapters that correspond to the 13 chapters found in *Microsoft Visual Basic .NET: RELOADED*. Each chapter in the Lab Manual consists of four labs. The first lab guides the student, step-by-step, through the process of creating an application that uses the concepts taught in the corresponding chapter in the book. The second and third labs also follow the tutorial-style format, but they provide less "hand-holding." The fourth lab in each chapter is called the "Beyond the Text" lab. The "Beyond the Text" labs teach a new concept and can be used to challenge readers to learn on their own.

APPROACH

There are many different approaches to teaching programming with Visual Basic .NET, and it's difficult to write one book that fits all of the approaches. Some instructors, for example, prefer a book that focuses on programming concepts only, while others want a book that combines programming concepts and tutorials, and allows the student to determine how much "tutorial-help" he or she needs to understand a particular concept. *Microsoft Visual Basic .NET: RELOADED* is designed to fit both of these approaches. The book itself focuses primarily on programming concepts. However, along with *Microsoft Visual Basic .NET: RELOADED – Lab Manual*, it can be used by instructors who want to combine both conceptual and tutorial-style teaching.

FEATURES

Microsoft Visual Basic .NET: RELOADED – Lab Manual is an exceptional Lab Manual because it also includes the following features:

- **"Read This Before You Begin"** This section is consistent with Course Technology's unequaled commitment to helping instructors introduce technology into the classroom. Technical considerations and assumptions about hardware, software, and default settings are listed in one place to help instructors save time and eliminate unnecessary aggravation.

- **Four labs** The first three labs in each chapter show readers how to use the concepts taught in the corresponding chapter in the *Microsoft Visual Basic .NET: RELOADED* book. The first lab guides the reader, step-by-step, through the process of creating an application. The second and third labs also follow the tutorial-style format, but they provide less "hand-holding." The fourth lab in each chapter teaches a new concept.

- **Beyond the Text lab** The "Beyond the Text" lab in each chapter teaches a new concept and can be assigned to students who have mastered the chapter material and now want to learn more.

- **Screenshots** Each chapter provides plenty of screenshots to help illustrate the material.

- **Scenario and Solution Discussion** Every lab begins with a Scenario followed by a Solution Discussion. The Scenario describes a programming-related problem. The Solution Discussion explains how to create an application that can be used to solve the problem.

- **Planning tools** For almost every lab, the student is shown the tools used to plan the application created in the lab. The planning tools include the following:

  - TOE chart
  - User interface
  - Objects, Properties, and Settings chart
  - Tab Order
  - Pseudocode

- **Tips** Tips are used to remind students about important concepts learned in the main text, *Microsoft Visual Basic .NET: RELOADED*.

TEACHING TOOLS

Data Files Data Files, which are necessary for completing many of the Labs, can be found on the Course Technology Web site at **www.course.com**.

Solution Files Solutions to the Labs can also be found on the Course Technology Web site at **www.course.com**. The solutions are password protected.

Figure Files Figure Files are available on the Course Technology Web site at **www.course.com** for your convenience.

ACKNOWLEDGMENTS

Writing a book is a team effort rather than an individual one. I would like to take this opportunity to thank my team, especially Tricia Boyle (Senior Product Manager), Melissa Panagos (Production Editor), Shawn Day (Quality Assurance), and the staff at Gex Publishing Services. Thank you for your support, enthusiasm, patience, and hard work. I could not have completed this project without you. Last, but certainly not least, I want to thank the following reviewers for their invaluable ideas and comments: James J. Ball, Indiana State University and Elaine Seeman, East Carolina University.

Diane Zak

Read This Before You Begin

TO THE USER

Data Files

To complete some of the labs in this book, you will need data files that have been created for this lab manual. Your instructor may provide the data files to you. You also can obtain the files electronically from the Course Technology Web site by connecting to **www.course.com**, and then searching for this lab manual title.

Each chapter in this lab manual has its own set of data files, which are stored in a separate folder within the VbDotNetLab folder; the only exception to this is Chapter 13. For example, the files for Chapter 1 are stored in the VbDotNetLab\Chap01 folder. Similarly, the files for Chapter 2 are stored in the VbDotNetLab\Chap02 folder. The files for Chapter 13 are stored in the VbDotNetLab\Chap13 and Inetpub\wwwroot\ Chap13Lab folders. Throughout this lab manual, you will be instructed to open files from or save files to these folders.

You can use a computer in your school lab or your own computer to complete the labs in this book.

Using Your Own Computer

To use your own computer to complete the material in this lab manual, you will need the following:

- A 486-level or higher personal computer running Microsoft Windows. This lab manual was written and Quality Assurance tested using Microsoft Windows XP.

- Microsoft Visual Studio .NET 2003 Professional Edition or Enterprise Edition, or Microsoft Visual Basic .NET 2003 Standard Edition, must be installed on your computer. This lab manual was written using Microsoft Visual Studio .NET 2003 Professional and Quality Assurance tested using Microsoft Visual Basic .NET 2003 Standard Edition.

Data Files

You will not be able to complete some of the labs in this book using your own computer unless you have the data files. You can get the data files from your instructor, or you can obtain the data files electronically from the Course Technology Web site by connecting to **www.course.com**, and then searching for this lab manual title.

Figures

The figures in this lab manual reflect how your screen will look if you are using a Microsoft Windows XP system. Your screen may appear slightly different in some instances if you are using another version of Microsoft Windows.

Visit Our World Wide Web Site

Additional materials designed especially for you might be available for your course on the World Wide Web. Go to **www.course.com**. Periodically search this site for more details.

To the Instructor

To complete some of the labs in this book, your users must use a set of data files. These files may be obtained electronically through the Course Technology Web site at **www.course.com**. Follow the instructions in the Help file to copy the data files to your server or standalone computer. You can view the Help file using a text editor such as WordPad or Notepad. Once the files are copied, you should instruct your users how to copy the files to their own computers or workstations. Or, you can direct them to visit the Web site and download these files on their own.

The labs in this book were Quality Assurance tested using Microsoft Visual Basic .NET 2003 Standard Edition on a Microsoft Windows XP operating system.

Course Technology Data Files

You are granted a license to copy the data files to any computer or computer network used by individuals who have purchased this lab manual.

An Introduction to Visual Basic .NET

Labs included in this chapter:

LAB 1.1 INTERLOCKING SOFTWARE – GETTING ACQUAINTED

Scenario Interlocking Software, a small firm specializing in custom programs, hires you as a programmer trainee. In that capacity, you learn to write applications using Microsoft Visual Basic .NET. On your first day of work, Chris Statton, the senior programmer at Interlocking Software, asks you to complete the following activity, which is designed to get you acquainted with the Visual Studio .NET IDE (Integrated Development Environment).

Activity

Before you can use Visual Basic .NET to create an application, you first must start Visual Studio .NET.

To start Visual Studio .NET:

1. Click the **Start** button on the Windows taskbar to open the Start menu.
2. Point to **All Programs**, then point to **Microsoft Visual Studio .NET 2003**, and then click **Microsoft Visual Studio .NET 2003**. The Microsoft Visual Studio .NET copyright screen appears momentarily, and then the Microsoft Development Environment window opens.
3. If the Start Page window is not open, click **Help** on the menu bar, and then click **Show Start Page**.
4. Click the **My Profile** tab on the Start Page window. The My Profile pane appears in the Start Page window, as shown in Figure 1.1. (Your screen might not look identical to Figure 1.1.)

My Profile pane

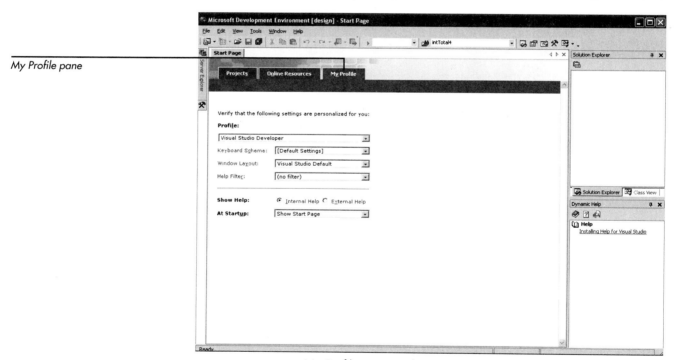

FIGURE 1.1   My Profile pane in the Start Page window

The My Profile pane allows you to customize various program settings in the IDE, such as the keyboard scheme, window layout, and help filter. A collection of customized preferences is called a profile. Visual Studio .NET provides a set of predefined profiles for your convenience.

5. If necessary, click the **Profile** list arrow, and then click **Visual Studio Developer** in the list.

6. If necessary, change the Keyboard Scheme, Window Layout, Help Filter, and At Startup list box selections on your screen to match those shown in Figure 1.1.

7. If necessary, click the **Internal Help** radio button to select it. If the "Changes will not take effect until Visual Studio is restarted" message appears in a dialog box, click the **OK** button to close the dialog box.

8. Click the **Projects** tab on the Start Page window. The Projects pane appears in the Start Page window, as shown in Figure 1.2. (Do not be concerned if your Projects pane shows project names and dates.)

Solution Explorer window

Start Page window

Server Explorer window

Toolbox window

Class View window

Dynamic Help window

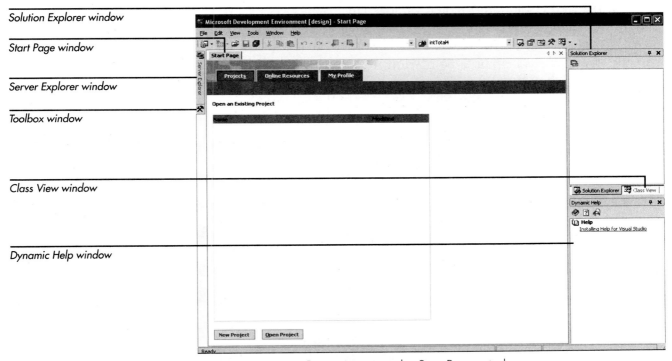

FIGURE 1.2   Projects pane in the Start Page window

HELP? If the Server Explorer window is not open, click View on the menu bar, and then click Server Explorer.

HELP? If the Toolbox window is not open, click View on the menu bar, and then click Toolbox.

HELP? If the Solution Explorer window is not open, click View on the menu bar, and then click Solution Explorer.

HELP? If the Class View window is not open, click View on the menu bar, and then click Class View.

HELP? If the Dynamic Help window is not open, click Help on the menu bar, and then click Dynamic Help.

As Figure 1.2 indicates, the IDE contains six windows: Server Explorer, Toolbox, Start Page, Solution Explorer, Class View, and Dynamic Help. In the next set of steps, you learn how to close, auto-hide, and display the windows in the IDE.

To close, auto-hide, and display the windows in the IDE:

1. Place your mouse pointer on the **Server Explorer** tab. When the Server Explorer window slides into view, which may take several moments, click the **Close** button on its title bar.

Now close the Start Page, Class View, and Dynamic Help windows.

2. Click the **Close** button on the Start Page window's title bar.

3. Click the **Class View** tab to make the Class View window the active window, and then click the **Close** button on its title bar.

4. Click the **Close** button on the Dynamic Help window's title bar.

Next, auto-hide the Solution Explorer window.

5. Click the **Auto Hide** button (the vertical pushpin) on the Solution Explorer window's title bar, then move the mouse pointer away from the window. The Solution Explorer window is minimized and appears as a tab on the right edge of the IDE.

HELP? If the Solution Explorer window remains on the screen when you move your mouse pointer away from the window, click another window's title bar.

Now temporarily display the Solution Explorer window.

6. Place your mouse pointer on the **Solution Explorer** tab. The Solution Explorer window slides into view.

7. Move your mouse pointer away from the Solution Explorer window. The window is minimized and appears as a tab again.

Next, use the Auto Hide button to permanently display the Toolbox window.

8. Place your mouse pointer on the **Toolbox** tab. When the Toolbox window slides into view, click the **Auto Hide** button (the horizontal pushpin) on its title bar. The vertical pushpin button replaces the horizontal pushpin button. Figure 1.3 shows the current status of the windows in the development environment.

Vertical pushpin

The Solution Explorer window is auto-hidden

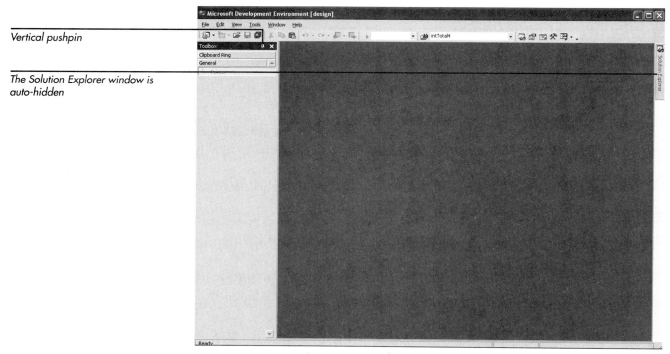

FIGURE 1.3   Current status of the windows in the development environment

Next, you learn how to return the layout of the windows in the IDE to the default layout that was provided during the initial setup of Visual Studio .NET.

To return the layout of the windows to the default layout:

1. Click **Tools** on the menu bar, and then click **Options**. The Options dialog box opens. If necessary, click the **Environment** folder to open it, and then click **General**. See Figure 1.4.

Reset Window Layout button

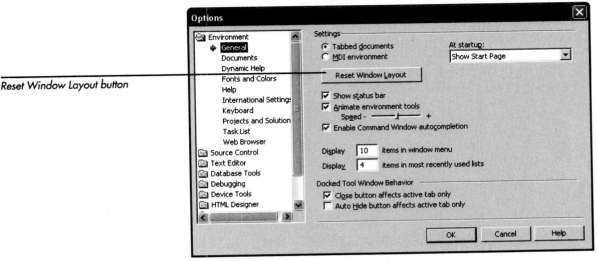

FIGURE 1.4   Options dialog box

2. Click the **Reset Window Layout** button. The Microsoft Development Environment dialog box shown in Figure 1.5 appears.

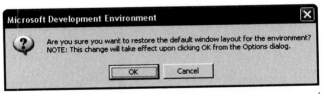

FIGURE 1.5   Microsoft Development Environment dialog box

3. Click the **OK** button to close the Microsoft Development Environment dialog box, and then click the **OK** button to close the Options dialog box.

4. If the Start Page window is not open, click **Help** on the menu bar, and then click **Show Start Page**. The screen should look similar to the one shown earlier in Figure 1.2.

In the next set of steps, you learn how to use Visual Basic .NET to create a Windows-based application.

To create a Visual Basic .NET Windows-based application:

1. Close the Server Explorer, Class View, Dynamic Help, and Start Page windows. Although it is not necessary to close these windows to create an application, doing so makes it easier to work in the IDE.

2. Click **File** on the Visual Studio .NET menu bar, point to **New**, and then click **Project**. The New Project dialog box opens.

3. If necessary, click **Visual Basic Projects** in the Project Types list box.

4. If necessary, click **Windows Application** in the Templates list box.

5. Type **Practice Project** in the Name text box.

6. Use the **Browse** button, which appears to the right of the Location text box, to open the **VbDotNetLab\Chap01** folder.

7. If necessary, click the **More** button.

8. Select the **Create directory for Solution** check box.

9. Type **Practice Solution** in the New Solution Name text box. See Figure 1.6.

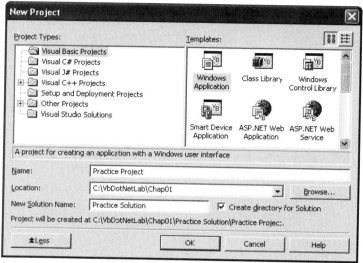

FIGURE 1.6   Completed New Project dialog box

10. Click the **OK** button to close the New Project dialog box. Visual Studio .NET creates a solution and adds a Visual Basic .NET project to the solution, as shown in Figure 1.7. Notice that two new windows appear in the IDE: the Windows Form Designer window and the Properties window.

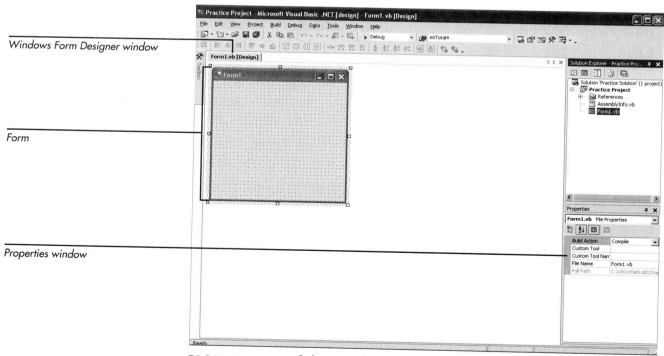

FIGURE 1.7   Solution and project created by Visual Studio .NET

HELP? If the Windows Form Designer window does not appear in the IDE, right-click Form1.vb in the Solution Explorer window, and then click View Designer.

HELP? If the Output window appears in the IDE, click the Close button on its title bar.

HELP? If the Properties window does not appear in the IDE, click View on the menu bar, and then click Properties Window.

HELP? If a plus box appears next to the project name in the Solution Explorer window, click the plus box.

HELP? If a minus box appears next to the References folder in the Solution Explorer window, click the minus box.

HELP? If the Solution Explorer window displays more folders and files than are shown in Figure 1.7, click the Show All Files button on the Solution Explorer window's toolbar.

HELP? If a Misc row appears in the Properties window, click the Alphabetic button on the Properties window's toolbar.

At times, you may want to change the size of the windows in the IDE. For example, you may want to widen the Solution Explorer window so that you can view the entire name of the solution and/or project. In the next set of steps, you learn how to size the windows in the IDE.

To size the windows in the IDE:

1. First, you will widen the Solution Explorer window. Position your mouse pointer on the Solution Explorer window's left border until the mouse pointer changes to ↔, then drag the border to the left until it reaches the desired width.

2. Next, you will lengthen the Properties window. Position your mouse pointer on the top border of the Properties window until the mouse pointer changes to ↕, then drag the border up until it reaches the desired height.

Only a form appears in the Windows Form designer window shown in Figure 1.7. A form is the foundation for the user interface in a Windows-based application. You create the user interface by adding other objects, such as buttons and text boxes, to the form. You add the objects, called controls, using the tools available in the Toolbox window. In the next set of steps, you add three controls to the current form. You also learn how to size, move, delete, and undelete a control.

To add and manipulate a control:

1. First, display the Toolbox window. Place your mouse pointer on the **Toolbox** tab. When the Toolbox window slides into view, click the **Auto Hide** button (the horizontal pushpin) on its title bar.

2. Click the **Label** tool in the toolbox, but do not release the mouse button. Hold down the mouse button as you drag the mouse pointer to the form. (You do not need to worry about the exact location.) As you drag the mouse pointer, both an outline of a rectangle and a plus box follow the mouse pointer.

3. Release the mouse button. A label control appears on the form, as shown in Figure 1.8. Notice that sizing handles appear around the label control. The sizing handles indicate that the control is selected. You can use the sizing handles to make a control bigger or smaller.

The asterisk indicates that the form has been changed since the last time it was saved

Sizing handle

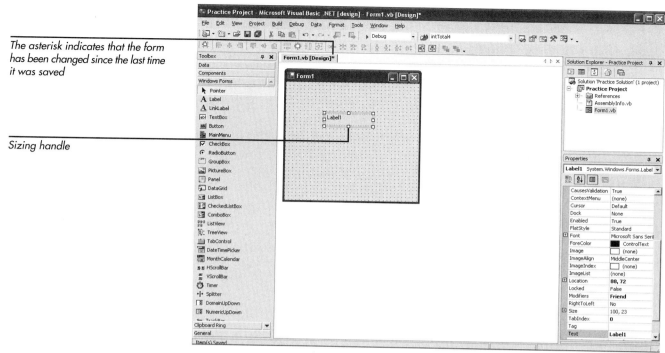

FIGURE 1.8   Label control added to the form

Notice that an asterisk (*) appears on the Form1.vb [Design] tab in the Windows Form designer window. The asterisk indicates that the form has been changed since the last time it was saved.

    4. Practice using the sizing handles to make the label control bigger and smaller.

TIP •••• You also can size a control by selecting it and then pressing and holding down the Shift key as you press one of the arrow keys on your keyboard. Additionally, you can set the control's Size property.

Now reposition the label control on the form.

    5. Place your mouse pointer on the center of the label control, then press the left mouse button and drag the control to another area of the form. Release the mouse button.

TIP •••• You also can move a control by selecting it and then pressing and holding down the Ctrl key as you press one of the arrow keys on your keyboard. Additionally, you can set the control's Location property.

Next, delete and then undelete the label control.

    6. Press the **Delete** key on your keyboard to delete the control.

TIP •••• To delete a control, the control must be selected and the Windows Form designer must be the active window.

    7. Click **Edit** on the menu bar, and then click **Undo** to reinstate the label control.

You also can add a control to a form by clicking the appropriate tool and then clicking the form.

    8. Click the **Label** tool in the toolbox, and then click the form. (You do not need to worry about the exact location.) Another label control, named Label2, appears on the form.

Additionally, you can click the appropriate tool, then place the mouse pointer on the form, and then press the left mouse button and drag the mouse pointer until the control is the desired size.

9. Click the **Button** tool in the toolbox, and then place the mouse pointer on the form. Press the left mouse button and drag the mouse pointer until the control is the desired size, then release the mouse button. (You do not need to worry about the exact location and size.) The form should contain two label controls and one button control, as shown in Figure 1.9.

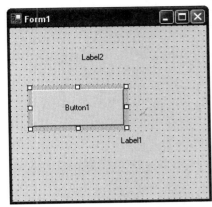

FIGURE 1.9   Controls added to the form

10. Click the **Auto Hide** button (the vertical pushpin) on the toolbox's title bar to auto-hide the toolbox.

Each object in Visual Basic .NET has a set of attributes that determine its appearance and behavior; the attributes are called properties. When an object is selected, its properties appear in the Properties window. In the next set of steps, you learn how to use the Properties window to change the default value assigned to the File Name property of the form file object.

To change the name of the form file object:

1. Click **Form1.vb** in the Solution Explorer window. The properties of the Form1.vb form file appear in the Properties window, as shown in Figure 1.10.

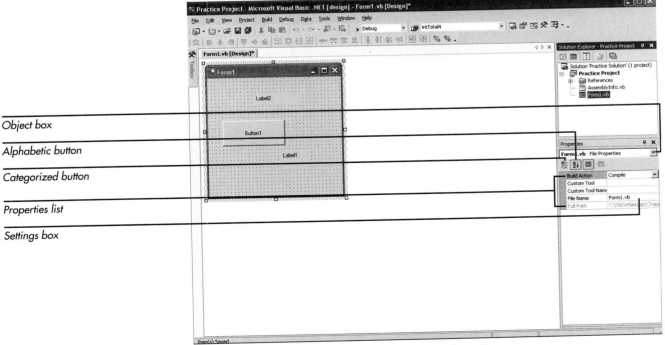

FIGURE 1.10   Properties of the Form1.vb form file

You can display the properties either alphabetically (as shown in Figure 1.10) or by category.

2. If the properties in your Properties window are listed by category, click the **Alphabetic** button. However, if the properties are listed alphabetically, click the **Categorized** button to view the category display, then click the **Alphabetic** button to return to the alphabetical list.

As indicated in Figure 1.10, the Properties window includes an Object box and a Properties list. The Object box contains the name of the selected object; in this case, it contains Form1.vb. The Properties list has two columns. The left column displays the names of the properties associated with the selected object, and the right column (called the Settings box) displays the current value, or setting, of each of the properties.

3. Click **File Name** in the Properties list, then type **Practice Form.vb** and press **Enter**. The Practice Form.vb filename appears in the Settings box in the Properties window. It also appears in the Solution Explorer window and on the Windows Form designer tab, as shown in Figure 1.11.

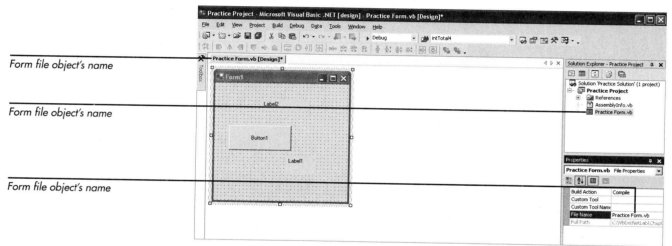

Form file object's name

Form file object's name

Form file object's name

FIGURE 1.11   Form file object's name displayed in the Properties, Solution Explorer, and Windows Form designer windows

Next, you change the default values assigned to some of the properties of the form object.

To change the values assigned to some of the properties of the form object:

1. Click the **form** (but not a control on the form) in the Windows Form designer window. The form's properties appear in the Properties window.

First, change the type and size of the font used to display text on the form.

2. Scroll the Properties window until you see Font listed in the Properties list. Click **Font** in the Properties list, then click the ... (ellipsis) button in the Settings box. When the Font dialog box opens, click **Tahoma** in the Font list box and **12** in the Size list box. See Figure 1.12.

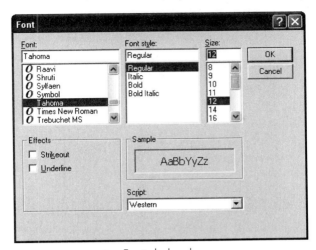

FIGURE 1.12 Font dialog box

3. Click the **OK** button. Notice that the changes made to the form's Font property affect the text displayed in the controls on the form.

A form's StartPosition property specifies where the form is positioned when the application is run and the form first appears on the screen.

4. Click **StartPosition** in the Properties list. Click the **list arrow** in the Settings box, and then click **CenterScreen**.

A form's Text property specifies the text to display in the form's title bar.

5. Click **Text** in the Properties list. Type **Practice Application** and press **Enter**. Notice that you do not have to erase the old value in the Settings box before entering the new value; the new value replaces the old value as you type.

Next, change the form's name from Form1 to frmFirst. The name is stored in the form's Name property.

6. Use the scroll bar in the Properties window to scroll to the top of the Properties list, then click **(Name)** in the Properties list.

7. Type **frmPractice** and press **Enter**. See Figure 1.13.

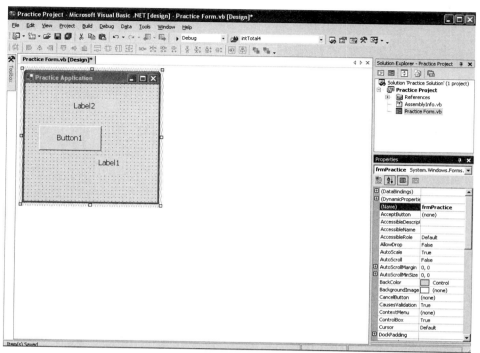

FIGURE 1.13 Current status of the interface

In the next set of steps, you assign values to some of the properties of the Label1 and Label2 controls.

To assign values to some of the properties of the Label1 and Label2 controls:

1. Click the **Label1** control in the form. Sizing handles appear around the Label1 control, and the control's properties appear in the Properties window.

First, change the label control's name from Label1 to lblFirst.

2. Click **(Name)** in the Properties list. Type **lblFirst** and press **Enter**.

Next, put a border around the lblFirst control.

3. Click **BorderStyle** in the Properties list. Click the **list arrow** in the Settings box, and then click **FixedSingle**.

Now remove the text that appears inside the lblFirst control. The text is stored in the control's Text property.

4. Click **Text** in the Properties list. Press the **Backspace** key on your keyboard, and then press **Enter**.

Now set the lblFirst control's Location and Size properties.

5. Click **Location** in the Properties list. Type **80, 40** and press **Enter**. (The first number is the distance from the left border of the form to the left border of the control. The second number is the distance from the top border of the form to the top border of the control.)

6. Click **Size** in the Properties list. Type **120, 23** and press **Enter**. (The first number is the width; the second number is the height.)

7. Click the **list arrow** in the Properties window's Object box, and then click **Label2** in the list. Sizing handles appear around the Label2 control, and the control's properties appear in the Properties window.

8. Change the Label2 control's **Name** property to **lblSecond**, and change its **Text** property to **Visual Basic .NET**.

Notice that only some of the text appears in the lblSecond control; this is because the text is longer than the width of the control. You can use the control's sizing handles to adjust the size of the control. Or, you can use the control's AutoSize property.

9. Click **AutoSize** in the Properties list. Click the **list arrow** in the Settings box, and then click **True**.

10. Click **Location** in the Properties list. Type **80, 80** and press **Enter**.

Next, you assign values to some of the properties of the button control.

To assign values to some of the properties of the button control:

1. Click the **Button1** control on the form. (If you cannot see the Button1 control on the form, click the list arrow in the Properties window's Object box, and then click Button1 in the list.) Sizing handles appear around the control, and the control's properties appear in the Properties window.

First, change the button's name from Button1 to btnExit.

2. Click **(Name)** in the Properties list. Type **btnExit** and press **Enter**.

Next, change the location and size of the btnExit control.

3. Set the btnExit control's **Location** property to **184, 200**.

4. Set the btnExit control's **Size** property to **80, 32**.

The Text property determines the caption that appears on a button control.

5. Set the btnExit control's **Text** property to **Exit**. See Figure 1.14.

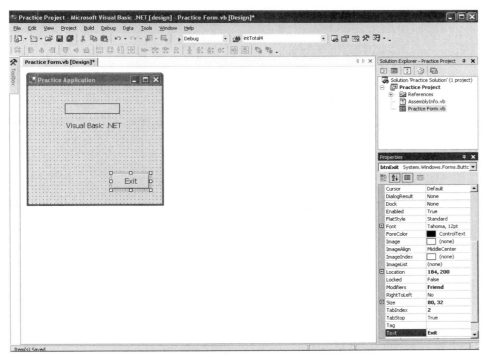

FIGURE 1.14 Completed interface

In the next set of steps, you learn how to lock and unlock the controls on the form. Locking the controls prevents them from being inadvertently moved as you work in the IDE.

To lock and unlock the controls on the form:

1. Click the **form** to make the Windows Form designer the active window.

You can use the Format menu to lock and unlock the controls.

2. Click **Format** on the menu bar, and then click **Lock Controls** to lock the controls.
3. Try dragging one of the controls to a different location on the form. You will not be able to.
4. Click **Format** on the menu bar, and then click **Lock Controls** to unlock the controls.
5. Drag one of the controls to a different location on the form.
6. Click **Edit** on the menu bar, and then click **Undo** to return the control to its previous position.

You also can lock and unlock the controls by right-clicking the form, and then clicking Lock Controls on the context menu.

7. Right-click the **form**, then click **Lock Controls**.
8. Try dragging one of the controls to a different location on the form. You will not be able to.

It is a good practice to save the current solution every 10 or 15 minutes so that you will not lose a lot of work if the computer loses power. You can save a solution by clicking File on the menu bar, and then clicking Save All. This saves any changes made to the files included in the solution. You also can save a solution by clicking the Save All button on the Standard toolbar.

To save the current solution:

1. Click **File** on the menu bar.
2. Click **Save All**. Notice that an asterisk (*) no longer appears on the Practice Form.vb [Design] tab. This indicates that the form has not been changed since the last time it was saved.

Now that the user interface is complete, you can start the application to see how it will look to the user. You can start an application by clicking Debug on the menu bar, and then clicking Start; or you can simply press the F5 key on your keyboard.

To start and also stop an application:

1. Right-click **Practice Project** in the Solution Explorer window, and then click **Properties**. The Practice Project Property Pages dialog box opens. If necessary, click the **Common Properties** folder to open it, and then click **General**.

When the application is started, the frmPractice form should be the first form that appears on the screen.

2. Click the **Startup object** list arrow, and then click **frmPractice** in the list. See Figure 1.15.

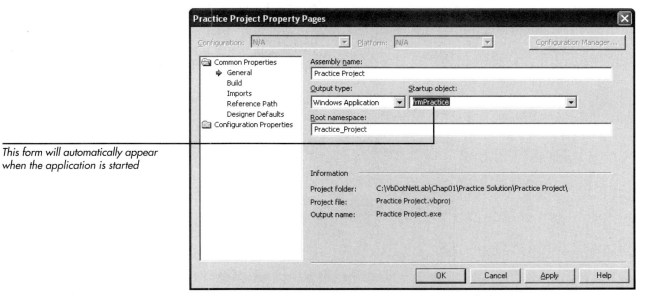

This form will automatically appear when the application is started

FIGURE 1.15 Practice Project Property Pages dialog box

3. Click the **OK** button to close the Practice Project Property Pages dialog box.

Now save the solution and then start the application. (You should always save the solution before starting the application.)

4. Click **File** on the menu bar, and then click **Save All**. Click **Debug** on the menu bar, and then click **Start**. See Figure 1.16. (Do not be concerned about the windows that appear at the bottom of the screen.)

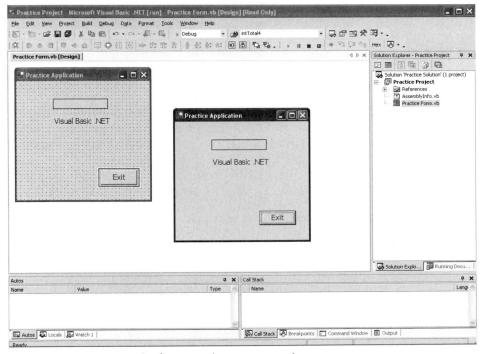

FIGURE 1.16 Result of starting the current application

5. Click the **Exit** button. Currently, the button does not perform any tasks when clicked. This is because you have not yet entered the instructions that tell it what tasks to perform.

At this point, you can stop the application by clicking the Close button on the form's title bar. You also can click the designer window to make it the active window, then click Debug on the menu bar, and then click Stop Debugging.

6. Click the **Close** button on the form's title bar. When the application ends, you are returned to the IDE, and an Output window appears at the bottom of the screen, as shown in Figure 1.17.

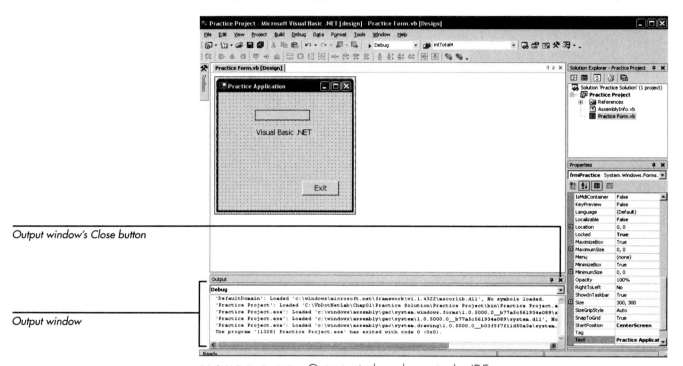

FIGURE 1.17 Output window shown in the IDE

7. Close the Output window by clicking the **Close** button on its title bar.

You use Visual Basic .NET code to tell a button how to respond when the user clicks it. You enter the code in the Code Editor window. You can use various methods to open the Code Editor window. For example, you can right-click anywhere on the form (except the form's title bar), and then click View Code on the context menu. You also can click View on the menu bar, and then click Code; or you can press the F7 key on your keyboard. (To use the View menu or the F7 key, the designer window should be the active window.)

To open the Code Editor window:

1. Right-click the **form**, then click **View Code**. The Code Editor window opens in the IDE.

2. Auto-hide the Solution Explorer and Properties windows by clicking each window's **Auto Hide** button; this will allow you to view more of the Code Editor window. Notice that the Code Editor window already contains some Visual Basic .NET code, as shown in Figure 1.18.

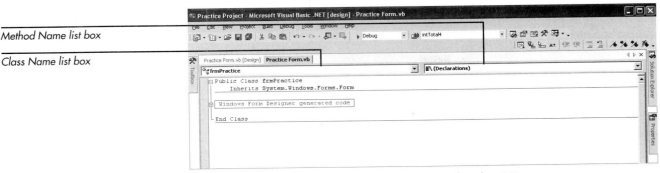

FIGURE 1.18   Code Editor window opened in the IDE

Method Name list box

Class Name list box

HELP?   If a minus box appears next to the `Windows Form Designer generated code` entry, click the minus box.

As Figure 1.18 indicates, the Code Editor window contains a Class Name list box and a Method Name list box. The Class Name list box lists the names of the objects included in the user interface. The Method Name list box, on the other hand, lists the events to which the selected object is capable of responding. You use the Class Name and Method Name list boxes to select the object and event, respectively, that you want to code.

To code the Exit button's Click event procedure:

1. Click the **Class Name** list arrow, and then click **btnExit** in the list. Click the **Method Name** list arrow, and then click **Click** in the list. See Figure 1.19.

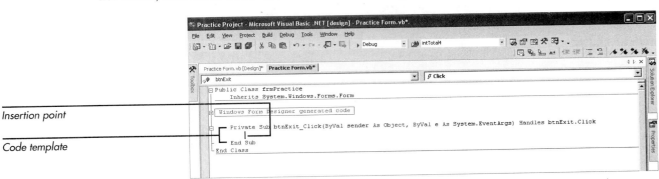

Insertion point

Code template

FIGURE 1.19   btnExit control's Click event procedure shown in the Code Editor window

Notice that, when you select an object and event, additional code automatically appears in the Code Editor window. To help you follow the rules of the Visual Basic .NET programming language, called syntax, the Code Editor provides you with a code template for every event procedure. The insertion point located in the event procedure indicates where you enter your code for the object. In this case, you want to instruct the button to end the application; you do so using the statement `Me.Close()`. You can type the statement on your own; or you can use the IntelliSense feature that is built into Visual Basic .NET. In this set of steps, you will use the IntelliSense feature.

2. Type **me.** (but don't press Enter). When you type the period, the IntelliSense feature displays a list of choices from which you can select. See Figure 1.20.

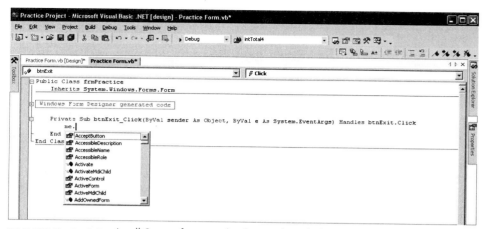

FIGURE 1.20 IntelliSense feature displays a list of choices

HELP? If the list of choices does not appear, the IntelliSense feature on your computer may have been turned off. To turn it on, click Tools on the menu bar, and then click Options. Open the Text Editor folder in the Options dialog box, and then open the Basic folder. Click General in the Basic folder, then select the Auto list members check box. Click the OK button to close the Options dialog box.

3. Type **clo** (but don't press Enter). The IntelliSense feature highlights the Close choice in the list, as shown in Figure 1.21.

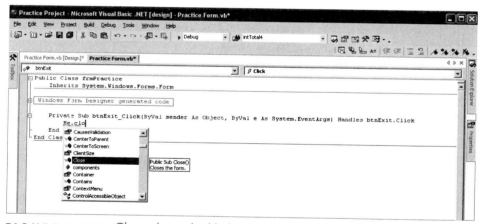

FIGURE 1.21 Close choice highlighted in the list

4. Press the **Tab** key on your keyboard to select the Close choice, and then press **Enter**. When the application is started and the user clicks the Exit button, the statement in the button's Click event procedure will terminate the application. See Figure 1.22.

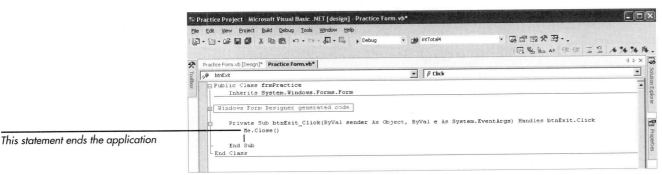

This statement ends the application

FIGURE 1.22 Completed Click event procedure for the btnExit control

Finally, close the Code Editor window, then save the solution and start the application.

To close the Code Editor window, then save the solution and start the application:

1. Click the **Close** button on the Code Editor window's title bar.
2. Click **File** on the menu bar, and then click **Save All**.
3. Click **Debug** on the menu bar, and then click **Start**.

Verify that the Exit button is working correctly.

4. Click the **Exit** button. The application ends and you are returned to the designer window.
5. Close the Output window.

When you are finished working on a solution, you should close the solution. You close a solution using the Close Solution option on the File menu. When you close a solution, all projects and files contained in the solution also are closed. If unsaved changes were made to the solution, project, or form, a dialog box opens and prompts you to save the appropriate files. The dialog box contains Yes, No, Cancel, and Help buttons. You click the Yes button to save the files before the solution is closed. You click the No button to close the solution without saving the files. You click the Cancel button to leave the solution open, and you click the Help button to display Help pertaining to the dialog box.

To close the current solution:

1. Click **File** on the menu bar, and then click **Close Solution**.

You can use the Solution Explorer window to verify that the solution is closed.

2. Temporarily display the Solution Explorer window to verify that no solutions are open in the IDE.

If you want to open an existing solution, you simply click File on the menu bar, and then click Open Solution. You then select the appropriate solution file in the Open Solution dialog box. You can recognize a solution file by the .sln extension on its filename. If a solution is already open in the IDE, it is closed before another solution is opened. In other words, only one solution can be open in the IDE at any one time.

To open the Practice Solution, then modify, save, and start it:

1. Click **File** on the menu bar, and then click **Open Solution**. The Open Solution dialog box opens.
2. Locate and then open the **VbDotNetLab\Chap01\Practice Solution** folder.
3. If necessary, click **Practice Solution** (Practice Solution.sln) in the list of filenames, and then click the **Open** button.
4. If the Windows Form Designer window is not displayed, click **View** on the menu bar, and then click **Designer**.

5. Temporarily display the Solution Explorer window to verify that the solution is open.

6. Type your first and last name in the **Text** property of the lblFirst control.

7. Set the lblFirst control's **AutoSize** property to **True**.

8. Save the solution, then start the application.

9. Click the **Exit** button to end the application, then close the Output window.

Lastly, you learn how to exit Visual Studio .NET. As in most Windows applications, you exit an application using either the Close button on the application window's title bar, or the Exit option on the File menu.

To exit Visual Studio .NET:

1. Click **File** on the menu bar, and then click **Close Solution** to close the current solution.

2. Click **File** on the menu bar, and then click **Exit** to exit Visual Studio .NET.

LAB 1.2 INTERLOCKING SOFTWARE – COPYRIGHT SCREEN

Scenario On your second day of work at Interlocking Software, Chris Statton assigns you your first application: a copyright screen. The copyright screen will serve as a splash screen for each custom application you create. The copyright screen will identify the application's author and copyright year.

Solution Discussion The user interface for this application will contain two label controls that display the author's name and the copyright year. It also will contain one button that allows the user to close the copyright screen.

User Interface

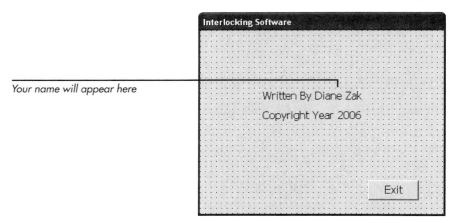

Your name will appear here

FIGURE 1.23

Activity

1. Start Visual Studio .NET.

2. Click **Tools** on the menu bar, and then click **Options** to open the Options dialog box. If necessary, click the **Environment** folder to open it, and then click **General**.

3. Click the **Reset Window Layout** button. The Microsoft Development Environment dialog box appears.

4. Click the **OK** button to close the Microsoft Development Environment dialog box, and then click the **OK** button to close the Options dialog box.

5. Close the Server Explorer, Class View, and Dynamic Help windows.

6. Click **File** on the Visual Studio .NET menu bar, point to **New**, and then click **Project**. Use Figure 1.24 to complete the New Project dialog box.

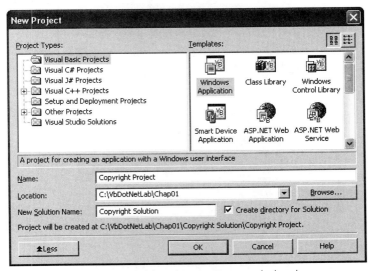

FIGURE 1.24 Completed New Project dialog box

7. Click the **OK** button to close the New Project dialog box.

8. Permanently display the Toolbox window.

9. Change the form file object's name from Form1.vb to **Copyright Form.vb**.

10. Change the form's name from Form1 to **frmCopyright**.

11. Right-click **Copyright Project** in the Solution Explorer window, and then click **Properties** to open the Copyright Project Property Pages dialog box. If necessary, click the **Common Properties** folder to open it, and then click **General**. Click the **Startup object** list arrow, and then click **frmCopyright** in the list. Click the **OK** button to close the Copyright Project Property Pages dialog box.

12. Change the form's Font property to **Tahoma, 12pt**.

13. Change the form's StartPosition property to **CenterScreen**.

14. Change the form's Text property to **Interlocking Software**.

15. Change the form's Size property to **370, 315**. The partially completed interface is shown in Figure 1.25.

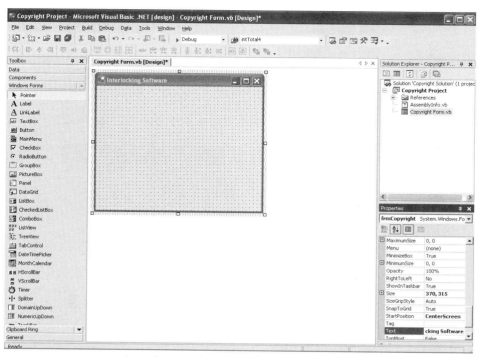

FIGURE 1.25   Partially completed interface

Next, add the two label controls and one button control to the interface.

To add the appropriate controls to the interface:

1. Use the Label tool in the toolbox to add two label controls to the form.
2. Use the Button tool in the toolbox to add a button control to the form.
3. Auto-hide the toolbox.
4. Set the following properties of the Label1 control:

Name	**lblAuthor**
AutoSize	**True**
Location	**90, 90**
Text	**Written By** *<type your name here>*

5. Set the following properties of the Label2 control:

Name	**lblYear**
AutoSize	**True**
Location	**90, 120**
Text	**Copyright Year 2006**

6. Set the following properties of the Button1 control:

Name	**btnExit**
Location	**250, 230**
Size	**75, 30**
Text	**Exit**

7. Lock the controls. The interface is shown in Figure 1.26.

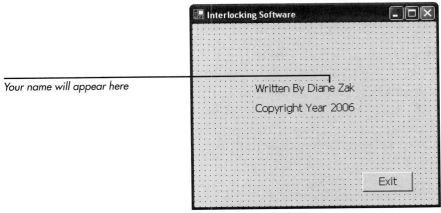

Your name will appear here

FIGURE 1.26   Controls added to the interface

8. Click **File** on the menu bar, and then click **Save All** to save the solution.

Now code the Exit button's Click event procedure, and then save the solution and start the application to verify that it is working correctly.

To code the Exit button's Click event procedure, then save the solution and start the application:

1. Right-click the **form**, and then click **View Code** to open the Code Editor window.
2. Display the code template for the btnExit control's Click event procedure. Type **me.close()** in the procedure and press **Enter**.
3. Close the Code Editor window.
4. Click **File** on the menu bar, and then click **Save All** to save the solution.
5. Click **Debug** on the menu bar, and then click **Start** to start the application. The copyright screen appears, as shown in Figure 1.27.

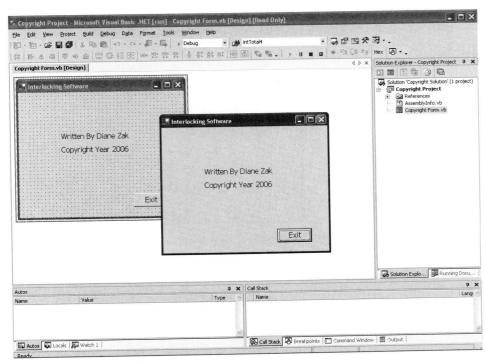

FIGURE 1.27   Copyright screen

6. Place your mouse pointer on the right border of the form until the mouse pointer becomes ↔, then drag the form's border to the left. Notice that you can size the form while the application is running. As a general rule, the user typically is not allowed to change the size of a splash screen. You can prevent the user from sizing the form by changing the form's FormBorderStyle property.

7. Click the **Exit** button to close the copyright screen.

8. Set the frmCopyright object's FormBorderStyle property to **FixedSingle**.

Splash screens also do not usually have Minimize, Maximize, and Close buttons. You can control the display of one or more of these buttons using the ControlBox, MinimizeBox, or MaximizeBox properties.

9. Set the frmCopyright object's ControlBox property to **False**. Notice that this removes the Minimize, Maximize, and Close buttons from the form's title bar.

10. Save the solution, then start the application.

11. Try to size the form by dragging one of its borders. You will notice that you cannot size the form using its borders.

12. Click the **Exit** button to close the copyright screen.

13. Close the Output window.

14. Click **File** on the menu bar, and then click **Close Solution** to close the solution.

LAB 1.3 TABATHA'S BED AND BREAKFAST

Scenario In this lab, you create an application for Tabatha's Bed and Breakfast. The application allows the user to display either the message "Welcome!" or the message "Good-bye".

Solution Discussion The user interface for this application will contain a label control that displays the appropriate message. It also will contain three buttons. Two of buttons will display a message, and the third button will close the application.

User Interface

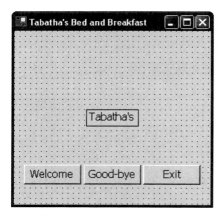

FIGURE 1.28

Activity

1. If necessary, start Visual Studio .NET.

2. Create a new Visual Basic .NET Windows application. Name the solution **Tabatha Solution**. Name the project **Tabatha Project**. Save the application in the VbDotNetLab\Chap01 folder.

3. Change the form file object's name from Form1.vb to **Tabatha Form.vb**.

4. Change the form's name from Form1 to **frmTabatha**.

5. Use the Tabatha Project Property Pages dialog box to set the Startup object to **frmTabatha**.

6. Change the form's Font property to **Tahoma, 12pt**.

7. The form should be centered on the screen when it first appears. Set the appropriate property.

8. The form's title bar should say **Tabatha's Bed and Breakfast**. Set the appropriate property.

9. Add a label control and three button controls to the form. Position the controls as shown in Figure 1.29.

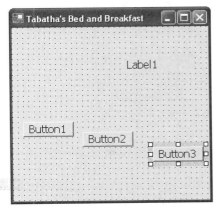

FIGURE 1.29   Controls positioned on the form

Now change the values assigned to some of the properties of the controls.

To change the values assigned to some of the properties of the controls:

1. The Label1 control should be named **lblMessage**. Set the appropriate property.

2. The Label1 control should have the FixedSingle border. Set the appropriate property.

3. The Label1 control should be automatically sized to fit its contents. Set the appropriate property.

4. The Label1 control should display the word **Tabatha's**. Set the appropriate property.

5. Click the **lblMessage** control on the form to select the control. Click **Format** on the menu bar. Point to **Center in Form**, and then click **Horizontally**.

6. Use the Format menu to center the lblMessage control vertically on the form.

7. Change the names of the Button1, Button2, and Button3 controls to **btnWelcome**, **btnBye**, and **btnExit**, respectively.

8. The words **Welcome**, **Good-bye**, and **Exit** should appear on the btnWelcome, btnBye, and btnExit controls, respectively. Set the appropriate properties.

9. Change the btnWelcome control's Size property to **85, 30**.

10. Change the btnWelcome control's Location property to **15, 205**.

Now you will select the three button controls, and then use the Format menu to make the btnBye and btnExit controls the same size as the btnWelcome control. When selecting a group of controls, the last control you select should always be the one whose size and/or location you want to match. In this case, you want the btnBye and btnExit controls to match the size of the btnWelcome control, so you will need to select the btnWelcome control last.

11. Click the **btnBye** control on the form. Press and hold down the **Ctrl** key as you click the **btnExit** control first and then the **btnWelcome** control, then release the Ctrl key. The three button controls are selected in the interface, as shown in Figure 1.30.

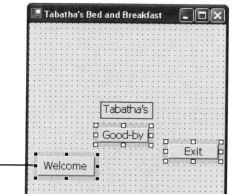

The reference control has black sizing handles

FIGURE 1.30   Button controls selected on the form

Notice that the sizing handles on the Welcome button, which was the last control selected, are black, whereas the sizing handles on the Good-bye and Exit buttons are white. The control with the black sizing handles is called the reference control.

12. Click **Format** on the menu bar. Point to **Make Same Size**, and then click **Both**. The Good-bye and Exit buttons are now the same size as the Welcome button.

13. Use the Format menu to align the top borders of the Good-bye and Exit buttons with the top border of the Welcome button.

14. Click the **form** to deselect the button controls.

15. Click the **btnExit** control on the form, then press the left arrow key on your keyboard to move the control one dot to the left.

16. Lock the controls. The completed interface is shown in Figure 1.31.

FIGURE 1.31   Completed interface

17. Save the solution.

Now code each button's Click event procedure, and then save the solution, start the application, and print the application's code.

To code each button's Click event procedure, then save the solution, start the application, and print the application's code:

1. Open the Code Editor window.

2. The btnExit control should close the application when it is clicked. Code the appropriate event procedure.

3. Display the code template for the btnWelcome control's Click event procedure. Type **me.lblmessage.text = "Welcome!"** in the procedure and press **Enter**.

4. Display the code template for the btnBye control's Click event procedure. Type **me.lblmessage.text = "Good-bye"** in the procedure and press **Enter**.

5. Save the solution, then start the application. The interface appears on the screen.

6. Click the **Welcome** button. The message "Welcome!" appears in the lblMessage control, as shown in Figure 1.32.

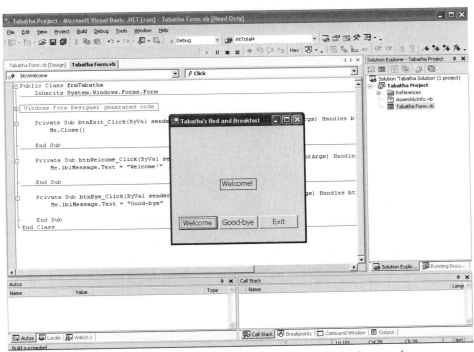

FIGURE 1.32 Welcome message displayed in the Tabatha interface

7. Click the **Good-bye** button. The message "Good-bye" appears in the lblMessage control.

8. Click the **Exit** button to close the application, then close the Output window.

9. Verify that the only plus box in the Code Editor window appears next to the `Windows Form Designer generated code` entry. If a plus box appears anywhere else in the Code Editor window, click the plus box. (You typically do not need to print the code generated by the designer.)

10. Click **File** on the menu bar, and then click **Print** to open the Print dialog box. If your computer is connected to a printer, click the **OK** button; otherwise, click the **Cancel** button.

11. Close the Code Editor window, then use the File menu to close the solution.

Beyond the Text

LAB 1.4 INTERLOCKING SOFTWARE – MODIFIED COPYRIGHT SCREEN

Scenario Chris Statton has asked you to include the Interlocking Software logo on the copyright screen you created in Lab 1.2. He also wants you to remove the Exit button, because he now wants the copyright screen to automatically close itself after five seconds.

Solution Discussion You will need to add both a picture box control and a timer control to the copyright screen you created in Lab 1.2. You will use the picture box control to display the Interlocking Software logo, and use the timer control to automatically close the copyright screen after five seconds.

User Interface

Your name will appear here

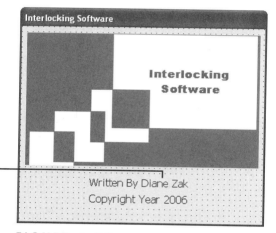

FIGURE 1.33

Activity

1. Use Windows to make a copy of the Copyright Solution folder, which is contained in the VbDotNetLab\Chap01 folder. Rename the copy Modified Copyright Solution.
2. If necessary, start Visual Studio .NET.
3. Open the Copyright Solution (Copyright Solution.sln) file contained in the VbDotNetLab\Chap01\Modified Copyright Solution folder.
4. Right-click **Copyright Form.vb** in the Solution Explorer window, then click **View Designer**.
5. Unlock the controls.
6. Set the frmCopyright object's Size property to **370, 335**.
7. Set the lblYear control's Location property to **55, 255**.
8. Set the lblAuthor control's Location property to **55, 230**.

First, add a picture box control to the interface.

To add a picture box control to the interface:

1. Use the PictureBox tool in the toolbox to add a picture box control to the form.

2. Set the picture box control's Location property to **8, 10**.

You use the picture box control's Image property to specify the image you want displayed inside the control.

3. Click **Image** in the Properties list, then click the ... (ellipsis) button in the Settings box. The Open dialog box opens.

The Interlocking Software logo is stored in the Logo (Logo.bmp) file, which is contained in the VbDotNetLab\Chap01 folder.

4. Open the VbDotNetLab\Chap01 folder. Click **Logo** (Logo.bmp) in the list of filenames, and then click the **Open** button.

5. Set the picture box control's SizeMode property to **AutoSize**. The picture box control automatically sizes to fit its current contents, as shown in Figure 1.34.

FIGURE 1.34   Picture box control added to the form

Next, delete the Exit button from the form.

To delete the Exit button from the form:

1. Click the **Exit** button on the form, then press **Delete**.

In addition to deleting the control on the form, you also must delete any code associated with the control in the Code Editor window.

2. Open the Code Editor window. Select the entire btnExit_Click procedure, as shown in Figure 1.35.

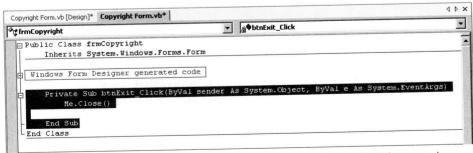

FIGURE 1.35   btnExit_Click procedure selected in the Code Editor window

3. Press **Delete** to delete the selected code.

You can use a timer control to process code at regular intervals. You simply set the control's Interval property to the length of the desired time interval, in milliseconds. You also set its Enabled property to True. The Enabled property determines whether an object can respond to an event; in this case, it determines whether the timer control can respond to the Tick event. In the control's Tick event procedure, you enter the code you want processed. The Tick event procedure tells the computer what to do after each time interval has elapsed. Now add a timer control to the interface.

To add a timer control to the interface:

1. Click the **Copyright Form.vb [Design]*** tab to return to the designer.
2. Use the Timer tool in the toolbox to add a timer control to the form. The timer control appears in the component tray, as shown in Figure 1.36.

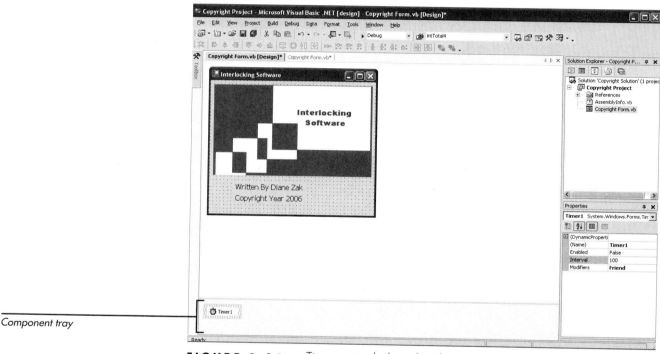

FIGURE 1.36 Timer control placed in the component tray

Unlike controls such as labels, picture boxes, and buttons, timer controls do not appear in the user interface when the application is started. Controls that do not appear in the interface are placed in the component tray.

3. Set the timer control's Name property to **tmrExit**.
4. Set the timer control's Enabled property to **True**.

The timer control should end the application after five seconds, which is 5000 milliseconds.

5. Set the timer control's Interval property to **5000**.
6. Click the **lblAuthor** control, then Ctrl+click the **lblYear** control. Both controls should be selected on the form.

HELP? Ctrl+click means to press and hold down the Ctrl key as you click.

7. Click **Format** on the menu bar. Point to **Center in Form**, and then click **Horizontally**.

8. Click the **form** to deselect the two label controls.

9. Lock the controls.

10. Save the solution.

Now code the timer control's Tick event procedure, and then save the solution and start the application to verify that it is working correctly.

To code the timer control's Tick event procedure, then save the solution and start the application:

1. Switch to the Code Editor window.

2. Display the code template for the tmrExit control's Tick event procedure. Type **me.close()** in the procedure and press **Enter**.

3. Close the Code Editor window.

4. Save the solution, then start the application. The modified copyright screen appears, as shown in Figure 1.37.

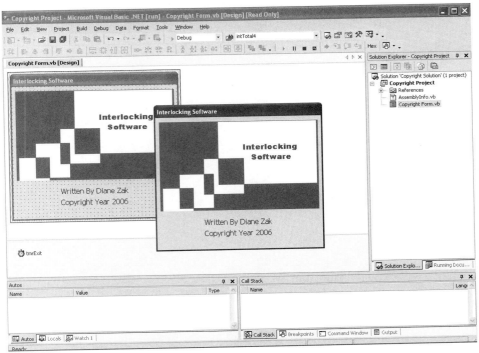

FIGURE 1.37   Modified copyright screen

After five seconds elapse, the application ends and the copyright screen is removed from view.

5. Close the Output window, then close the solution.

6. Exit Visual Studio .NET.

Creating a User Interface

Labs included in this chapter:

- Lab 2.1 Typing Haven
- Lab 2.2 Foster Industries
- Lab 2.3 Harborlights
- Lab 2.4 Sellers Warehouse

LAB 2.1 TYPING HAVEN

Scenario Typing Haven charges 5¢ per typed envelope and 15¢ per typed page. The company accountant wants an application to help her prepare bills. She will enter the number of typed envelopes and the number of typed pages. The application should calculate and display the total amount due.

Solution Discussion The Typing Haven application needs to provide areas for the user to enter the number of typed envelopes and the number of typed pages; you will use text boxes for this purpose. The application also needs to display the total amount due; you will use a label control for this purpose, because the user should not be able to change the amount after it has been displayed. You also will use three button controls that allow the user to calculate the total amount due, clear the screen for the next calculation, and exit the application.

TOE Chart

Task	Object	Event
1. Calculate the total amount due 2. Display the total amount due in the lblTotal control	btnCalc	Click
Clear the screen for the next calculation	btnClear	Click
End the application	btnExit	Click
Display the total amount due (from btnCalc)	lblTotal	None
Get and display the number of typed envelopes and the number of typed pages	txtEnvelopes, txtPages	None

FIGURE 2.1

User Interface

Typing Haven

Bill Calculator

Envelopes: [   ]   Calculate

Pages: [   ]   Clear

Total due: [   ]   Exit

FIGURE 2.2

The information in the user interface shown in Figure 2.2 is arranged vertically. The controls are positioned two dots away from the edges of the form, and related controls are placed on succeeding dots. The buttons are stacked vertically and are the same height and the same width. The borders of the controls are aligned wherever possible to minimize the number of different margins used in the interface. Labels that identify controls are left-aligned and, in this case, positioned to the left of the control they identify. The identifying labels end with a colon and are entered using sentence capitalization. The button captions, on the other hand, do not end with a colon and are entered using book title capitalization. In this case, each identifying label and button caption contain either one word or two words; additionally, each is meaningful and appears on one line in its respective control. All of the controls use the same font type, which is Tahoma. Only two font sizes are used in the interface: approximately 20pt for the "Bill Calculator" text, and 12pt for the text in the remaining controls. Access keys are assigned to each of the controls that can accept user input.

Activity

1. Start Visual Studio .NET.
2. If necessary, close the Start Page, Server Explorer, Class View, and Dynamic Help windows.
3. Click **File** on the Visual Studio .NET menu bar, point to **New**, and then click **Project**. The New Project dialog box opens.
4. If necessary, click **Visual Basic Projects** in the Project Types list box, and click **Windows Application** in the Templates list box.
5. Type **Typing Haven Project** in the Name text box.
6. Use the **Browse** button, which appears to the right of the Location text box, to open the **VbDotNetLab\Chap02** folder.
7. If necessary, click the **More** button.
8. If necessary, select the **Create directory for Solution** check box.
9. Type **Typing Haven Solution** in the New Solution Name text box.
10. Click the **OK** button to close the New Project dialog box.

Now set the appropriate properties of the form file object and form object.

To set the appropriate properties of the form file object and form object:

1. Right-click **Form1.vb** in the Solution Explorer window, then click **Rename**. Change the form file object's name from Form1.vb to **Typing Haven.vb**.
2. Click the **form**, then click **(Name)** in the Properties window. Change the form object's name from Form1 to **frmTyping**.
3. Right-click **Typing Haven Project** in the Solution Explorer window, then click **Properties**. Click the **Startup object** list arrow, and then click **frmTyping** in the list. Click the **OK** button.
4. Click the **form**, then change the values assigned to the following properties:

Font	**Tahoma, 12 pt**
Size	**360, 250**
StartPosition	**CenterScreen**
Text	**Typing Haven**

5. Save the solution by clicking **File** on the menu bar, and then clicking **Save All**.

Next, use the toolbox to add five label controls, two text boxes, and three buttons to the interface.

To add the appropriate controls:

1. Use the Label tool to add five label controls to the form.
2. Use the TextBox tool to add two text boxes to the form.
3. Use the Button tool to add three buttons to the form.
4. Position the controls as shown in Figure 2.3.

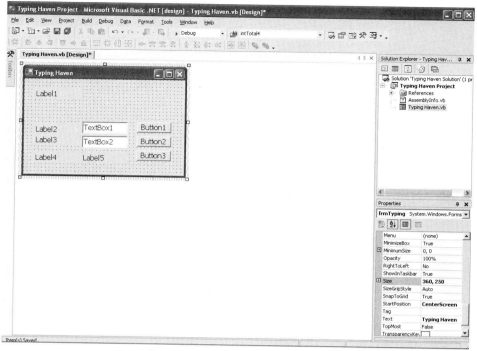

FIGURE 2.3   Controls added to the form

In the next set of steps, you change the values assigned to some of the properties of the controls.

To change the values assigned to some of the properties of the controls:

1. Click the **Label1** control in the form. Sizing handles appear around the Label1 control, and the control's properties appear in the Properties window.

2. Change the values assigned to the following properties:

   AutoSize   **True**
   Font   **Tahoma, 20pt**
   Text   **Bill Calculator**

3. Click the **Label1** control in the form. Click **Format** on the menu bar, point to **Center in Form**, and then click **Horizontally**.

4. Click the **Label2** control in the form, then change the values assigned to the following properties:

   AutoSize   **True**
   Location   **24, 105**
   Text   **&Envelopes:**

5. Click the **Label3** control in the form, then change the values assigned to the following properties:

   AutoSize   **True**
   Location   **24, 136**
   Text   **&Pages:**

6. Click the **Label4** control in the form, then change the values assigned to the following properties:

   AutoSize   **True**
   Location   **24, 170**
   Text   **Total due:**

7. Click the **TextBox1** control in the form, then change the values assigned to the following properties:

(Name)	**txtEnvelopes**
Location	**112, 105**
Size	**32, 27**
Text	(empty)

8. Click the **TextBox2** control in the form, then change the values assigned to the following properties:

(Name)	**txtPages**
Location	**112, 136**
Size	**32, 27**
Text	(empty)

9. Click the **Label5** control in the form, then change the values assigned to the following properties:

(Name)	**lblTotal**
BorderStyle	**FixedSingle**
Location	**112, 170**
Size	**100, 25**
Text	(empty)
TextAlign	**MiddleCenter**

10. Click the **Button1** control in the form, then change the values assigned to the following properties:

(Name)	**btnCalc**
Location	**248, 105**
Size	**85, 25**
Text	**&Calculate**

11. Click the **Button2** control in the form, then change the values assigned to the following properties:

(Name)	**btnClear**
Location	**248, 136**
Text	**C&lear**

12. Click the **Button3** control in the form, then change the values assigned to the following properties:

(Name)	**btnExit**
Location	**248, 170**
Text	**E&xit**

13. Click the **btnExit** control in the form, then Ctrl+click the **btnClear** control, and then Ctrl+click the **btnCalc** control. This selects the three button controls, making the btnCalc control the reference control.

14. Click **Format** on the menu bar, point to **Make Same Size**, and then click **Both**. Click the **form** to deselect the selected controls.

15. Right-click the **form**, then click **Lock Controls**.

16. Save the solution. The completed interface is shown in Figure 2.4.

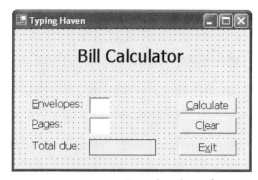

FIGURE 2.4   Completed interface

Now set the appropriate tab order for the controls. You specify the desired order using the TabIndex property. You can use the Properties list to set the TabIndex property; or, you can use the Tab Order option on the View menu.

To set the appropriate tab order:

1. Click **View** on the menu bar, and then click **Tab Order**. The current TabIndex value for each control appears in blue boxes on the form. The TabIndex values reflect the order in which each control was added to the form.

2. Place the mouse pointer on the **Envelopes:** label. A rectangle surrounds the label and the mouse pointer becomes a crosshair, as shown in Figure 2.5.

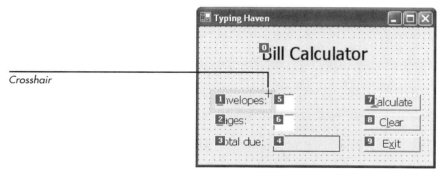

FIGURE 2.5   Crosshair positioned on the Envelopes: label

3. Click the **Envelopes:** label (or click the box containing the number 1). The number 0 replaces the number 1 in the box, and the color of the box changes from blue to white to indicate that you have set the control's TabIndex value.

4. Click the **txtEnvelopes** control, which appears to the immediate right of the Envelopes: label. The number 1 replaces the number 5 in the box, and the color of the box changes from blue to white.

5. Use Figure 2.6 to set the tab order for the remaining controls in the interface.

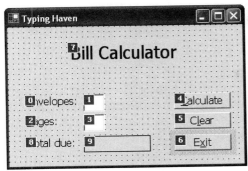

FIGURE 2.6   Correct TabIndex values shown in the form

HELP? If you make a mistake when setting the TabIndex values, press the Esc key on your keyboard and then repeat steps 1 through 5.

6. Press **Esc** to remove the TabIndex boxes from the form.

7. Save the solution.

Next, you code the Exit button's Click event procedure. (You learn how to code the Calculate and Clear buttons in Chapter 3.)

To code the Exit button's Click event procedure:

1. Right-click the **form**, then click **View Code** to open the Code Editor window.

2. If necessary, auto-hide the Solution Explorer and Properties windows so that you can view more of the Code Editor window.

3. Click the **Class Name** list arrow, and then click **btnExit** in the list.

4. Click the **Method Name** list arrow, and then click **Click** in the list.

5. Type **me.close()** and press **Enter**. See Figure 2.7.

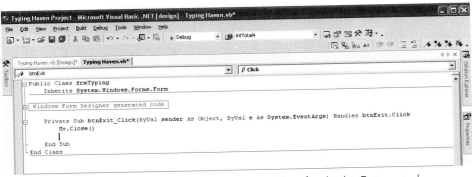

FIGURE 2.7   Completed Click event procedure for the btnExit control

You can use the Options dialog box to change the type, size, and color of the font used to display text in the Code Editor window.

6. Click **Tools** on the menu bar, and then click **Options**. If necessary, open the **Environment** folder, and then click **Fonts and Colors**. See Figure 2.8. (Do not be concerned if your settings are different from those shown in Figure 2.8.)

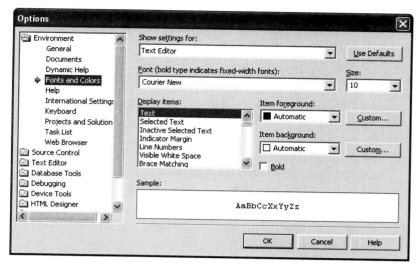

FIGURE 2.8   Options dialog box

7. Click the **Size** list arrow, and then click **12** in the list. Click the **OK** button to close the Options dialog box. The text in the Code Editor window appears in a larger size, as shown in Figure 2.9.

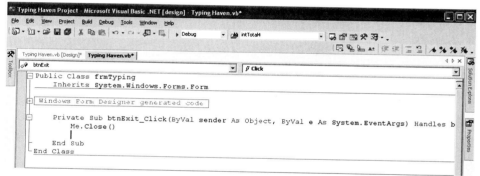

FIGURE 2.9   Code shown in a larger size font

8. Use the Options dialog box to return the font size to its original value.

Finally, close the Code Editor window, then save the solution and start the application.

To close the Code Editor window, then save the solution and start the application:

1. Click the **Close** button on the Code Editor window's title bar.
2. Click **File** on the menu bar, and then click **Save All**.
3. Click **Debug** on the menu bar, and then click **Start**. The blinking insertion point indicates that the txtEnvelopes control has the focus. See Figure 2.10.

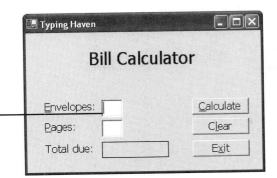

The blinking insertion point indicates that the text box has the focus

FIGURE 2.10 Typing Haven application

Verify that the TabIndex values and access keys work correctly.

4. Press the **Tab** key four times. The focus moves from the txtEnvelopes control to the txtPages control, and then to the btnCalc, btnClear, and btnExit controls.

5. Press and hold down the **Alt** key as you press the letter **e** on your keyboard, then release the Alt key. The focus moves to the txtEnvelopes control.

6. Press **Alt+p** to move the focus to the txtPages control.

7. Press **Alt+x** to select the Exit button. The computer processes the code in the Exit button's Click event procedure, which ends the application.

8. Close the Output window.

Now close the solution.

9. Click **File** on the menu bar, and then click **Close Solution**. Temporarily display the Solution Explorer window to verify that no solutions are open in the IDE.

LAB 2.2 FOSTER INDUSTRIES

Scenario The sales manager at Foster Industries wants an application that allows him to enter three monthly sales amounts. The application should calculate and display the average monthly sales amount.

Solution Discussion The Foster Industries application needs to provide areas for the user to enter the three monthly sales amounts; you will use text boxes for this purpose. The application also needs to display the average monthly sales amount; you will use a label control for this purpose, because the user should not be able to change the amount after it has been displayed. You also will use two button controls that allow the user to calculate the average monthly sales amount and exit the application.

TOE Chart

Task	Object	Event
1. Calculate the average monthly sales amount 2. Display the average monthly sales amount in the lblAvg control	btnCalc	Click
End the application	btnExit	Click
Display the average monthly sales amount (from btnCalc)	lblAvg	None
Get and display three monthly sales amounts	txtMonth1, txtMonth2, txtMonth3	None

FIGURE 2.11

User Interface

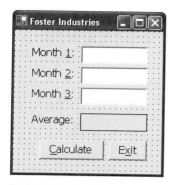

FIGURE 2.12

The information in the user interface shown in Figure 2.12 is arranged vertically. The controls are positioned two dots away from the edges of the form, and related controls are placed on succeeding dots. The buttons are positioned horizontally and are the same height. The borders of the controls are aligned wherever possible to minimize the number of different margins used in the interface. Labels that identify controls are left-aligned and, in this case, positioned to the left of the control they identify. The identifying labels end with a colon and are entered using sentence capitalization. The button captions, on the other hand, do not end with a colon and are entered using book title capitalization. Each identifying label and button caption contains either one word or a word followed by a number; additionally, each is meaningful and appears on one line in its respective control. All of the controls use the same font type and font size: Tahoma and 12pt. Access keys are assigned to each of the controls that can accept user input.

Activity

1. If necessary, start Visual Studio .NET.
2. Click **File** on the Visual Studio .NET menu bar, point to **New**, and then click **Project**. Use Figure 2.13 to complete the New Project dialog box.

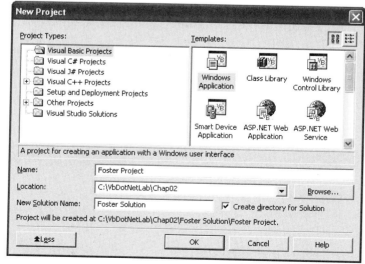

FIGURE 2.13

3. Click the **OK** button to close the New Project dialog box.

4. Change the form file object's name from Form1.vb to **Foster Form.vb**.

5. Change the form's name from Form1 to **frmFoster**.

6. Right-click **Foster Project** in the Solution Explorer window, and then click **Properties**. Change the Startup object to **frmFoster**, then click the **OK** button to close the Foster Project Property Pages dialog box.

7. Change the values assigned to the following properties of the form:

Font	**Tahoma, 12 pt**
Size	**255, 250**
StartPosition	**CenterScreen**
Text	**Foster Industries**

8. Save the solution.

Next, use the toolbox to add five label controls, three text boxes, and two buttons to the interface.

To add the appropriate controls:

1. Use the Label tool to add five label controls to the form.

2. Use the TextBox tool to add three text boxes to the form.

3. Use the Button tool to add two buttons to the form.

4. Position the controls as shown in Figure 2.14.

FIGURE 2.14   Controls added to the form

In the next set of steps, you change the values assigned to some of the properties of the controls.

To change the values assigned to some of the properties of the controls:

1. Click the **Label1** control, then Ctrl+click the **Label2**, **Label3**, and **Label4** controls. The four controls are now selected. Click **AutoSize** in the Properties window, then click the **list arrow** in the Settings box, and then click **True**. Click the **form** to deselect the controls.

2. Change the values assigned to the following properties of the Label1 control:

Location	**24, 24**
Text	**Month &1:**

3. Change the values assigned to the following properties of the Label2 control:

Location	**24, 56**
Text	**Month &2:**

4. Change the values assigned to the following properties of the Label3 control:

Location	**24, 88**
Text	**Month &3:**

5. Change the values assigned to the following properties of the Label4 control:

Location	**24, 128**
Text	**Average:**

6. Change the values assigned to the following properties of the Label5 control:

(Name)	**lblAvg**
BorderStyle	**FixedSingle**
Location	**100, 128**
Size	**100, 27**
Text	(empty)
TextAlign	**MiddleCenter**

7. Change the values assigned to the following properties of the TextBox1 control:

(Name)	**txtMonth1**
Location	**100, 24**
Size	**100, 27**
Text	(empty)

8. Change the values assigned to the following properties of the TextBox2 control:

(Name)	**txtMonth2**
Location	**100, 56**
Size	**100, 27**
Text	(empty)

9. Change the values assigned to the following properties of the TextBox3 control:

(Name)	**txtMonth3**
Location	**100, 88**
Size	**100, 27**
Text	(empty)

10. Change the values assigned to the following properties of the Button1 control:

(Name)	**btnCalc**
Location	**40, 170**
Size	**96, 30**
Text	**&Calculate**

11. Change the values assigned to the following properties of the Button2 control:

(Name)	**btnExit**
Location	**144, 170**
Size	**56, 30**
Text	**E&xit**

12. Change the form's Size property to **230, 255**.

13. Right-click the **form**, then click **Lock Controls**.

14. Save the solution. The completed interface is shown in Figure 2.15.

FIGURE 2.15   Completed interface

Now set the appropriate tab order for the controls.

To set the appropriate tab order:

1. Click **View** on the menu bar, and then click **Tab Order**. The current TabIndex value for each control appears in blue boxes on the form. The TabIndex values reflect the order in which each control was added to the form.

2. Use Figure 2.16 to set the tab order for the controls in the interface.

FIGURE 2.16   Correct TabIndex values shown in the form

HELP? If you make a mistake when setting the TabIndex values, press the Esc key on your keyboard and then repeat steps 1 and 2.

3. Press **Esc** to remove the TabIndex boxes from the form.

4. Save the solution.

Next, you code the Exit button's Click event procedure. (You learn how to code the Calculate button in Chapter 3.)

To code the Exit button's Click event procedure, then save the solution and start the application:

1. Right-click the **form**, then click **View Code** to open the Code Editor window.

2. If necessary, auto-hide the Solution Explorer and Properties windows so that you can view more of the Code Editor window.

3. Display the code template for the btnExit control's Click event procedure, then enter the statement that directs the computer to end the application. See Figure 2.17.

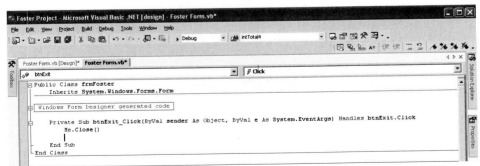

FIGURE 2.17   Completed Click event procedure for the btnExit control

4. Close the Code Editor window.

5. Save the solution, then start the application. See Figure 2.18.

FIGURE 2.18   Foster Industries application

Verify that the TabIndex values and access keys work correctly.

6. Press the **Tab** key four times. The focus moves from the txtMonth1 control to the txtMonth2 control, and then to the txtMonth3, btnCalc, and btnExit controls.

7. Press and hold down the **Alt** key as you press the number **1** on your keyboard, then release the Alt key. The focus moves to the txtMonth1 control.

8. Press **Alt+2** to move the focus to the txtMonth2 control, then press **Alt+3** to move the focus to the txtMonth3 control.

9. Press **Alt+x** to select the Exit button. The computer processes the code in the Exit button's Click event procedure, which ends the application.

10. Close the Output window, then close the solution. Temporarily display the Solution Explorer window to verify that no solutions are open in the IDE.

LAB 2.3 HARBORLIGHTS

Scenario The store manager of Harborlights wants an application that allows her to enter a sales amount. The application should calculate and display the sales tax (5%) and the total amount due.

Solution Discussion The Harborlights application needs to provide an area for the user to enter the sales amount; you will use a text box for this purpose. The application also needs to display the sales tax and the total amount due; you will use label controls for this purpose, because the user should not be able to change the amounts after they have been displayed. You also will provide a button control for calculating both the sales tax and total amount due, and a button control for exiting the application.

TOE Chart

Task	Object	Event
1. Calculate the sales tax 2. Calculate the total amount due 3. Display the sales tax in the lblTax control 4. Display the total amount due in the lblTotal control	btnCalc	Click
End the application	btnExit	Click
Display the sales tax (from btnCalc)	lblTax	None
Display the total amount due (from btnCalc)	lblTotal	None
Get and display the sales amount	txtSales	None

FIGURE 2.19

User Interface

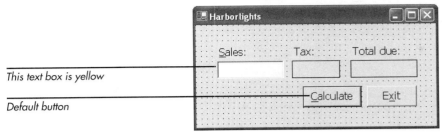

This text box is yellow

Default button

FIGURE 2.20

The information in the user interface shown in Figure 2.20 is arranged horizontally. The controls are positioned three dots away from the edges of the form, and related controls are placed on succeeding dots. The buttons are positioned horizontally and are the same height. The Calculate button is the default button. The borders of the controls are aligned wherever possible to minimize the number of different margins used in the interface. Labels that identify controls are left-aligned and, in this case, positioned above the control they identify. The identifying labels end with a colon and are entered using sentence capitalization. The button captions, on the other hand, do not end with a colon and are entered using book title capitalization. Each identifying label and button caption contains either one or two words; additionally, each is meaningful and appears on one line in its respective control. All of the controls use the same font type and font size: Tahoma and 12pt. Color is used sparingly in the interface, and serves only to bring attention to the text box used to enter the sales amount. Access keys are assigned to each of the controls that can accept user input.

Activity

1. If necessary, start Visual Studio .NET.
2. Create a new Visual Basic .NET Windows application. Name the solution **Harborlights Solution**. Name the project **Harborlights Project**. Save the application in the VbDotNetLab\ Chap02 folder.
3. Change the form file object's name from Form1.vb to **Harborlights Form.vb**.
4. Change the form object's name from Form1 to **frmHarborlights**.
5. Use the Harborlights Project Property Pages dialog box to set the Startup object to **frmHarborlights**.
6. Create the interface shown earlier in Figure 2.20. The interface contains five label controls, one text box, and two buttons. The control names are listed in Figure 2.19.
7. Click the **txtSales** control, then click **BackColor**. Click the **list arrow** in the Settings box, and then click the **Custom** tab. Click a **light yellow square** in the color palette.
8. Lock the controls in place on the form.
9. Set the appropriate tab order for the controls.
10. Code the Exit button's Click event procedure so that it ends the application.
11. Close the Code Editor window, then save the solution and start the application. See Figure 2.21.

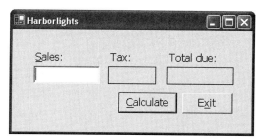

FIGURE 2.21   Harborlights application

12. Verify that the TabIndex values work correctly. Also verify that Alt+s sends the focus to the txtSales control.

13. Click the **Exit** button to close the application, then close the Output window.

14. Close the solution. Temporarily display the Solution Explorer window to verify that no solutions are open in the IDE.

BEYOND THE TEXT

LAB 2.4 SELLERS WAREHOUSE

Scenario   In this lab, you learn how to select (highlight) the existing text in a text box control when the control receives the focus.

Solution Discussion   You can use the SelectAll method to select the existing text in a text box. You enter the method in a text box's Enter event, which occurs when a text box receives the focus.

User Interface

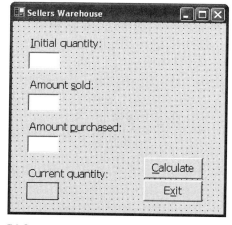

FIGURE 2.22

Activity

1. If necessary, start Visual Studio .NET.

2. Open the Sellers Warehouse Solution (Sellers Warehouse Solution.sln) file, which is contained in the VbDotNetLab\Chap02\Sellers Warehouse Solution folder.

HELP? If the designer window is not open, right-click Sellers Warehouse Form.vb in the Solution Explorer window, then click View Designer.

3. Start the application.

4. Type **35** in the Initial quantity box, and then press **Tab** to move the focus to the Amount sold box.

5. Type **10** in the Amount sold box, and then press **Tab** to move the focus to the Amount purchased box.

6. Type **15** in the Amount purchased box, and then press **Tab** three times to move the focus to the Initial quantity box. Notice that the insertion point appears after the number 35 in the box. See Figure 2.23.

Insertion point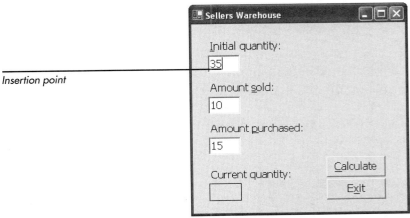

F I G U R E 2 . 2 3   Insertion point shown in the Initial quantity box

7. Press **Tab** to move the focus to the Amount sold box. Notice that the insertion point appears after the number 10 in the box.

8. Press **Tab** to move the focus to the Amount purchased box. Notice that the insertion point appears after the number 15 in the box.

9. Click the **Exit** button to end the application.

It is customary in Windows applications to have a text box's existing text selected (highlighted) when the text box receives the focus. You can select a text box's existing text by entering the SelectAll method in the text box's Enter event.

To code each text box's Enter event, then save the solution and start the application:

1. Open the Code Editor window.

2. Display the code template for the txtInitial control's Enter event procedure. Type **me.txtinitial.selectall()** in the procedure and press **Enter**.

3. Display the code template for the txtSold control's Enter event procedure. Type **me.txtsold.selectall()** in the procedure and press **Enter**.

4. Display the code template for the txtPurchased control's Enter event procedure. Type **me.txtpurchased.selectall()** in the procedure and press **Enter**. See Figure 2.24.

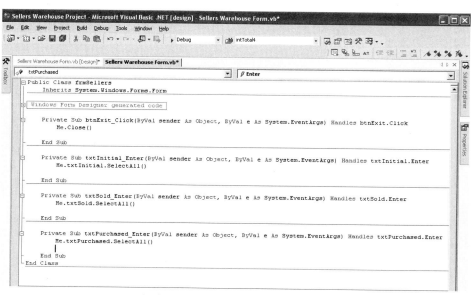

FIGURE 2.24 Code for the Sellers Warehouse application

5. Close the Code Editor window, then save the solution and start the application.

6. Type **35** in the Initial quantity box, **10** in the Amount sold box, and **15** in the Amount purchased box.

7. Press **Tab** three times to move the focus to the Initial quantity box. When the Initial quantity box receives the focus, the code in the txtInitial control's Enter event tells the computer to select (highlight) the control's existing text. See Figure 2.25.

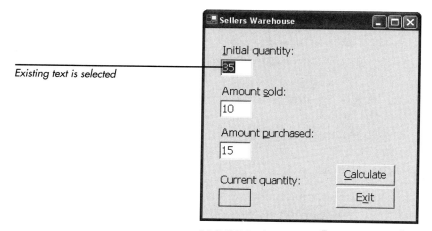

Existing text is selected

FIGURE 2.25 Existing text selected in the Initial quantity box

8. Type **2** in the Initial quantity box. Notice that the number 2 replaces the selected text in the box.

9. Press **Tab** to move the focus to the Amount sold box. The computer selects the existing text in the box.

10. Press **Tab** to move the focus to the Amount purchased box. The computer selects the existing text in the box.

11. Click the **Exit** button to end the application.

12. Close the Output window, then close the solution.

13. Exit Visual Studio .NET.

Variables, Constants, Methods, and Calculations

Labs included in this chapter:

LAB 3.1 TYPING HAVEN

Scenario In this lab, you complete the Typing Haven application you created in Lab 2.1 in Chapter 2. Recall that Typing Haven charges 5¢ per typed envelope and 15¢ per typed page. The company accountant wants an application to help her prepare bills. She will enter the number of typed envelopes and the number of typed pages. The application should calculate and display the total amount due.

Solution Discussion The user interface for the Typing Haven application contains two text boxes for entering the number of typed envelopes and the number of typed pages. It also contains a label control for displaying the total amount due. Additionally, it contains three buttons that allow the user to calculate the total amount due, clear the screen for the next calculation, and exit the application.

Only the Click event procedures for the three button controls need to be coded. The btnCalc control's Click event procedure will calculate the total amount due by adding together the charge for the typed envelopes and the charge for the typed pages. It will display the total amount due, formatted using the "C2" format, in the lblTotal control. The charge for the typed envelopes is calculated by multiplying the number of envelopes by 5¢, which is the charge per envelope. The charge for the typed pages is calculated by multiplying the number of pages by 15¢, which is the charge per page. After displaying the total amount due in the lblTotal control, the procedure will send the focus to the btnClear control, which, in most cases, is the next control the user will want to select.

The btnClear control's Click event procedure is responsible for clearing the screen for the next calculation. To clear the screen, the procedure will remove the user input—in this case, the number of typed envelopes and the number of typed pages—from the text boxes. It also will remove the contents of the label control that displays the total amount due. After removing the contents of the text boxes and label control, the procedure will send the focus to the txtEnvelopes control so that the user can begin entering the data for the next calculation.

The btnExit control's Click event procedure is responsible for ending the application. You coded this procedure in Lab 2.1 in Chapter 2.

TOE Chart

Task	Object	Event
1. Calculate the total amount due 2. Display the total amount due in the lblTotal control	btnCalc	Click
Clear the screen for the next calculation	btnClear	Click
End the application	btnExit	Click
Display the total amount due (from btnCalc)	lblTotal	None
Get and display the number of typed envelopes and the number of typed pages	txtEnvelopes, txtPages	None

FIGURE 3.1

User Interface

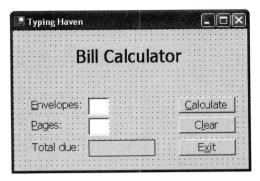

FIGURE 3.2

Pseudocode

btnCalc Click event procedure

1. calculate the total charge for the typed envelopes by multiplying the number of typed envelopes by .05
2. calculate the total charge for the typed pages by multiplying the number of typed pages by .15
3. calculate the total amount due by adding together the total charge for the typed envelopes and the total charge for the typed pages
4. display the total amount due in the lblTotal control
5. send the focus to the btnClear control

btnClear Click event procedure

1. clear the contents of the txtEnvelopes, txtPages, and lblTotal controls
2. send the focus to the txtEnvelopes control

btnExit Click event procedure

1. close the application

FIGURE 3.3

Activity

1. Use Windows to copy the Typing Haven Solution folder from the VbDotNetLab\Chap02 folder to the VbDotNetLab\Chap03 folder.
2. Start Visual Studio .NET.
3. Click **File** on the Visual Studio .NET menu bar, and then click **Open Solution**. The Open Solution dialog box opens.
4. Open the **VbDotNetLab\Chap03\Typing Haven Solution** folder. If necessary, click **Typing Haven Solution** (Typing Haven Solution.sln) in the list of filenames.
5. Click the **Open** button.
6. Right-click **Typing Haven.vb** in the Solution Explorer window, and then click **View Designer**. The user interface shown in Figure 3.2 appears on the screen.

First, enter the appropriate comments and Option statements in the Code Editor window. Recall that the `Option Explicit On` statement tells the computer to warn you if your code contains the name of an undeclared variable. The `Option Strict On` statement, on the other hand, tells the computer not to perform any implicit type conversions that might result in a loss of data.

To enter the appropriate comments and Option statements:

1. Right-click the **form**, and then click **View Code**. The Code Editor window opens and displays the btnExit control's Click event procedure, which you coded in Chapter 2.

2. The blinking insertion point should be positioned before the `Public Class frmTyping` line. Press **Enter** to insert a blank line above that line, and then press the **up arrow** on your keyboard to position the insertion point in the blank line.

3. Type the comments shown in Figure 3.4, replacing `<enter your name and date here>` with your name and the current date. Also type the Option statements shown in the figure.

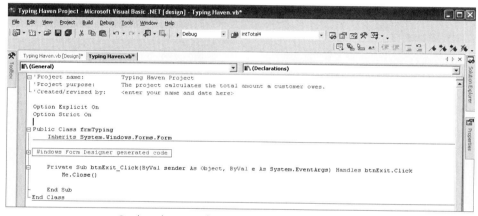

FIGURE 3.4   Code Editor window showing comments and Option statements

TIP •••• An easy way to enter the `Option Explicit On` statement is to type `option e` and then press the Spacebar. Then type `on` and press Enter. To type the `Option Strict On` statement, type `option s` and then press the Spacebar. Then type `on` and press Enter.

Now use the pseudocode shown earlier in Figure 3.3 to code the btnClear control's Click event procedure.

To code the btnClear control's Click event procedure:

1. Click the **Class Name** list arrow, and then click **btnClear** in the list.

2. Click the **Method Name** list arrow, and then click **Click** in the list. The code template for the btnClear_Click procedure appears in the Code Editor window.

According to the pseudocode, the btnClear_Click procedure should clear the contents of the txtEnvelopes, txtPages, and lblTotal controls. It then should send the focus to the txtEnvelopes control.

3. Type '**prepares the screen for the next calculation** and press **Enter** twice.

4. Type **me.txtenvelopes.text** = "" and press **Enter**.

TIP •••• An easy way to enter the `Me.txtEnvelopes.Text = " "` statement is to type `me.tx` and then press the period followed by the equal sign. Then type `" "` and press Enter.

5. Type **me.txtpages.text = ""** and press **Enter**.

6. Type **me.lbltotal.text = ""** and press **Enter**.

7. Type **me.txtenvelopes.focus()** and press **Enter**. The completed btnClear_Click procedure is shown in Figure 3.5.

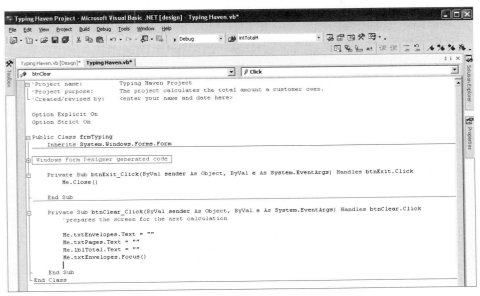

FIGURE 3.5 Completed btnClear_Click procedure

8. Save the solution by clicking **File** on the menu bar and then clicking **Save All**.

Next, use the pseudocode shown earlier in Figure 3.3 to code the btnCalc control's Click event procedure.

To code the btnCalc control's Click event procedure:

1. Click the **Class Name** list arrow, and then click **btnCalc** in the list.

2. Click the **Method Name** list arrow, and then click **Click** in the list. The code template for the btnCalc_Click procedure appears in the Code Editor window.

3. Type '**calculates the total amount due** and press **Enter** twice.

First, you will declare the procedure's constants and variables.

4. Type '**declare constants and variables** and press **Enter**.

The charge per typed envelope is .05 and the charge per typed page is .15. Because both charges will be the same for each calculation, you will assign the amounts to named constants. Recall that a named constant is a computer memory location whose contents cannot be changed while the application is running.

5. Type **const decCHARGE_PER_ENVELOPE as decimal = .05d** and press **Enter**. Recall that the letter d that follows the number .05 in the statement is one of the literal type characters in Visual Basic .NET. A literal type character forces a literal constant to assume a data type other than the one its form indicates. In this case, the d forces the Double number .05 to assume the Decimal data type.

6. Type **const decCHARGE_PER_PAGE as decimal = .15d** and press **Enter**.

You will use variables to store the number of typed envelopes, the number of typed pages, the total charge for the typed envelopes, the total charge for the typed pages, and the total due, because these amounts will be different for each calculation. Like a named constant, a variable is a computer memory location that can store data. Unlike a named constant, however, the contents of a variable can be changed while the application is running.

7. Type **dim decEnvelopes as decimal** and press **Enter**.

8. Type **dim decPages as decimal** and press **Enter**.

9. Type **dim decTotalEnvelopeCharge as decimal** and press **Enter**.

10. Type **dim decTotalPageCharge as decimal** and press **Enter**.

11. Type **dim decTotalDue as decimal** and press **Enter** twice.

Next, assign the input data to variables. In this case, the input data is the number of typed envelopes and the number of typed pages. The number of typed envelopes is stored in the Text property of the txtEnvelopes control; you will assign this value to the decEnvelopes variable. The number of typed pages is stored in the Text property of the txtPages control; you will assign this value to the decPages variable. When assigning the Text property of the controls to the Decimal variables, you will need to convert the Text property (which is a String) to Decimal.

12. Type **'assign input to variables** and press **Enter**.

13. Type **decenvelopes = convert.todecimal(me.txtenvelopes.text)** and press **Enter**.

14. Type **decpages = convert.todecimal(me.txtpages.text)** and press **Enter** twice.

The first step in the pseudocode for the btnCalc Click event procedure is to calculate the total charge for the typed envelopes. You calculate the amount by multiplying the number of typed envelopes by .05, which is the charge per typed envelope. The number of typed envelopes is stored in the decEnvelopes variable, and the charge per typed envelope is stored in the decCHARGE_PER_ENVELOPE named constant. You will assign the result to the decTotalEnvelopeCharge variable.

15. Type **'calculate the total charge for typed envelopes** and press **Enter**.

16. Type **dectotalenvelopecharge = decenvelopes * deccharge_per_envelope** and press **Enter**.

The second step is to calculate the total charge for the typed pages. You calculate the amount by multiplying the number of typed pages by .15, which is the charge per typed page. The number of typed pages is stored in the decPages variable, and the charge per typed page is stored in the decCHARGE_PER_PAGE named constant. You will assign the result to the decTotalPageCharge variable.

17. Type **'calculate the total charge for typed pages** and press **Enter**.

18. Type **dectotalpagecharge = decpages * deccharge_per_page** and press **Enter**.

The third step is to calculate the total amount due by adding together the total charge for the typed envelopes and the total charge for the typed pages. The total charge for the typed envelopes is stored in the decTotalEnvelopeCharge variable, and the total charge for the typed pages is stored in the decTotalPageCharge variable. You will store the sum of both amounts in the decTotalDue variable.

19. Type **'calculate the total due** and press **Enter**.

20. Type **dectotaldue = dectotalenvelopecharge + dectotalpagecharge** and press **Enter** twice.

The fourth step is to display in the lblTotal control the total amount due, which is stored in the decTotalDue variable. To display the variable's value in the control, you will need to convert the value to the String data type. You also will format the number with a dollar sign and two decimal places.

21. Type **'display the total due** and press **Enter**.

22. Type **me.lbltotal.text = dectotaldue.tostring("c2")** and press **Enter** twice.

The last step in the pseudocode for the btnCalc Click event procedure is to send the focus to the btnClear control.

23. Type **'set the focus** and press **Enter**.

24. Type **me.btnclear.focus()** and press **Enter**. The completed btnCalc_Click procedure is shown in Figure 3.6.

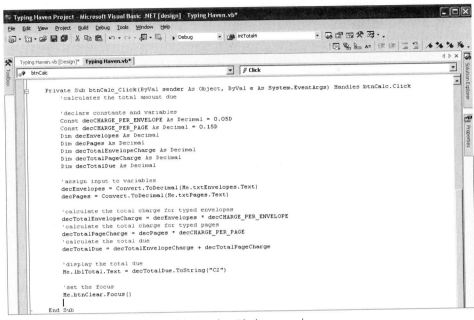

FIGURE 3.6   Completed btnCalc_Click procedure

Now that you have finished coding the application, you can test the application to verify that the code is working correctly.

To test the application:

1. Click **File** on the menu bar, and then click **Save All**.
2. Click **Debug** on the menu bar, and then click **Start**. The blinking insertion point indicates that the txtEnvelopes control has the focus.
3. Type **4** in the txtEnvelopes control and then press **Tab**.
4. Type **20** in the txtPages control and then click the **Calculate** button. The btnCalc_Click procedure calculates the total amount due and then displays the amount in the lblTotal control. The procedure also sends the focus to the Clear button, as shown in Figure 3.7.

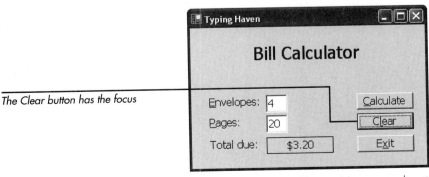

The Clear button has the focus

FIGURE 3.7   Typing Haven application

5. Click the **Clear** button. The btnClear_Click procedure removes the contents of the txtEnvelopes, txtPages, and lblTotal controls.

6. Click the **Exit** button. The btnExit_Click procedure ends the application.

7. Close the Output window, then close the Code Editor window.

You are finished with the solution, so you can close it.

8. Click **File** on the menu bar, and then click **Close Solution**. Temporarily display the Solution Explorer window to verify that the solution is closed.

LAB 3.2 FOSTER INDUSTRIES

Scenario In this lab, you complete the Foster Industries application you created in Lab 2.2 in Chapter 2. Recall that the sales manager at Foster Industries wants an application that allows him to enter three monthly sales amounts. The application should calculate and display the average monthly sales amount.

Solution Discussion The user interface for the Foster Industries application contains three text boxes for entering the three monthly sales amounts. It also contains a label control for displaying the average monthly sales amount. Additionally, it contains two buttons that allow the user to calculate the average monthly sales amount and exit the application.

Only the Click event procedures for the two button controls need to be coded. The btnCalc control's Click event procedure will calculate the average monthly sales amount by first adding together the three monthly sales amounts and then dividing the sum by three; it will display the quotient, formatted with a dollar sign and two decimal places, in the lblAvg control.

The btnExit control's Click event procedure is responsible for ending the application. You coded this procedure in Lab 2.2 in Chapter 2.

TOE Chart

Task	Object	Event
1. Calculate the average monthly sales amount 2. Display the average monthly sales amount in the lblAvg control	btnCalc	Click
End the application	btnExit	Click
Display the average monthly sales amount (from btnCalc)	lblAvg	None
Get and display three monthly sales amounts	txtMonth1, txtMonth2, txtMonth3	None

FIGURE 3.8

User Interface

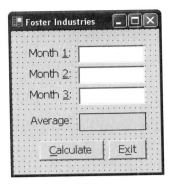

FIGURE 3.9

Pseudocode

---

btnCalc Click event procedure

1. calculate the average monthly sales amount by adding together the three monthly sales amounts, and then dividing the sum by 3
2. display the average monthly sales amount in the lblAvg control

btnExit Click event procedure

1. close the application

FIGURE 3.10

Activity

1. Use Windows to copy the Foster Solution folder from the VbDotNetLab\Chap02 folder to the VbDotNetLab\Chap03 folder.
2. If necessary, start Visual Studio .NET.
3. Open the **Foster Solution** (Foster Solution.sln) file contained in the VbDotNetLab\ Chap03\Foster Solution folder.
4. Right-click **Foster Form.vb** in the Solution Explorer window, and then click **View Designer**. The user interface shown in Figure 3.9 appears on the screen.

First, enter the appropriate comments and Option statements in the Code Editor window.

To enter the appropriate comments and Option statements:

1. Open the Code Editor window.
2. Insert a blank line above the `Public Class frmFoster` line. Type the following comments in the blank line, replacing *<enter your name and date here>* with your name and the current date. After typing the last comment, press **Enter** twice.

   'Project name: **Foster Project**
   'Project purpose: **The project calculates the average monthly sales amount.**
   'Created/revised by: *<enter your name and date here>*

3. Type the Option statement that tells the computer to warn you if your code contains the name of an undeclared variable, and then press **Enter**.

4. Type the Option statement that tells the computer not to perform any implicit type conversions that might result in a loss of data, and then press **Enter**.

Now use the pseudocode shown earlier in Figure 3.10 to code the btnCalc control's Click event procedure.

To code the btnCalc control's Click event procedure:

1. Display the code template for the btnCalc control's Click event procedure.

2. Type '**calculates the average monthly sales amount** and press **Enter** twice.

First, you will declare the variables that the procedure will use.

3. Type '**declare variables** and press **Enter**.

You will use variables to store the three monthly sales amounts and the average monthly sales amount, because these amounts will be different for each calculation.

4. Type the Dim statement to declare a Decimal variable named **decMonth1**, and then press **Enter**.

5. Type the Dim statement to declare a Decimal variable named **decMonth2**, and then press **Enter**.

6. Type the Dim statement to declare a Decimal variable named **decMonth3**, and then press **Enter**.

7. Type the Dim statement to declare a Decimal variable named **decAvg**, and then press **Enter** twice.

Next, assign the input data to variables. In this case, the input data is the three monthly sales amounts, which are stored in the Text property of the txtMonth1, txtMonth2, and txtMonth3 controls. You will assign the three values to the decMonth1, decMonth2, and decMonth3 variables. When assigning the values to the Decimal variables, you will need to convert the Text property (which is a String) to Decimal.

8. Type '**assign input to variables** and press **Enter**.

9. Type the statement that first converts the Text property of the txtMonth1 control to Decimal and then assigns the result to the decMonth1 variable, and then press **Enter**.

10. Type the statement that first converts the Text property of the txtMonth2 control to Decimal and then assigns the result to the decMonth2 variable, and then press **Enter**.

11. Type the statement that first converts the Text property of the txtMonth3 control to Decimal and then assigns the result to the decMonth3 variable, and then press **Enter** twice.

The first step in the pseudocode for the btnCalc Click event procedure is to calculate the average monthly sales amount. You calculate the amount by adding together the three monthly sales amounts—which are stored in the decMonth1, decMonth2, and decMonth3 variables—and then dividing the sum by 3. You will assign the result to the decAvg variable.

12. Type '**calculate the average monthly sales amount** and press **Enter**.

13. Type the statement that first adds together the contents of the decMonth1, decMonth2, and decMonth3 variables, and then divides the sum by three. The statement should assign the result to the decAvg variable. (Keep in mind that the division operator has a higher precedence than does the addition operator.) After entering the statement, press **Enter** twice.

The last step in the pseudocode is to display in the lblAvg control the average monthly sales amount, which is stored in the decAvg variable. To display the variable's value in the control, you will need to convert the value to the String data type. You also will format the value to display a dollar sign and two decimal places.

14. Type '**display the average monthly sales amount** and press **Enter**.

15. Type the statement that first converts the contents of the decAvg variable to the String data type, and then assigns the result to the lblAvg control. Format the result to display a dollar sign and two decimal places. After typing the statement, press **Enter**.

In Lab 2.4 in Chapter 2, you learned how to select (highlight) the existing text in a text box control when the control receives the focus.

To select the existing text in each text box control:

1. Display the code template for the txtMonth1 control's Enter event, then enter the appropriate statement.
2. Display the code template for the txtMonth2 control's Enter event, then enter the appropriate statement.
3. Display the code template for the txtMonth3 control's Enter event, then enter the appropriate statement.

Now that you have finished coding the application, you can test the application to verify that the code is working correctly.

To test the application:

1. Save the solution, then start the application.
2. Type **1500** as the sales amount for Month 1, **3000** as the sales amount for Month 2, and **2000** as the sales amount for Month 3.
3. Click the **Calculate** button. The btnCalc_Click procedure calculates the average monthly sales amount and then displays the amount in the lblAvg control, as shown in Figure 3.11.

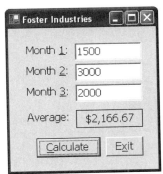

FIGURE 3.11   Foster Industries application

4. Press **Tab** twice to move the focus to the txtMonth1 control. The txtMonth1_Enter procedure selects the text box's existing text.
5. Press **Tab** to move the focus to the txtMonth2 control. The txtMonth2_Enter procedure selects the text box's existing text.
6. Press **Tab** to move the focus to the txtMonth3 control. The txtMonth3_Enter procedure selects the text box's existing text.
7. Click the **Exit** button. The btnExit_Click procedure ends the application.
8. Close the Output window, then close the Code Editor window.

You are finished with the solution, so you can close it.

9. Close the solution. Temporarily display the Solution Explorer window to verify that the solution is closed.

LAB 3.3 HARBORLIGHTS

Scenario In this lab, you complete the Harborlights application you created in Lab 2.3 in Chapter 2. Recall that the store manager of Harborlights wants an application that allows her to enter a sales amount. The application should calculate and display the sales tax and the total amount due. The sales tax rate is 5%.

Solution Discussion The user interface for the Harborlights application contains one text box for entering the sales amount. It also contains two label controls for displaying the sales tax and the total amount due. Additionally, it contains a button for calculating both the sales tax and the total amount due, and a button for exiting the application.

Only the Click event procedures for the two button controls need to be coded. The btnCalc control's Click event procedure will calculate the sales tax by multiplying the sales amount by the sales tax rate, which is 5%. It will calculate the total amount due by adding together the sales amount and the sales tax. It will display the sales tax, formatted with two decimal places, in the lblTax control. It will display the total amount due, formatted with a dollar sign and two decimal places, in the lblTotal control.

The btnExit control's Click event procedure is responsible for ending the application. You coded this procedure in Lab 2.3 in Chapter 2.

TOE Chart

Task	Object	Event
1. Calculate the sales tax 2. Calculate the total amount due 3. Display the sales tax in the lblTax control 4. Display the total amount due in the lblTotal control	btnCalc	Click
End the application	btnExit	Click
Display the sales tax (from btnCalc)	lblTax	None
Display the total amount due (from btnCalc)	lblTotal	None
Get and display the sales amount	txtSales	None

FIGURE 3.12

User Interface

FIGURE 3.13

Pseudocode

btnCalc Click event procedure

1. calculate the sales tax by multiplying the sales amount by 5%
2. calculate the total amount due by adding together the sales amount and the sales tax
3. display the sales tax in the lblTax control
4. display the total amount due in the lblTotal control

btnExit Click event procedure

1. close the application

FIGURE 3.14

Activity

1. Use Windows to copy the Harborlights Solution folder from the VbDotNetLab\Chap02 folder to the VbDotNetLab\Chap03 folder.
2. If necessary, start Visual Studio .NET.
3. Open the **Harborlights Solution** (Harborlights Solution.sln) file contained in the VbDotNetLab\Chap03\Harborlights Solution folder.
4. View the form in the designer window. The user interface shown in Figure 3.13 appears on the screen.

First, enter the appropriate comments and Option statements in the Code Editor window.

To enter the appropriate comments and Option statements:

1. Open the Code Editor window.
2. Insert a blank line above the `Public Class frmHarborlights` line. In the blank line, enter comments to identify the project's name and purpose. Also enter a comment that contains your name and the current date.
3. Enter the Option statement that tells the computer to warn you if your code contains the name of an undeclared variable.
4. Enter the Option statement that tells the computer not to perform any implicit type conversions that might result in a loss of data.

Now use the pseudocode shown earlier in Figure 3.14 to code the btnCalc control's Click event procedure.

To code the btnCalc control's Click event procedure:

1. Display the code template for the btnCalc control's Click event procedure.
2. Type '**calculates the sales tax and the total amount due** and press **Enter** twice.
3. Type '**declare the constant and variables** and press **Enter**.
4. Enter the statement to declare a named constant for the sales tax rate.
5. Enter the statements to declare the appropriate variables.

Next, assign the input data to a variable.

6. Type '**assign input to variable** and press **Enter**.

7. Enter the statement to assign to a variable the sales amount entered by the user.

The first step in the pseudocode for the btnCalc Click event procedure is to calculate the sales tax.

8. Type '**calculate the sales tax** and press **Enter**.

9. Enter the statement that calculates the sales tax and assigns the result to a variable.

The second step in the pseudocode is to calculate the total amount due.

10. Type '**calculate the total amount due** and press **Enter**.

11. Enter the statement that calculates the total amount due and assigns the result to a variable.

The third step in the pseudocode is to display the sales tax in the lblTax control.

12. Type '**display the sales tax** and press **Enter**.

13. Enter the statement that displays the sales tax, formatted with two decimal places, in the lblTax control.

The last step in the pseudocode is to display the total amount due in the lblTotal control.

14. Type '**display the total amount due** and press **Enter**.

15. Enter the statement that displays the total amount due, formatted with a dollar sign and two decimal places, in the lblTotal control.

Now that you have finished coding the application, you can test the application to verify that the code is working correctly.

To test the application:

1. Save the solution, then start the application.

2. Type **160** as the sales amount, and then press **Enter** to select the Calculate button, which is the default button in the interface. The btnCalc_Click procedure calculates the sales tax and the total due and then displays both amounts in the interface, as shown in Figure 3.15.

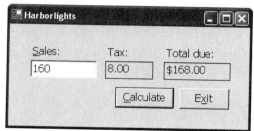

FIGURE 3.15 Harborlights application

3. Click the **Exit** button to end the application.

4. Close the Output window, then close the Code Editor window.

You are finished with the solution, so you can close it.

5. Close the solution. Temporarily display the Solution Explorer window to verify that the solution is closed.

BEYOND THE TEXT

LAB 3.4 SELLERS WAREHOUSE

Scenario In this lab, you learn how to use functions to convert a value to a specified data type.

Solution Discussion Rather than using the Convert class methods to convert a value to the desired data type, you can use the Conversion functions listed in Figure 3.16.

Function	Purpose
CDbl(*value*)	convert *value* to the Double data type
CInt(*value*)	convert *value* to the Integer data type
CSng(*value*)	convert *value* to the Single data type
CStr(*value*)	convert *value* to the String data type

FIGURE 3.16 Conversion functions

TOE Chart

Task	Object	Event
1. Calculate the current quantity 2. Display the current quantity in the lblInstock control	btnCalc	Click
End the application	btnExit	Click
Display the current quantity (from btnCalc)	lblInstock	None
Get and display the initial quantity	txtInitial	None
Get and display the quantity sold	txtSold	None
Get and display the quantity purchased	txtPurchased	None

FIGURE 3.17

User Interface

Sellers Warehouse

Initial quantity:

Amount sold:

Amount purchased:

Current quantity: Calculate

                       Exit

FIGURE 3.18

Pseudocode

btnCalc Click event procedure

1. calculate the current quantity by subtracting the quantity sold from the initial quantity, and then adding the quantity purchased to the result
2. display the current quantity in the lblInstock control

btnExit Click event procedure

1. close the application

F I G U R E   3 . 1 9

Activity

1. If necessary, start Visual Studio .NET.
2. Open the **Sellers Warehouse Solution** (Sellers Warehouse Solution.sln) file, which is contained in the VbDotNetLab\Chap03\Sellers Warehouse Solution folder. The user interface shown in Figure 3.18 appears on the screen.
3. Open the Code Editor window.
4. Use the pseudocode shown in Figure 3.19, and the conversion functions shown in Figure 3.16, to code the btnCalc_Click procedure.
5. Close the Code Editor window, then save the solution and start the application.
6. Type **15** in the Initial quantity box, **2** in the Amount sold box, and **12** in the Amount purchased box.
7. Click the **Calculate** button. The btnCalc_Click procedure calculates the current quantity in stock and then displays the amount in the lblInstock control, as shown in Figure 3.20.

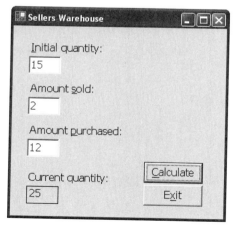

F I G U R E   3 . 2 0   Sellers Warehouse application

8. Click the **Exit** button to end the application.
9. Close the Output window, then close the solution.
10. Exit Visual Studio .NET.

Making Decisions in a Program

Labs included in this chapter:

LAB 4.1 JACOB HEATERS

Scenario Jacob Heaters wants an application that the store clerks can use to calculate the total amount due on an order. The clerk will enter the number of units ordered. The application should calculate the total amount due by multiplying the number of units ordered by the price per unit. The price per unit depends on the number of units ordered, as follows:

Number of units ordered	Price per unit
1 – 4	$10
5 – 10	9
Over 10	7

Solution Discussion The Jacob Heaters application needs to provide an area for the user to enter the number of units ordered; you will use a text box for this purpose. The application also needs to display the total amount due; you will use a label control for this purpose, because the user should not be able to change the amount after it has been displayed. You also will use a button control that allows the user to calculate the total amount due, and a button control for exiting the application.

TOE Chart

Task	Object	Event
1. Calculate the total amount due 2. Display the total amount due in the lblDue control	btnCalc	Click
End the application	btnExit	Click
Display the total amount due (from btnCalc)	lblDue	None
Get and display the number of units ordered	txtUnits	None

FIGURE 4.1

User Interface

lblDue

txtUnits

btnExit

btnCalc

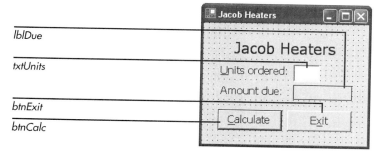

FIGURE 4.2

Objects, Properties, and Settings

Object	Property	Setting
Label1	AutoSize Font Text	True Tahoma, 18pt Jacob Heaters
Label2	AutoSize Text	True &Units ordered:
Label3	AutoSize Text	True Amount due:
Label4	Name BorderStyle Text TextAlign	lblDue FixedSingle (empty) MiddleCenter
TextBox1	Name Text	txtUnits (empty)
Button1	Name Text	btnCalc &Calculate
Button2	Name Text	btnExit E&xit

FIGURE 4.3

Tab Order

FIGURE 4.4

Pseudocode

btnCalc Click event procedure

1. if the txtUnits control contains data, and the data can be converted to a number

   assign the number of units ordered to a variable

   else

   assign 0 to the variable

   end if

2. calculate the total amount due as follows:

   if the number of units ordered is greater than or equal to 1 and less than or equal to 4

   total amount due = number of units ordered * 10

   else if the number of units ordered is greater than or equal to 5 and less than or equal to 10

   total amount due = number of units ordered * 9

   else if the number of units ordered is greater than 10

   total amount due = number of units ordered * 7

   else

   total amount due = 0

   display a message requesting the user to re-enter the number of units ordered

   end ifs

3. display the total amount due in the lblDue control

4. send the focus to the txtUnits control

btnExit Click event procedure

1. close the application

FIGURE 4.5

Activity

1. Start Visual Studio .NET.

2. Click **File** on the Visual Studio .NET menu bar, point to **New**, and then click **Project**. The New Project dialog box opens.

3. If necessary, click **Visual Basic Projects** in the Project Types list box, and click **Windows Application** in the Templates list box.

4. Type **Jacob Heaters Project** in the Name text box.

5. Use the **Browse** button, which appears to the right of the Location text box, to open the **VbDotNetLab\Chap04** folder.

6. If necessary, click the **More** button.

7. If necessary, select the **Create directory for Solution** check box.

8. Type **Jacob Heaters Solution** in the New Solution Name text box.

9. Click the **OK** button to close the New Project dialog box.

Now set the appropriate properties of the form file object and form object.

To set the appropriate properties of the form file object and form object:

1. Right-click **Form1.vb** in the Solution Explorer window, then click **Rename**. Change the form file object's name from Form1.vb to **Jacob Heaters Form.vb**.

2. Click the **form**, then click **(Name)** in the Properties window. Change the form object's name from Form1 to **frmJacob**.

3. Right-click **Jacob Heaters Project** in the Solution Explorer window, then click **Properties**. Click the **Startup object** list arrow, and then click **frmJacob** in the list. Click the **OK** button.

4. Click the **form**, then change the values assigned to the following properties:

Font	**Tahoma, 12 pt**
Size	**256, 224**
StartPosition	**CenterScreen**
Text	**Jacob Heaters**

5. Save the solution by clicking **File** on the menu bar, and then clicking **Save All**.

Next, add the appropriate controls to the interface, and then set the values of some of their properties.

To add the appropriate controls, then set the values of some of their properties:

1. Use the Label tool to add four label controls to the form.

2. Use the TextBox tool to add one text box to the form.

3. Use the Button tool to add two buttons to the form.

4. Use the chart shown in Figure 4.3 to set the properties of each control.

5. Position the controls as shown in Figure 4.2.

6. Lock the controls in place on the form.

7. Use Figure 4.4 to set the appropriate tab order.

8. Designate the Calculate button as the default button by setting the form's AcceptButton property to **btnCalc**.

9. Save the solution.

Now that the interface is complete, you can begin coding the application. First you will enter the appropriate comments and Option statements.

To enter the appropriate comments and Option statements:

1. Right-click the **form**, and then click **View Code** to open the Code Editor window.

2. Type the comments shown in Figure 4.6, replacing <enter your name and date here> with your name and the current date. Also type the Option statements shown in the figure.

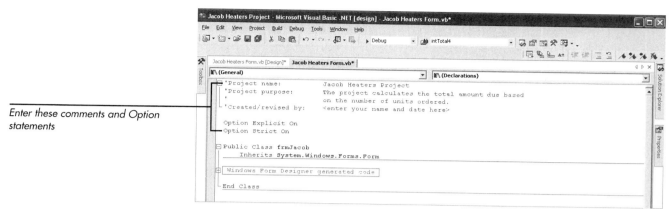

Enter these comments and Option statements

FIGURE 4.6   Code Editor window showing comments and Option statements

TIP •••• The font size used to display the code shown in Figure 4.6 was changed to 11 point for readability. As you learned in Lab 2.1 in Chapter 2, you can use the Options dialog box to change the type, size, and color of the font used to display text in the Code Editor window. You simply click Tools on the menu bar, and then click Options. You then open the Environment folder and click Fonts and Colors.

Now use the pseudocode shown earlier in Figure 4.5 to code the btnCalc control's Click event procedure.

To code the btnCalc control's Click event procedure:

1. Click the **Class Name** list arrow, and then click **btnCalc** in the list.
2. Click the **Method Name** list arrow, and then click **Click** in the list. The code template for the btnCalc_Click procedure appears in the Code Editor window.
3. Type '**calculates the total amount due** and press **Enter** twice.

First, you will declare the procedure's variables.

4. Type '**declare variables** and press **Enter**.

You will use a variable named intUnits to store the number of units ordered, and a variable named intDue to store the total amount due. A variable is appropriate in each case because the amount will be different for each calculation.

5. Type **dim intUnits as integer** and press **Enter**.
6. Type **dim intDue as integer** and press **Enter** twice.

The first step in the pseudocode for the btnCalc Click event procedure is to determine whether the txtUnits control contains data, and whether the data can be converted to a number. If the control contains data that can be converted to a number, the procedure will assign the data, which represents the number of units ordered, to the intUnits variable; otherwise, it will assign the number zero to the intUnits variable.

7. Type the comments and If/Else selection structure shown in Figure 4.7, and then position the insertion point as shown in the figure.

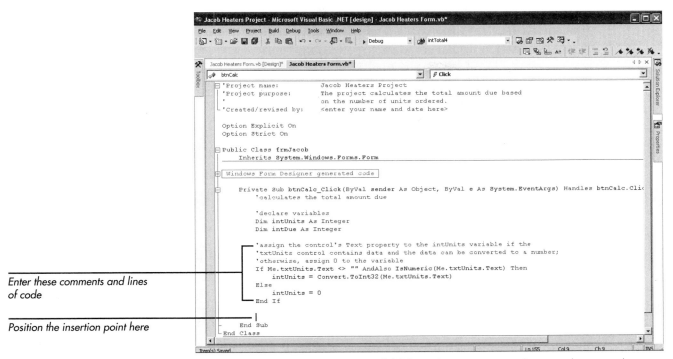

Enter these comments and lines of code

Position the insertion point here

FIGURE 4.7   Comments and If/Else selection structure shown in the procedure

The second step in the pseudocode is to calculate the total amount due, which is based on the number of units ordered. For example, if the number of units ordered is from one through four, the total amount due is calculated by multiplying the number of units ordered by $10. However, if the number of units ordered is from five through 10, the total amount due is calculated by multiplying the number of units ordered by $9. Similarly, if the number of units ordered is over 10, then the total amount due is calculated by multiplying the number of units ordered by $7. The number of units ordered is stored in the intUnits variable. You will assign the total amount due to the intDue variable.

8. Type the comments and partial If/ElseIf/Else selection structure shown in Figure 4.8, and then position the insertion point as shown in the figure.

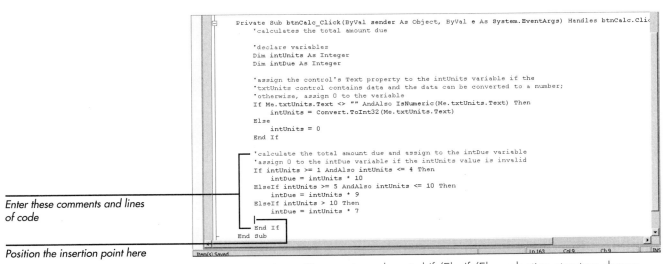

Enter these comments and lines of code

Position the insertion point here

FIGURE 4.8   Comments and partial If/ElseIf/Else selection structure shown in the procedure

If the intUnits variable contains a value that is not greater than or equal to one, the value is considered invalid. In that case, the procedure should assign the number zero to the intDue variable and then display a message requesting the user to re-enter the number of units ordered.

9. Type **Else** and press **Enter**, then type **intdue = 0** and press **Enter**.

10. Type **messagebox.show("Please re-enter the number of units.", "Jacob Heaters", messageboxbuttons.ok, messageboxicon.information, messageboxdefaultbutton. button1)**.

11. Insert line continuation characters in the MessageBox.Show method, as shown in Figure 4.9, and then position the insertion point as shown in the figure.

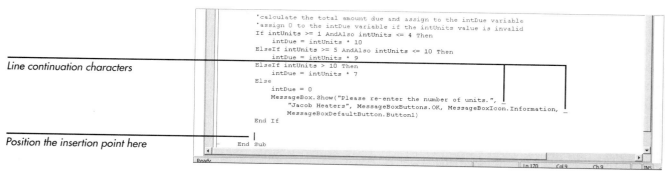

Line continuation characters

Position the insertion point here

FIGURE 4.9   Line continuation characters inserted in the MessageBox.Show method

The third step in the pseudocode is to display the total amount due in the lblDue control. The total amount due is stored in the intDue variable. To display the variable's value in the control, you will need to convert the value to the String data type. You also will format the number with a dollar sign and zero decimal places.

12. Type **'display the total amount due** and press **Enter**.

13. Type **me.lbldue.text = intdue.tostring("c0")** and press **Enter** twice.

The last step in the pseudocode for the btnCalc Click event procedure is to send the focus to the txtUnits control, which is the control that the user most likely will access after making a calculation.

14. Type **'set the focus** and press **Enter**.

15. Type **me.txtunits.focus()** and press **Enter**.

Next, you will code the btnExit control's Click event procedure. The procedure is responsible for ending the application.

To code the btnExit control's Click event procedure:

1. Display the code template for the btnExit control's Click event procedure.

2. Type **'ends the application** and press **Enter**.

3. Type **me.close()** and press **Enter**.

Now that you have finished coding the application, you can test the application to verify that the code is working correctly.

To test the application:

1. Save the solution by clicking **File** on the menu bar, and then clicking **Save All**.

2. Start the application by clicking **Debug** on the menu bar, and then clicking **Start**. The blinking insertion point indicates that the txtUnits control has the focus.

First, calculate the total amount due for five units. The amount should be $45, which is the number of units (5) multiplied by the price per unit ($9).

   3. Type **5** in the txtUnits control and then click the **Calculate** button. The btnCalc_Click procedure calculates the total amount due and then displays the amount ($45) in the lblDue control. The procedure also sends the focus to the txtUnits control, as shown in Figure 4.10.

Insertion point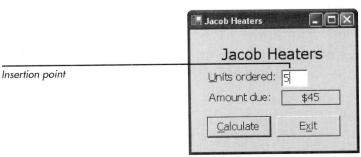

FIGURE 4.10 Location of insertion point shown in the interface

Notice that the blinking insertion point appears after the number 5 in the txtUnits control. Recall that it is customary in Windows applications to have a text box's existing text selected (highlighted) when the text box receives the focus. You will fix this problem in the next set of steps.

   4. Press **Tab** three times to move the focus from the txtUnits control to the Calculate button, the Exit button, and then back to the txtUnits control. Here again, notice that the text is not automatically selected when the text box receives the focus.

   5. Click the **Exit** button. The btnExit_Click procedure ends the application.

   6. Close the Output window.

As you learned in Lab 2.4 in Chapter 2, you can use the SelectAll method to select the existing text in a text box. To select the text when the text box receives the focus, you enter the SelectAll method in the text box's Enter event.

To enter the SelectAll method in the txtUnits control's Enter event, and then continue testing the application:

   1. Display the code template for the txtUnits control's Enter event.

   2. Type **'selects the existing text** and press **Enter**.

   3. Type **me.txtunits.selectall()** and press **Enter**.

   4. Save the solution, and then start the application.

   5. Type **5** in the txtUnits control and then click the **Calculate** button. The btnCalc_Click procedure calculates the total amount due and then displays the amount ($45) in the lblDue control. The procedure also sends the focus to the txtUnits control. Notice that the text box's existing text is automatically selected, as shown in Figure 4.11.

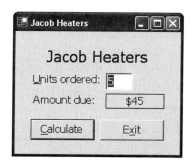

FIGURE 4.11   Existing text selected in the text box

6. Press **Tab** three times to move the focus from the txtUnits control to the Calculate button, the Exit button, and then back to the txtUnits control. Here again, notice that the text is automatically selected when the text box receives the focus.

Now calculate the total amount due for two units. The amount should be $20, which is the number of units (2) multiplied by the price per unit ($10).

7. Type **2** in the txtUnits control and then click the **Calculate** button. The btnCalc_Click procedure calculates the total amount due and then displays the amount ($20) in the lblDue control.

Finally, calculate the total amount due for 30 units. The amount should be $210, which is the number of units (30) multiplied by the price per unit ($7).

8. Type **30** in the txtUnits control and then press **Enter** to select the Calculate button, which is the default button on the form. The btnCalc_Click procedure calculates the total amount due and then displays the amount ($210) in the lblDue control, as shown in Figure 4.12. Notice that the text box's existing text is not selected.

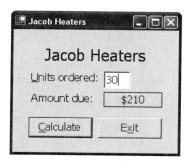

FIGURE 4.12   Existing text is not selected in the text box

When you use the Enter key to select the default button on a form, the button does not receive the focus; rather, the focus remains in the current control. In this case, for example, when you press the Enter key after typing the number of units in the txtUnits control, the Calculate button does not receive the focus; in this case, the focus remains in the txtUnits control. Because the txtUnits control does not lose the focus when you press the Enter key, the `Me.txtUnits.Focus()` statement in the btnCalc_Click procedure does not trigger the control's Enter event. As a result, the `Me.txtUnits.SelectAll()` statement in the control's Enter event procedure is not processed. You can fix this problem by entering the `Me.txtUnits.SelectAll()` statement in the btnCalc_Click procedure; you do this in the next set of steps.

9. Click the **Exit** button to end the application.

10. Close the Output window.

In the next set of steps, you enter the `Me.txtUnits.SelectAll()` statement in the btnCalc control's Click event procedure. You then continue testing the application's code.

To enter the SelectAll method in the btnCalc_Click procedure, and then continue testing the application:

1. In the blank line below the `Me.txtUnits.Focus()` statement, type '**select the existing text** and press **Enter**.
2. Type **me.txtunits.selectall()** and press **Enter**. The completed code for the Jacob Heaters application is shown in Figure 4.13.

```
'Project name:          Jacob Heaters Project
'Project purpose:       The project calculates the total amount due based
'                       on the number of units ordered.
'Created/revised by:    <enter your name and date here>

Option Explicit On
Option Strict On

Public Class frmJacob
    Inherits System.Windows.Forms.Form

[Windows Form Designer generated code]

    Private Sub btnCalc_Click(ByVal sender As Object, ByVal e As System.EventArgs)
        Handles btnCalc.Click
        'calculates the total amount due

        'declare variables
        Dim intUnits As Integer
        Dim intDue As Integer

        'assign the control's Text property to the intUnits variable if the
        'txtUnits control contains data and the data can be converted to a number;
        'otherwise, assign 0 to the variable
        If Me.txtUnits.Text <> "" AndAlso IsNumeric(Me.txtUnits.Text) Then
            intUnits = Convert.ToInt32(Me.txtUnits.Text)
        Else
            intUnits = 0
        End If

        'calculate the total amount due and assign to the intDue variable
        'assign 0 to the intDue variable if the intUnits value is invalid
        If intUnits >= 1 AndAlso intUnits <= 4 Then
            intDue = intUnits * 10
        ElseIf intUnits >= 5 AndAlso intUnits <= 10 Then
            intDue = intUnits * 9
        ElseIf intUnits > 10 Then
            intDue = intUnits * 7
        Else
            intDue = 0
            MessageBox.Show("Please re-enter the number of units.", _
                "Jacob Heaters", MessageBoxButtons.OK, MessageBoxIcon.Information, _
                MessageBoxDefaultButton.Button1)
        End If

        'display the total amount due
        Me.lblDue.Text = intDue.ToString("C0")
```

(Figure is continued on next page)

```
          'set the focus
          Me.txtUnits.Focus()
          'select the existing text
          Me.txtUnits.SelectAll()

    End Sub

    Private Sub btnExit_Click(ByVal sender As Object, ByVal e As System.EventArgs)
          Handles btnExit.Click
          'ends the application
          Me.Close()

    End Sub

    Private Sub txtUnits_Enter(ByVal sender As Object, ByVal e As System.EventArgs)
          Handles txtUnits.Enter
          'selects the existing text
          Me.txtUnits.SelectAll()

    End Sub
End Class
```

FIGURE 4.13   Completed code for the Jacob Heaters application

3. Save the solution, and then start the application.

4. Type **30** in the txtUnits control and then press **Enter** to select the Calculate button, which is the default button on the form. The btnCalc_Click procedure calculates the total amount due and then displays the amount ($210) in the lblDue control. Notice that the existing text is automatically selected in the text box.

5. Click the **Exit** button to end the application.

6. Close the Output window, and then close the Code Editor window.

You are finished with the solution, so you can close it.

7. Click **File** on the menu bar, and then click **Close Solution**.

LAB 4.2 WESTERN VETERINARIANS

Scenario Western Veterinarians wants an application that the receptionist can use to look up the doctor's fee for performing a specific medical procedure. The receptionist will need to enter a two-letter code that represents the procedure. The application should display the doctor's fee. The two-letter codes, along with their corresponding procedure names and fees, are as follows:

Code	Procedure	Fee
TC	Teeth Cleaning	$50
RV	Rabies Vaccination	15
OS	Other Shots	5
HW	Heartworm Test	15
FC	Fecal Check	5
OV	Office Visit	15

Solution Discussion The Western Veterinarians application needs to provide an area for the user to enter a two-letter code; you will use a text box for this purpose. You will set the text box's MaxLength property to two to prevent the user from entering more than two characters. You also will set its CharacterCasing property to Upper; this will ensure that the code is uppercase.

The application also needs to display the doctor's fee; you will use a label control for this purpose, because the user should not be able to change the fee after it has been displayed. You also will use a button control that allows the user to display the doctor's fee, and a button control for exiting the application.

TOE Chart

Task	Object	Event
Display the doctor's fee in the lblFee control	btnDisplay	Click
End the application	btnExit	Click
Display the doctor's fee (from btnDisplay)	lblFee	None
Get and display a two-letter code	txtCode	None

FIGURE 4.14

User Interface

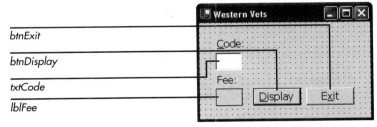

FIGURE 4.15

Objects, Properties, and Settings

Object	Property	Setting
frmVets	AcceptButton Font Size StartPosition Text	btnDisplay Tahoma, 12pt 265, 185 CenterScreen Western Vets
Label1	AutoSize Text	True &Code:
Label2	AutoSize Text	True Fee:
Label3	Name BorderStyle Text	lblFee FixedSingle (empty)
TextBox1	Name CharacterCasing MaxLength Text	txtCode Upper 2 (empty)
Button1	Name Text	btnDisplay &Display
Button2	Name Text	btnExit E&xit

FIGURE 4.16

Tab Order

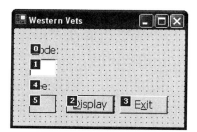

FIGURE 4.17

Pseudocode

btnDisplay Click event procedure
1. assign the code to a variable
2. assign the doctor's fee to a variable, as follows:
   code value:
TC	assign 50
RV, HW, OV	assign 15
OS, FC	assign 5
other	assign 0
	display an error message
3. display the doctor's fee in the lblFee control
4. send the focus to the txtCode control

btnExit Click event procedure
1. close the application

FIGURE 4.18

Activity

1. If necessary, start Visual Studio .NET.
2. Click **File** on the Visual Studio .NET menu bar, point to **New**, and then click **Project**. Use Figure 4.19 to complete the New Project dialog box.

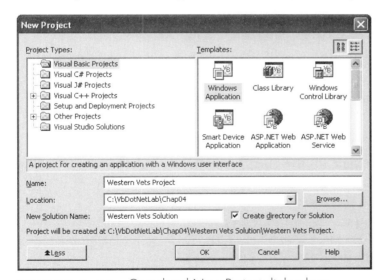

FIGURE 4.19 Completed New Project dialog box

3. Click the **OK** button to close the New Project dialog box.
4. Change the form file object's name from Form1.vb to **Western Vets Form.vb**.
5. Change the form's name from Form1 to **frmVets**.

6. Right-click **Western Vets Project** in the Solution Explorer window, and then click **Properties**. Change the Startup object to **frmVets**, then click the **OK** button to close the Western Vets Project Property Pages dialog box.

Next, add the appropriate controls to the interface, and then set the values of some of their properties.

7. Use the Label tool to add three label controls to the form.

8. Use the TextBox tool to add one text box to the form.

9. Use the Button tool to add two buttons to the form.

10. Use the chart shown in Figure 4.16 to set the properties of the form and each control.

11. Position the controls as shown in Figure 4.15.

12. Lock the controls in place on the form.

13. Use Figure 4.17 to set the appropriate tab order.

14. Save the solution.

Now that the interface is complete, you can begin coding the application. First you will enter the appropriate comments and Option statements.

To enter the appropriate comments and Option statements:

1. Open the Code Editor window.

2. Insert a blank line above the `Public Class frmVets` line. Type the following comments in the blank line, replacing *<enter your name and date here>* with your name and the current date. After typing the last comment, press **Enter** twice.

'**Project name:**	**Western Vets Project**
'**Project purpose:**	**The project displays the doctor's fee**
'	**corresponding to the code entered by the user.**
'**Created/revised by:**	*<enter your name and date here>*

3. Type the Option statement that tells the computer to warn you if your code contains the name of an undeclared variable, and then press **Enter**.

4. Type the Option statement that tells the computer not to perform any implicit type conversions that might result in a loss of data, and then press **Enter**.

Now use the pseudocode shown earlier in Figure 4.18 to code the btnDisplay control's Click event procedure.

To code the btnDisplay control's Click event procedure:

1. Display the code template for the btnDisplay control's Click event procedure.

2. Type '**displays the doctor's fee** and press **Enter** twice.

First, you will declare the procedure's variables.

3. Type '**declare variables** and press **Enter**.

You will use a variable named strCode to store the two-letter code entered by the user, and a variable named intFee to store the doctor's fee.

4. Type the statement to declare a String variable named **strCode**, and then press **Enter**.

5. Type the statement to declare an Integer variable named **intFee**, and then press **Enter** twice.

The first step in the pseudocode for the btnDisplay Click event procedure is to assign to a variable the code entered by the user.

6. Type '**assign input to variable** and press **Enter**.

7. Type the statement that assigns the contents of the txtCode control to the strCode variable, and then press **Enter** twice.

The second step in the pseudocode is to assign the doctor's fee to a variable. The fee is based on the code entered by the user and stored, using uppercase letters, in the strCode variable. The btnDisplay_Click procedure will use the strCode variable as the *selectorExpression* in a Select Case statement to determine the appropriate fee. The Select Case statement will compare the value stored in the variable to the following valid codes: TC, RV, HW, OV, OS, and FC. If the value matches one of the valid codes, the procedure will assign the corresponding fee to the intFee variable. However, if the value does not match one of the valid codes, the procedure will assign the number zero to the intFee variable and then display a message alerting the user that the code he or she entered is invalid.

7. Type the comment and Case selection structure shown in Figure 4.20, and then position the insertion point as shown in the figure.

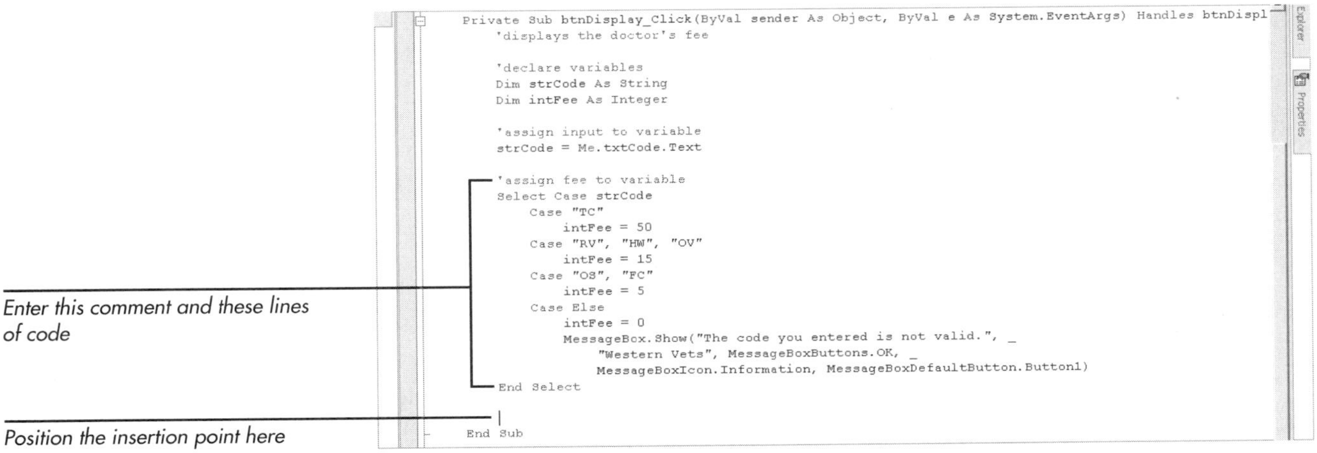

FIGURE 4.20 Comment and Case selection structure shown in the procedure

The third step in the pseudocode is to display the doctor's fee in the lblFee control. The fee is stored in the intFee variable.

8. Type '**display the fee** and press **Enter**.

9. Type the statement to assign the doctor's fee to the lblFee control. Format the fee to display a dollar sign and zero decimal places. After typing the statement, press **Enter** twice.

The last step in the pseudocode for the btnDisplay Click event procedure is to send the focus to the txtCode control, which is the control that the user most likely will access after displaying the fee.

10. Type '**set the focus** and press **Enter**.

11. Type the statement to send the focus to the txtCode control. After typing the statement, press **Enter**.

Next, code the btnExit control's Click event procedure. According to the pseudocode, the procedure is responsible for ending the application.

To code the btnExit control's Click event procedure:

1. Display the code template for the btnExit control's Click event procedure.

2. Type '**ends the application** and press **Enter**.

3. Type the statement that directs the computer to end the application, and then press **Enter**.

Now that you have finished coding the application, you can test the application to verify that the code is working correctly.

To test the application:

1. Save the solution, then start the application.

First, display the fee for an office visit. The fee should be $15.

2. Type **ov** as the code. Notice that the CharacterCasing property of the text box changes the two letters to uppercase.

3. Click the **Display** button. The btnDisplay_Click procedure displays the doctor's fee ($15) in the lblFee control, and then sends the focus to the txtCode control, as shown in Figure 4.21. Notice that the control's existing text is not automatically selected. You fix this problem in the next set of steps.

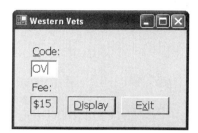

FIGURE 4.21 Western Veterinarians application

Next, try to enter more than two characters in the txtCode control.

4. Type the letter **a**. Notice that the txtCode control does not accept more then two characters.

5. Press **Tab** three times to move the focus from the txtCode control to the btnDisplay control, the btnExit control, and then back to the txtCode control. Here again, notice that the text box's existing text is not automatically selected.

Next, display the fee for Teeth Cleaning. The fee should be $50.

6. Press **Backspace** two times to delete the letters OV, type **tc** as the code, and then press **Enter** to select the Display button, which is the default button on the form. The btnDisplay_Click procedure displays the doctor's fee ($50) in the lblFee control, and then sends the focus to the txtCode control. Here again, notice that the text box's existing text is not automatically selected.

7. Click the **Exit** button. The btnExit_Click procedure ends the application.

8. Close the Output window.

In the next set of steps, you enter the code to automatically select the text box's existing text when the text box receives the focus. You also enter the code to automatically select the existing text when the user presses the Enter key to choose the default button.

To select the existing text in the txtCode control, and then continue testing the application:

1. Enter the statement to automatically select the txtCode control's existing text when the control receives the focus. Include an appropriate comment above the statement.

2. Enter the statement to automatically select the txtCode control's existing text when the user presses the Enter key to choose the Display button, which is the default button. Include an appropriate comment above the statement.

3. Save the solution, then start the application.

First, display the fee for Rabies Vaccination. The fee should be $15.

4. Type **rv** as the code, and then click the **Display** button. The btnDisplay_Click procedure displays the doctor's fee ($15) in the lblFee control, and then sends the focus to the txtCode control. The control's existing text should be automatically selected.

5. Press **Tab** three times to move the focus from the txtCode control to the btnDisplay control, the btnExit control, and then back to the txtCode control. The text box's existing text should be automatically selected.

Next, display the fee for Other Shots. The fee should be $5.

6. Type **os** as the code, and then press **Enter** to select the Display button, which is the default button. The btnDisplay_Click procedure displays the doctor's fee ($5) in the lblFee control. The existing text in the txtCode control should be automatically selected.

7. On your own, display the fee for HW (Heartworm Test). The fee should be $15.

8. On your own, display the fee for FC (Fecal Check). The fee should be $5.

Now test the application using an invalid code.

9. Type **ty** as the code, and then press **Enter**. The message box shown in Figure 4.22 appears on the screen.

FIGURE 4.22 Message box resulting from an invalid code entry

10. Click the **OK** button to close the message box, then click the **Exit** button to end the application.

11. Close the Output window, then close the Code Editor window.

You are finished with the solution, so you can close it.

12. Close the solution. Temporarily display the Solution Explorer window to verify that the solution is closed.

LAB 4.3 MARINE PACKING COMPANY

Scenario Marine Packing Company wants an application that the order department can use to calculate the price of an order. The order clerks will enter the number of units ordered, and whether the customer is a wholesaler or a retailer. The application should calculate the total amount due. The price per unit depends on both the customer type (wholesaler or retailer) and the number of units ordered, as follows:

Wholesaler:		Retailer:	
Number of units	Price per unit	Number of units	Price per unit
1 – 4	$10	1 – 3	$15
over 4	9	4 – 8	14
		over 8	12

Solution Discussion The Marine Packing Company application needs to provide areas for the user to enter the number of units ordered and a letter (either W or R) that identifies the customer as either a wholesaler or a retailer; you will use text boxes for this purpose. You will set to one the MaxLength property of the text box that contains the letter; this will prevent the user from entering more than one character. You also will set the text box's CharacterCasing property to Upper to ensure that the letter entry is uppercase.

The application also needs to display the total amount due; you will use a label control for this purpose, because the user should not be able to change the amount after it has been displayed. You also will use a button control that allows the user to calculate the total amount due, and a button control for exiting the application.

TOE Chart

Task	Object	Event
1. Calculate the total amount due 2. Display the total amount due in the lblDue control	btnCalc	Click
End the application	btnExit	Click
Display the total amount due (from btnCalc)	lblDue	None
Get and display a letter (either W or R)	txtType	None
Get and display the number of units	txtUnits	None

FIGURE 4.23

User Interface

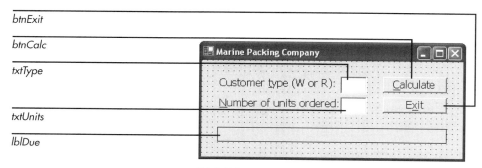

FIGURE 4.24

Objects, Properties, and Settings

Object	Property	Setting
frmMarine	Font Size StartPosition Text	Tahoma, 12pt 400, 185 CenterScreen Marine Packing Company
Label1	AutoSize Text	True Customer &type (W or R):
Label2	AutoSize Text	True &Number of units ordered:
Label3	Name BorderStyle Text TextAlign	lblDue FixedSingle (empty) MiddleCenter
TextBox1	Name CharacterCasing MaxLength Text	txtType Upper 1 (empty)
TextBox2	Name Text	txtUnits (empty)
Button1	Name Text	btnCalc &Calculate
Button2	Name Text	btnExit E&xit

FIGURE 4.25

Tab Order

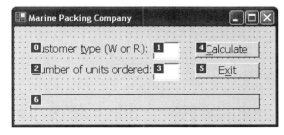

FIGURE 4.26

Pseudocode

btnCalc Click event procedure
1. assign the customer type to a variable
2. if the txtUnits control contains data, and the data can be converted to a number
        assign the number of units to a variable
    else
        assign 0 to the variable
    end if
3. determine the price per unit, as follows:
    customer type:
        W   assign the price per unit, as follows:
               if the number of units is greater than or equal to 1 and less than or equal to 4
                  assign 10 as the price per unit
               else if the number of units is greater than 4
                  assign 9 as the price per unit
               else
                  assign 0 as the price per unit
               end ifs
        R   assign the price per unit, as follows
               if the number of units is greater than or equal to 1 and less than or equal to 3
                  assign 15 as the price per unit
               else if the number of units is greater than or equal to 4 and less than or equal to 8
                  assign 14 as the price per unit
               else if the number of units is greater than 8
                  assign 12 as the price per unit
               else
                  assign 0 as the price per unit
               end ifs
        Other   assign 0 as the price per unit
                display an error message
4. calculate the total amount due by multiplying the number of units by the price per unit
5. display the message "Total amount due:" and the total amount due in the lblDue control
6. send the focus to the txtType control

btnExit Click event procedure
1. close the application

F I G U R E   4 . 2 7

Activity

1. If necessary, start Visual Studio .NET.
2. Create a new Visual Basic .NET Windows application. Name the solution **Marine Packing Solution**. Name the project **Marine Packing Project**. Save the application in the VbDotNetLab\Chap04 folder.
3. Change the form file object's name from Form1.vb to **Marine Packing Form.vb**.
4. Change the form object's name from Form1 to **frmMarine**.
5. Use the Marine Packing Project Property Pages dialog box to set the Startup object to **frmMarine**.
6. Add three label controls, two text boxes, and two buttons to the form.
7. Use the chart shown in Figure 4.25 to set the properties of the form and each control.
8. Position the controls as shown in Figure 4.24.
9. Lock the controls in place on the form.
10. Use Figure 4.26 to set the appropriate tab order.
11. Save the solution.

Now that the interface is complete, you can code the application.

To code the application:

1. Open the Code Editor window.
2. Insert a blank line above the `Public Class frmMarine` line. In the blank line, enter comments to identify the project's name and purpose. Also enter a comment that contains your name and the current date.
3. Enter the Option statement that tells the computer to warn you if your code contains the name of an undeclared variable.
4. Enter the Option statement that tells the computer not to perform any implicit type conversions that might result in a loss of data.
5. Display the code template for the btnCalc control's Click event procedure.
6. Type **'calculates the total amount due** and press **Enter** twice.
7. Type **'declare variables** and press **Enter**.
8. Enter the statements to declare the appropriate variables.
9. Use the pseudocode shown in Figure 4.27 to finish coding the btnCalc Click event procedure. Include meaningful comments in the code. Display the total amount due with a dollar sign and two decimal places.
10. Display the code template for the btnExit control's Click event procedure.
11. Type **'ends the application** and press **Enter**.
12. Type the statement that directs the computer to end the application, and then press **Enter**.
13. Enter (in the appropriate event procedure) the statement to automatically select the existing text in the txtType control when the control receives the focus. Include a meaningful comment above the statement.
14. Enter (in the appropriate event procedure) the code to automatically select the existing text in the txtUnits control when the control receives the focus. Include a meaningful comment above the statement.

Now that you have finished coding the application, you can test the application to verify that the code is working correctly.

To test the application:

1. Save the solution, then start the application.

First, display the total amount due for a retailer that orders 10 units. The message "Total amount due: $120.00" should appear in the lblDue control.

2. Type **r** as the customer type. Notice that the CharacterCasing property of the text box changes the letter to uppercase.

3. Type **10** as the number of units ordered, then click the **Calculate** button. The btnCalc_Click procedure displays the message "Total amount due: $120.00" in the lblDue control, and then sends the focus to the txtType control, as shown in Figure 4.28.

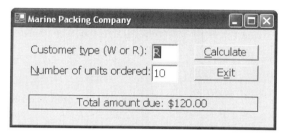

FIGURE 4.28   Marine Packing Company application

Next, try to enter more than one character in the txtType control.

4. Type **wh** as the customer type. Notice that the txtType control does not accept more than one character.

Now display the total amount due for a wholesaler that orders two units.

5. Press **Tab** to move the focus to the txtUnits control. The text box's existing text should be automatically selected. Type **2** and then click the **Calculate** button. The message "Total amount due: $20.00" appears in the lblDue control, which is correct.

Next, enter a negative number of units ordered.

6. Press **Tab** to move the focus to the txtUnits control. Type **-3** and then click the **Calculate** button. The message "Total amount due: $0.00" appears in the lblDue control, which is correct.

Now enter an invalid customer type.

7. Type **p** as the customer type, and then type **5** as the number of units. Click the **Calculate** button. A message box similar to the one shown in Figure 4.29 appears on the screen. (Your message box may not be identical to the one shown in the figure.)

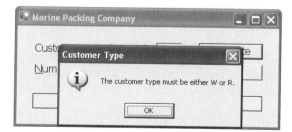

FIGURE 4.29   Message box resulting from an invalid customer type entry

8. Click the **OK** button to close the message box.

9. On your own, test the application using the following data:

Customer type	Units ordered
R	3
R	5
W	5

10. Click the **Exit** button to end the application.

11. Close the Output window, then close the Code Editor window.

You are finished with the solution, so you can close it.

12. Close the solution. Temporarily display the Solution Explorer window to verify that the solution is closed.

Beyond the Text

LAB 4.4 HARRINGTON PRIMARY CENTER

Scenario Susan Michaels teaches second grade at Harrington Primary Center. She wants an application that her students can use to practice adding numbers. The application should display the addition problem on the screen, then allow the student to enter the answer, and then verify that the answer is correct. If the student's answer is not correct, the application should give him or her as many chances as necessary to answer the problem correctly. In this lab, you will learn how to generate random numbers for the addition problems.

Solution Discussion Visual Studio .NET provides a pseudo-random number generator, which is a device that produces a sequence of numbers that meet certain statistical requirements for randomness. Pseudo-random numbers are chosen with equal probability from a finite set of numbers. The chosen numbers are not completely random because a definite mathematical algorithm is used to select them, but they are sufficiently random for practical purposes. To use the pseudo-random number generator in a procedure, you first create a Random object, typically using the syntax **Dim** *objectname* **As New Random**. The Random object represents the pseudo-random number generator in the procedure.

After creating a Random object, you can generate random integers using the Random.Next method. The syntax of the Random.Next method is *randomObject*.**Next**(*minValue, maxValue*), where *randomObject* is the name of a Random object. The *minValue* and *maxValue* arguments in the syntax must be integers, and *minValue* must be less than *maxValue*. The Random.Next method returns an integer that is greater than or equal to *minValue*, but less than *maxValue*. Figure 4.30 shows an example of using a Random object and the Random.Next method to generate random integers.

```
Dim rndGenerator As New Random
intNum = rndGenerator.Next(0, 51)
```

creates a Random object named rndGenerator, then assigns (to the intNum variable) a random integer that is greater than or equal to 0, but less than 51

FIGURE 4.30 Example of generating random integers

TOE Chart

Task	Object	Event
1. Generate two random numbers from 1 through 10 2. Display random numbers in lblNum1 and lblNum2	btnDisplay	Click
1. Calculate the correct answer to the addition problem 2. If the user's answer matches the correct answer, display "Great Job!" in lblResult 3. If the user's answer does not match the correct answer, display "Try again." in lblResult	btnCheck	Click
End the application	btnExit	Click
Display the first random number (from btnDisplay)	lblNum1	None
Display the second random number (from btnDisplay)	lblNum2	None
Display "Great Job!" or "Try again" message (from btnCheck)	lblResult	None
Get and display the user's answer	txtAnswer	None

FIGURE 4.31

User Interface

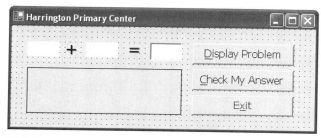

FIGURE 4.32

Pseudocode

btnDisplay Click event procedure

1. generate two random numbers that are greater than or equal to 1 but less than or equal to 10; assign the random numbers to variables
2. display the random numbers in the lblNum1 and lblNum2 controls
3. clear the contents of the lblResult control
4. send the focus to the txtAnswer control

btnCheck Click event procedure

1. if the lblNum1 control does not contain data

    display a message requesting the user to click the Display Problem button

else

    calculate the correct answer to the addition problem by adding together the random numbers in the controls

    if the txtAnswer control contains data, and the data can be converted to a number

        assign the user's answer to a variable

        if the user's answer is correct

          display "Great Job!" in the lblResult control

          clear the lblNum1, lblNum2, and txtAnswer controls

        else

          display "Try again." in the lblResult control

        end if

    else

        display a message requesting the user to re-enter the answer

    end if

end if

2. send the focus to the txtAnswer control

btnExit Click event procedure

1. close the application

FIGURE 4.33

Activity

1. If necessary, start Visual Studio .NET.
2. Open the **Harrington Solution** (Harrington Solution.sln) file, which is contained in the VbDotNetLab\Chap04\Harrington Solution folder. The user interface shown in Figure 4.32 appears on the screen.
3. Open the Code Editor window. Notice that the btnExit_Click and txtAnswer_Enter procedures have been coded for you.
4. Use the pseudocode shown in Figure 4.33 to code the btnDisplay control's Click event procedure.

5. Use the pseudocode shown in Figure 4.33 to code the btnCheck control's Click event procedure.

6. Save the solution, and then start the application.

7. Click the **Display Problem** button. The btnDisplay_Click procedure displays two random numbers in the lblNum1 and lblNum2 controls, and then places the focus in the txtAnswer control, as shown in Figure 4.34. (Because the numbers are random, your addition problem may be different from the one shown in the figure.)

Your numbers may be different

The blinking insertion point indicates that the text box has the focus

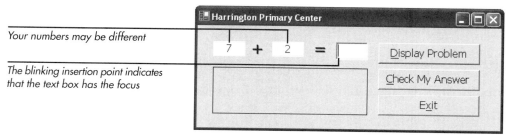

FIGURE 4.34 Harrington Primary Center application

8. Type the correct answer to the addition problem, and then click the **Check My Answer** button. The btnCheck_Click procedure displays the message "Great Job!" in the lblResult control. The procedure also removes the contents of the lblNum1, lblNum2, and txtAnswer controls, and then places the focus in the txtAnswer control.

9. Click the **Display Problem** button to display another addition problem.

10. This time, type an incorrect answer to the addition problem, and then click the **Check My Answer** button. The btnCheck_Click procedure displays the message "Try again." in the lblResult control, and then places the focus in the txtAnswer control. Notice that the procedure keeps the current addition problem on the screen, allowing you to enter another answer.

11. Type the correct answer to the addition problem, and then click the **Check My Answer** button. The btnCheck_Click procedure displays the message "Great Job!" in the lblResult control. The procedure also removes the contents of the lblNum1, lblNum2, and txtAnswer controls, and then places the focus in the txtAnswer control.

Now observe what happens when you click the Check My Answer button before displaying an addition problem on the screen.

12. Click the **Check My Answer** button. A message box similar to the one shown in Figure 4.35 appears on the screen. (Your message box may not be identical to the one shown in the figure.)

FIGURE 4.35 Message box that displays when the interface does not contain an addition problem

13. Click the **OK** button to close the message box.

Finally, observe what happens when you display an addition problem on the screen, but then click the Check My Answer button before entering a value in the txtAnswer control.

14. Click the **Display Problem** button, then click the **Check My Answer** button. A message box similar to the one shown in Figure 4.36 appears on the screen. (Your message box may not be identical to the one shown in the figure.)

FIGURE 4.36 Message box that displays when the txtAnswer control is empty

15. Click the **OK** button to close the message box.
16. Click the **Exit** button to end the application.
17. Close the Output window, and then close the Code Editor window.
18. Close the solution, and then exit Visual Studio .NET.

Repeating Program Instructions

Labs included in this chapter:

LAB 5.1 SHOPPERS HAVEN

Scenario The manager of Shoppers Haven wants an application that the store clerks can use to calculate the discounted price of an item, using discount rates from 10% through 30% in increments of 5%. The clerks will enter the item's original price. The application should display the discount rates and discounted prices in the interface.

Solution Discussion The Shoppers Haven application needs to provide an area for the user to enter the original price of the item; you will use a text box for this purpose. The application also needs to display the discount rates and discounted prices; you will use a label control for this purpose, because the user should not be able to change the rates and prices after they have been displayed. You also will use a button control that allows the user to calculate and display the discounted prices, and a button control for exiting the application.

TOE Chart

Task	Object	Event
1. Calculate the discounted prices using rates of 10% through 30%, in increments of 5% 2. Display the discount rates and discounted prices in the lblDiscountPrice control	btnCalc	Click
End the application	btnExit	Click
Display the discount rates and discounted prices (from btnCalc)	lblDiscountPrice	None
Get and display the item's original price	txtOriginal	None
Select the existing text		Enter

FIGURE 5.1

User Interface

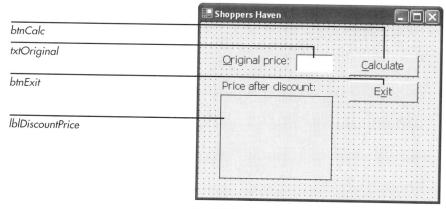

FIGURE 5.2

Objects, Properties, and Settings

Object	Property	Setting
Label1	AutoSize Text	True &Original price:
Label2	AutoSize Text	True Price after discount:
Label3	Name BorderStyle Size Text	lblDiscountPrice FixedSingle 168, 128 (empty)
TextBox1	Name Text	txtOriginal (empty)
Button1	Name Text	btnCalc &Calculate
Button2	Name Text	btnExit E&xit

FIGURE 5.3

Tab Order

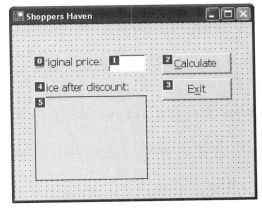

FIGURE 5.4

Pseudocode

btnCalc Click event procedure
1. clear the contents of the lblDiscountPrice control
2. if txtOriginal contains data, and the data can be converted to a number
    assign the contents of txtOriginal to a variable
    repeat for discount rates of 10% through 30% in increments of 5%
        calculate the discounted price by multiplying the original price by the current discount rate, and then subtracting the result from the original price
        display the discount rate and discounted price in lblDiscountPrice
    end repeat
  else
    display a message requesting the user to re-enter the original price
  end if
3. send the focus to the txtOriginal control

btnExit Click event procedure
1. close the application

txtOriginal Enter event procedure
1. select the existing text

F I G U R E   5 . 5

Activity

1. Start Visual Studio .NET.
2. Click **File** on the Visual Studio .NET menu bar, point to **New**, and then click **Project**. The New Project dialog box opens.
3. If necessary, click **Visual Basic Projects** in the Project Types list box, and click **Windows Application** in the Templates list box.
4. Type **Shoppers Haven Project** in the Name text box.
5. Use the **Browse** button to open the **VbDotNetLab\Chap05** folder.
6. If necessary, click the **More** button.
7. If necessary, select the **Create directory for Solution** check box.
8. Type **Shoppers Haven Solution** in the New Solution Name text box.
9. Click the **OK** button to close the New Project dialog box.

Now set the appropriate properties of the form file object and form object.

To set the appropriate properties of the form file object and form object:

1. Right-click **Form1.vb** in the Solution Explorer window, then click **Rename**. Change the form file object's name from Form1.vb to **Shoppers Haven Form.vb**.
2. Click the **form** and then click **(Name)** in the Properties window. Change the form object's name from Form1 to **frmShoppers**.

3. Right-click **Shoppers Haven Project** in the Solution Explorer window, then click **Properties**. Click the **Startup object** list arrow, and then click **frmShoppers** in the list. Click the **OK** button.

4. Click the **form**, then change the values assigned to the following properties:

Font	**Tahoma, 12 pt**
Size	**368, 304**
StartPosition	**CenterScreen**
Text	**Shoppers Haven**

5. Save the solution by clicking **File** on the menu bar, and then clicking **Save All**.

Next, add the appropriate controls to the interface, and then set the values of some of their properties.

To add the appropriate controls, then set the values of some of their properties:

1. Use the Label tool to add three label controls to the form.

2. Use the TextBox tool to add one text box to the form.

3. Use the Button tool to add two buttons to the form.

4. Use the chart shown in Figure 5.3 to set the properties of each control.

5. Position the controls as shown in Figure 5.2.

6. Lock the controls in place on the form.

7. Use Figure 5.4 to set the appropriate tab order.

8. Save the solution.

Now that the interface is complete, you can begin coding the application. First you will enter the appropriate comments and Option statements.

To enter the appropriate comments and Option statements:

1. Right-click the **form**, and then click **View Code** to open the Code Editor window.

2. Type the comments shown in Figure 5.6, replacing `<enter your name and date here>` with your name and the current date. Also type the Option statements shown in the figure.

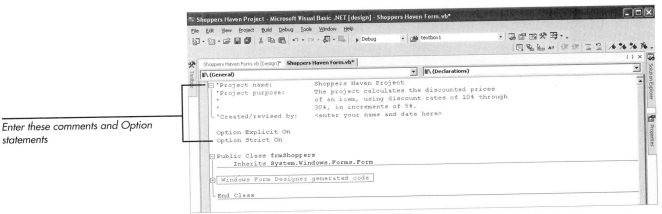

Enter these comments and Option statements

FIGURE 5.6 Code Editor window showing comments and Option statements

Now use the pseudocode shown earlier in Figure 5.5 to code the btnCalc control's Click event procedure.

To code the btnCalc control's Click event procedure:

1. Click the **Class Name** list arrow, and then click **btnCalc** in the list.

2. Click the **Method Name** list arrow, and then click **Click** in the list. The code template for the btnCalc_Click procedure appears in the Code Editor window.

3. Type '**calculates the discounted prices using discount rates of 10% through** and press **Enter**, then type '**30%, in increments of 5%** and press **Enter** twice.

First, you will declare the procedure's variables.

4. Type '**declare variables** and press **Enter**.

You will use a variable named decOriginalPrice to store the original price of the item, and a variable named decDiscountPrice to store each discounted price. You will use a variable named decDiscountRate as the counter variable in a loop that repeats its instructions for discount rates of 10% through 30% (in increments of 5%). A variable is appropriate in each case because the amount will be different for each calculation.

5. Type **dim decOriginalPrice as decimal** and press **Enter**.

6. Type **dim decDiscountPrice as decimal** and press **Enter**.

7. Type **dim decDiscountRate as decimal** and press **Enter** twice.

The first step in the pseudocode for the btnCalc Click event procedure is to clear the contents of the lblDiscountPrice control.

8. Type '**clear the contents of the lblDiscountPrice control** and press **Enter**, then type **me.lbldiscountprice.text = ""** and press **Enter** twice.

The next step is to determine whether the txtOriginal control contains data, and whether the data can be converted to a number. If the control contains data that can be converted to a number, the procedure will assign the data, which represents the original price, to the decOriginalPrice variable; otherwise, it will display a message requesting the user to re-enter the data.

9. Type the comments and If/Else selection structure shown in Figure 5.7, and then position the insertion point as shown in the figure.

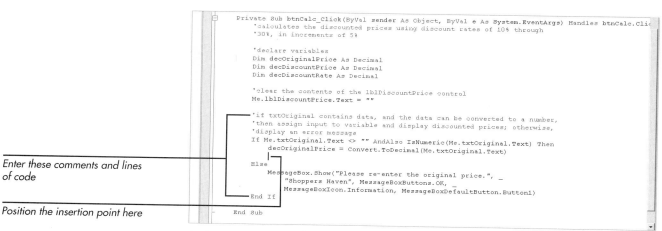

Enter these comments and lines of code

Position the insertion point here

```
Private Sub btnCalc_Click(ByVal sender As Object, ByVal e As System.EventArgs) Handles btnCalc.Cli
    'calculates the discounted prices using discount rates of 10% through
    '30%, in increments of 5%

    'declare variables
    Dim decOriginalPrice As Decimal
    Dim decDiscountPrice As Decimal
    Dim decDiscountRate As Decimal

    'clear the contents of the lblDiscountPrice control
    Me.lblDiscountPrice.Text = ""

    'if txtOriginal contains data, and the data can be converted to a number,
    'then assign input to variable and display discounted prices; otherwise,
    'display an error message
    If Me.txtOriginal.Text <> "" AndAlso IsNumeric(Me.txtOriginal.Text) Then
        decOriginalPrice = Convert.ToDecimal(Me.txtOriginal.Text)

    Else
        MessageBox.Show("Please re-enter the original price.", _
            "Shoppers Haven", MessageBoxButtons.OK, _
            MessageBoxIcon.Information, MessageBoxDefaultButton.Button1)
    End If

    End Sub
```

FIGURE 5.7   Comments and If/Else selection structure shown in the procedure

According to the pseudocode, after assigning the contents of the txtOriginal control to a variable, the procedure should use a loop that repeats its instructions for discount rates from 10% through 30%, in increments of 5%. You will use a For…Next statement to code the loop.

10. Type **for decdiscountrate = 0.1d to 0.3d step 0.05d** and press **Enter**.

The first instruction in the loop should calculate the discounted price by multiplying the original price by the current discount rate, and then subtracting the result from the original price. The original price is stored in the decOriginalPrice variable, and the current discount rate is stored in the decDiscountRate variable. The procedure should assign the discounted price to the decDiscountPrice variable.

11. Type **decdiscountprice = decoriginalprice - decoriginalprice * decdiscountrate** and press **Enter**.

The last instruction in the loop should display both the discount rate and discounted price in the lblDiscountPrice control. You will use the "P0" format to display a percent sign and zero decimal places in the discount rate, and the "N2" format to display two decimal places in the discounted price.

12. Type the additional lines of code indicated in Figure 5.8. Also change the Next clause to **Next decDiscountRate**, and then position the insertion point as shown in the figure.

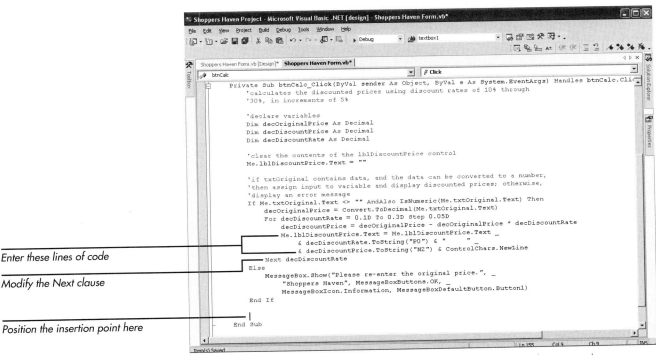

FIGURE 5.8   Completed For…Next statement shown in the procedure

The last step in the pseudocode for the btnCalc Click event procedure is to send the focus to the txtOriginal control, which is the control that the user most likely will access after making a calculation.

13. Type '**set the focus** and press **Enter**.

14. Type **me.txtoriginal.focus()** and press **Enter**.

Next, you will code the btnExit control's Click event procedure (which is responsible for ending the application) and the txtOriginal control's Enter event procedure (which is responsible for selecting the existing text).

To code the btnExit control's Click event procedure and the txtOriginal control's Enter event procedure:

1. Display the code template for the btnExit control's Click event procedure.
2. Type **'ends the application** and press **Enter**.
3. Type **me.close()** and press **Enter**.
4. Display the code template for the txtOriginal control's Enter event procedure.
5. Type **'selects the existing text** and press **Enter**.
6. Type **me.txtoriginal.selectall()** and press **Enter**.

Now that you have finished coding the application, you can test the application to verify that the code is working correctly.

To test the application:

1. Save the solution by clicking **File** on the menu bar, and then clicking **Save All**.
2. Start the application by clicking **Debug** on the menu bar, and then clicking **Start**. The blinking insertion point indicates that the txtOriginal control has the focus.

First, calculate the discounted prices for an item costing $100. The discounted prices should be 90.00, 85.00, 80.00, 75.00, and 70.00; these prices represent the original price ($100) multiplied by the discount rates (10%, 15%, 20%, 25%, and 30%).

3. Type **100** in the txtOriginal control, and then click the **Calculate** button. The btnCalc_Click procedure calculates the discounted prices and then displays the prices in the lblDiscountPrice control. The procedure also sends the focus to the txtOriginal control, whose Enter event selects the existing text, as shown in Figure 5.9.

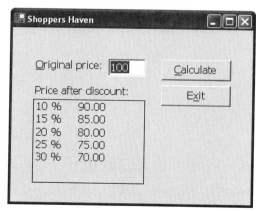

FIGURE 5.9   Shoppers Haven application

Now test the application using invalid data.

4. Type **k** in the txtOriginal control and then click the **Calculate** button. The btnCalc_Click procedure displays the message box shown in Figure 5.10.

FIGURE 5.10 Message box resulting from invalid data entry

5. Click the **OK** button to close the message box.

6. Click the **Exit** button. The btnExit_Click procedure ends the application.

7. Close the Output window, and then close the Code Editor window.

You are finished with the solution, so you can close it.

8. Click **File** on the menu bar, and then click **Close Solution**.

LAB 5.2 POWDER SKATING RINK

Scenario Powder Skating Rink holds a weekly ice skating competition. Competing skaters must perform a two-minute program in front of a panel of judges. The number of judges varies from week to week. At the end of a skater's program, each judge assigns a score of zero through 10 to the skater. The manager of the ice rink wants an application that can be used to calculate and display a skater's average score. The application also should display the skater's total score and the number of scores entered.

Solution Discussion The Powder Skating Rink application needs to provide an area for the user to enter each judge's score. Because the number of judges varies from week to week, you will use a dialog box rather than text boxes to get the scores. The dialog box, which will be displayed by the InputBox function, will allow the user to enter any number of scores. The user can click the Cancel button in the dialog box to indicate that he or she is finished entering scores.

The application also needs to display a skater's average score, as well as his or her total score and the number of scores entered; you will use label controls for this purpose, because the user should not be able to change these values after they have been displayed. You also will use a button control that allows the user to calculate and display the total and average scores and the number of scores entered. Additionally, you will use a button control for exiting the application.

TOE Chart

Task	Object	Event
1. Get each judge's score, which must be from zero through 10 2. Calculate the total score 3. Calculate the number of scores entered 4. Calculate the average score 5. Display the total score in lblTotalScores 6. Display the number of scores entered in lblNumberOfScores 7. Display the average score in lblAvg	btnCalc	Click
End the application	btnExit	Click
Display the total score (from btnCalc)	lblTotalScores	None
Display the number of scores entered (from btnCalc)	lblNumberOfScores	None
Display the average score (from btnCalc)	lblAvg	None

FIGURE 5.11

User Interface

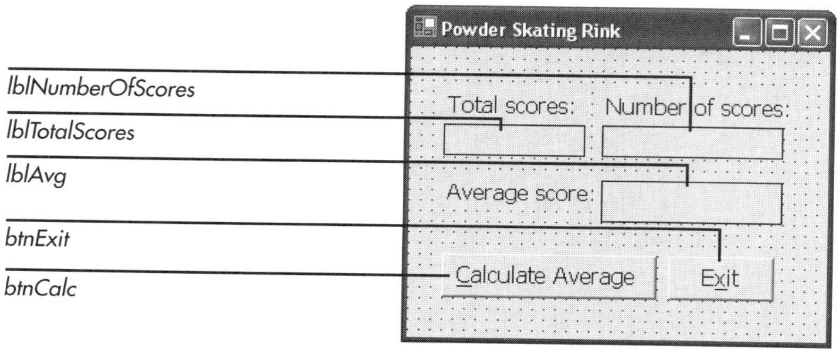

FIGURE 5.12

Objects, Properties, and Settings

Object	Property	Setting
frmPowder	Font	Tahoma, 12pt
	Size	304, 248
	StartPosition	CenterScreen
	Text	Powder Skating Rink
Label1	AutoSize	True
	Text	Total scores:
Label2	AutoSize	True
	Text	Number of scores:
Label3	AutoSize	True
	Text	Average score:
Label4	Name	lblTotalScores
	BorderStyle	FixedSingle
	Text	(empty)
	TextAlign	MiddleCenter
Label5	Name	lblNumberOfScores
	BorderStyle	FixedSingle
	Text	(empty)
	TextAlign	MiddleCenter
Label6	Name	lblAvg
	BorderStyle	FixedSingle
	Font	Tahoma, 24pt
	Text	(empty)
	TextAlign	MiddleCenter
Button1	Name	btnCalc
	Text	&Calculate Average
Button2	Name	btnExit
	Text	E&xit

FIGURE 5.13

Tab Order

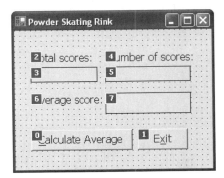

FIGURE 5.14

Pseudocode

btnCalc Click event procedure
1. clear the contents of the lblTotalScores, lblNumberOfScores, and lblAvg controls
2. use the InputBox function to get the first score; assign the score to the strScore variable
3. repeat until the user clicks the Cancel button in the InputBox function's dialog box
    if the score is numeric
        assign the score to the intScore variable
        if the score is greater than or equal to zero and less than 11
            add the score to the intTotalScores accumulator variable
            add 1 to the intNumberOfScores counter variable
        else
            assign True to the blnDataError variable to indicate that the score is invalid
        end if
    else
        assign True to the blnDataError variable to indicate that the score is invalid
    end if

    if the blnDataError variable contains True, which indicates that the score is invalid
        display a message informing the user that the score must be from 0 through 10
        reset the blnDataError variable to False
    end if

    use the InputBox function to get another score; assign the score to the strScore variable
    end repeat
4. display the contents of the intTotalScores accumulator variable in lblTotalScores
5. display the contents of the intNumberOfScores counter variable in lblNumberOfScores
6. if the intNumberOfScores counter variable contains a value that is greater than 0
    calculate the average score by dividing the intTotalScores accumulator variable by the intNumberOfScores counter variable; assign the result to the decAvg variable
    end if
7. display the contents of the decAvg variable in lblAvg

btnExit Click event procedure
1. close the application

FIGURE 5.15

Activity

1. If necessary, start Visual Studio .NET.
2. Click **File** on the Visual Studio .NET menu bar, point to **New**, and then click **Project**. Use Figure 5.16 to complete the New Project dialog box.

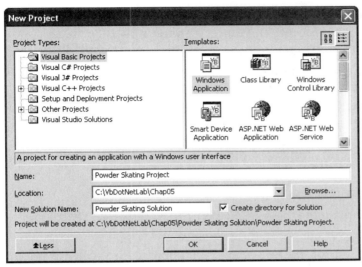

FIGURE 5.16 Completed New Project dialog box

3. Click the **OK** button to close the New Project dialog box.
4. Change the form file object's name from Form1.vb to **Powder Skating Form.vb**.
5. Change the form's name from Form1 to **frmPowder**.
6. Right-click **Powder Skating Project** in the Solution Explorer window, and then click **Properties**. Change the Startup object to **frmPowder**, then click the **OK** button to close the Powder Skating Project Property Pages dialog box.

Next, add the appropriate controls to the interface, and then set the values of some of their properties.

7. Use the Label tool to add six label controls to the form.
8. Use the Button tool to add two buttons to the form.
9. Use the chart shown in Figure 5.13 to set the properties of the form and each control.
10. Position the controls as shown in Figure 5.12.
11. Lock the controls in place on the form.
12. Use Figure 5.14 to set the appropriate tab order.
13. Save the solution.

Now that the interface is complete, you can begin coding the application. First you will enter the appropriate comments and Option statements.

To enter the appropriate comments and Option statements:

1. Open the Code Editor window.

2. Insert a blank line above the `Public Class frmPowder` line. Type the following comments in the blank line, replacing *<enter your name and date here>* with your name and the current date. After typing the last comment, press **Enter** twice.

   'Project name: **Powder Skating Project**

   'Project purpose: **The project calculates a skater's average score.**

   'Created/revised by: *<enter your name and date here>*

3. Type the Option statement that tells the computer to warn you if your code contains the name of an undeclared variable, and then press **Enter**.

4. Type the Option statement that tells the computer not to perform any implicit type conversions that might result in a loss of data, and then press **Enter**.

Now use the pseudocode shown earlier in Figure 5.15 to code the btnCalc control's Click event procedure.

To code the btnCalc control's Click event procedure:

1. Display the code template for the btnCalc control's Click event procedure.

2. Type '**calculates the average score** and press **Enter** twice.

First, you will declare the procedure's variables. The procedure will use six variables named strScore, intScore, intNumberOfScores, intTotalScores, blnDataError, and decAvg.

3. Type '**declare variables** and press **Enter**.

4. Type the statement to declare a String variable named **strScore**, and then press **Enter**. The strScore variable will store the string returned by the InputBox function. The string might be a valid score, an invalid score, or a zero-length string (if the user clicks the Cancel button).

5. Type the statement to declare an Integer variable named **intScore**, and then press **Enter**. The intScore variable will store the score after it is converted to an integer.

6. Type the statement to declare an Integer variable named **intNumberOfScores**, and then press **Tab**. Type '**counter** and press **Enter**. The intNumberOfScores variable will be used as a counter variable to keep track of the number of scores entered.

7. Type the statement to declare an Integer variable named **intTotalScores**, and then press **Tab**. Type '**accumulator** and press **Enter**. The intTotalScores variable will be used as an accumulator variable to keep track of the skater's total score.

8. Type the statement to declare a Boolean variable named **blnDataError**, and then press **Enter**. The procedure will use the Boolean variable blnDataError to keep track of whether the score entered by the user is valid.

9. Type the statement to declare a Decimal variable named **decAvg**, and then press **Enter** twice. The decAvg variable will be used to store the skater's average score.

The first step in the pseudocode for the btnCalc Click event procedure is to clear the contents of three label controls.

10. Type '**clear the labels** and press **Enter**.

11. Type the statements to clear the contents of the lblTotalScores, lblNumberOfScores, and lblAvg controls. After typing the last statement, press **Enter** twice.

The second step in the pseudocode is to use the InputBox function to get the first score, and assign the score to the strScore variable. (Recall that the InputBox function returns a string.) The syntax of the InputBox function is **InputBox(***prompt*[, *title*][, *defaultResponse*]**)**. In the syntax, *prompt* is the message you want displayed inside the dialog box, *title* is the text you want displayed in the dialog box's title bar, and *defaultResponse* is the text you want displayed in the input area of the dialog box. The *title* and *defaultResponse* arguments are optional.

In this case, you will use the concatenated string "Score " & Convert.ToString (intNumberOfScores + 1) for the *prompt* argument; this will display the message "Score 1" in the dialog box. You will use the string "Powder Skating Rink" for the *title* argument, and the string "0" for the *defaultResponse* argument.

12. Type '**get first score** and press **Enter**.

13. Type **strScore = inputbox("Score " & convert.tostring(intnumberofscores + 1), _** and press **Enter**. Press **Tab**, then type **"Powder Skating Rink", "0")** and press **Enter**.

The third step in the pseudocode is a loop that repeats its instructions until the user clicks the Cancel button in the InputBox function's dialog box. Recall that when the user clicks the Cancel button, the InputBox function returns a zero-length (or empty) string.

14. Type '**process the loop until the user clicks Cancel** and press **Enter**.

15. Type **do until strscore = ""** and press **Enter**.

The first instruction in the loop should determine whether the score entered by the user is numeric.

16. Type **if isnumeric(strscore) then** and press **Enter**.

If the score is numeric, the selection structure's true path should convert the score to an integer and then assign the result to the intScore variable. Otherwise, its false path should assign the Boolean value True to the blnDataError variable to indicate that the score is invalid; in this case, the score is invalid because it is not numeric.

17. Type the additional comment and lines of code shown in Figure 5.17, then position the insertion point as indicated in the figure.

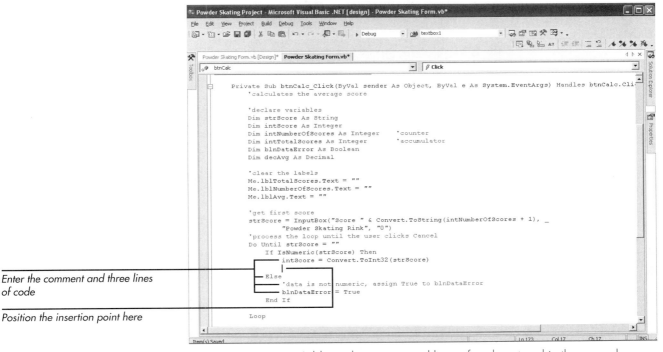

FIGURE 5.17 Additional comment and lines of code entered in the procedure

After assigning the score to the intScore variable, the selection structure's true path should use a nested selection structure to determine whether the score is in the appropriate range. In this case, the appropriate range is the numbers zero through 10. If the score is in-range, then the nested selected structure's true path should add the score to the intTotalScores accumulator variable, and add the number one to the intNumberOfScores counter variable. If the score is not in-range, then the nested selection structure's false path should assign the Boolean value True to the blnDataError variable to indicate that the score is invalid; in this case, the score is invalid because it is not in-range.

18. Enter the appropriate nested selection structure. Include comments to explain the code in both paths.

The second instruction in the loop is another selection structure that checks the value stored in the blnDataError variable. If the blnDataError variable contains the Boolean value True, it indicates that the score entered by the user is invalid. In that case, the selection structure's true path should display a message informing the user that the score must be from 0 through 10. It then should reset the blnDataError variable to False.

19. Position the insertion point two lines below the last End If clause, but above the Loop clause. Type '**display a message if the data is not valid, then reset the** and press **Enter**. Type '**blnDataError variable to False** and press **Enter**.

20. Enter the appropriate selection structure. Use the MessageBox.Show method to display the message.

The last instruction in the loop is to use the InputBox function to get another score, and assign the score to the strScore variable.

21. Position the insertion point two lines below the last End If clause, but above the Loop clause. Type '**get another score** and press **Enter**.

22. Type **strScore = inputbox("Score " & convert.tostring(intnumberofscores + 1), _** and press **Enter**. Press **Tab**, then type **"Powder Skating Rink", "0")**. You have now finished coding the third step in the procedure's pseudocode.

The fourth and fifth steps in the pseudocode are to display the contents of the intTotalScores accumulator variable and the contents of the intNumberOfScores counter variable in the lblTotalScores and lblNumberOfScores controls, respectively.

23. Position the insertion point two lines below the Loop clause, but above the End Sub clause. Type '**display accumulator and counter in label controls** and press **Enter**.

24. Type the statement to display the contents of the intTotalScores variable in the lblTotalScores control, and then press **Enter**.

25. Type the statement to display the contents of the intNumberOfScores variable in the lblNumberOfScores control, and then press **Enter** twice.

The sixth step in the pseudocode is a selection structure that determines whether the intNumberOfScores counter variable contains a value that is greater than zero. (Recall that division by zero is undefined and will cause the application to end abruptly with an error.) If the value is greater than zero, the selection structure's true path should calculate the average score by dividing the intTotalScores accumulator variable by the intNumberOfScores counter variable. The result should be assigned to the decAvg variable.

26. Type '**if intNumberOfScores is greater than zero, then calculate the average score** and press **Enter**.

27. Type the statement to calculate the average score and assign the result to the decAvg variable, and then press **Enter** twice.

The last step in the pseudocode for the btnCalc Click event procedure is to display the contents of the decAvg variable in the lblAvg control.

28. Type '**display the average score** and press **Enter**.
29. Type the statement to display the average score in the lblAvg control. Use the "N1" format style. You now have finished coding the btnCalc Click event procedure.

Next, code the btnExit control's Click event procedure. According to the pseudocode, the procedure is responsible for ending the application.

To code the btnExit control's Click event procedure:

1. Display the code template for the btnExit control's Click event procedure.
2. Type '**ends the application** and press **Enter**.
3. Type the statement that directs the computer to end the application, and then press **Enter**.

Now that you have finished coding the application, you can test the application to verify that the code is working correctly.

To test the application:

1. Save the solution, then start the application.

First, display the average score for a skater earning scores of 10, 8, 6, and 8.

2. Click the **Calculate Average** button. The btnCalc_Click procedure displays the dialog box shown in Figure 5.18.

FIGURE 5.18   *Dialog box displayed by the btnCalc_Click procedure*

3. Type **10** as Score 1 and then click the **OK** button. The procedure adds the number 10 to the intTotalScores accumulator, giving 10. It also adds the number 1 to the intNumberOfScores counter variable, giving 1.
4. Type **8** as Score 2 and then press **Enter** to select the OK button. The procedure adds the number 8 to the intTotalScores accumulator, giving 18. It also adds the number 1 to the intNumberOfScores counter variable, giving 2.
5. Type **6** as Score 3 and then press **Enter**. The procedure adds the number 6 to the intTotalScores accumulator, giving 24. It also adds the number 1 to the intNumberOfScores counter variable, giving 3.

Before entering the last score, observe what happens when you enter a letter rather than a number, and when you enter a number that is not in-range.

6. Type **a** as Score 4 and then press **Enter**. The procedure displays a message box similar to the one shown in Figure 5.19.

FIGURE 5.19   *Message box resulting from entering invalid data*

7. Press **Enter** to select the OK button, which closes the message box.

8. Type **25** as Score 4 and then press **Enter**. The procedure displays a message box similar to the one shown in Figure 5.19. Press **Enter** to close the message box.

Now enter the skater's fourth score, which is 8.

9. Type **8** as Score 4 and then press **Enter**. The procedure adds the number 8 to the intTotalScores accumulator, giving 32. It also adds the number 1 to the intNumberOfScores counter variable, giving 4.

10. Click the **Cancel** button to indicate that you are finished entering the scores. The btnCalc_Click procedure displays the contents of the intTotalScores and intNumberOfScores variables in the interface. It then calculates the average score and displays the score in the lblAvg control, as shown in Figure 5.20.

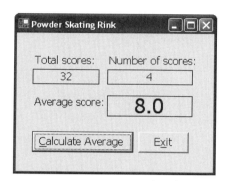

FIGURE 5.20 Powder Skating Rink application

11. Click the **Exit** button. The btnExit_Click procedure ends the application.

12. Close the Output window, then close the Code Editor window.

You are finished with the solution, so you can close it.

13. Close the solution. Temporarily display the Solution Explorer window to verify that the solution is closed.

LAB 5.3 GUESSING GAME

Scenario In this lab, you code an application that allows the user 10 chances to guess a random number generated by the computer. Each time the user makes an incorrect guess, the application will display a message that tells the user either to guess a higher number or to guess a lower number. If the user guesses the random number, the application will display a "Congratulations!" message. However, if the user is not able to guess the random number after 10 tries, the application will display the random number in a message.

Solution Discussion The Guessing Game application needs to provide an area for the user to enter each guess; you will use the InputBox function to display a dialog box for this purpose. The application also will use a label control to display the values that the user has already guessed. Additionally, the application will use two button controls: one for starting the game and the other for exiting the application.

TOE Chart

Task	Object	Event
1. Generate a random number between 1 and 100 2. Get from 1 to 10 guesses from the user 3. Display the user's guesses in lblGuesses 4. If the current guess is greater than the random number, display a message requesting the user to enter a lower number 5. If the current guess is less than the random number, display a message requesting the user to enter a higher number 6. If the current guess is equal to the random number, display a "Congratulations!" message 7. If the user does not guess the random number after 10 tries, display a message containing the random number	btnPlay	Click
End the application	btnExit	Click
Display the user's guesses (from btnPlay)	lblGuesses	None

FIGURE 5.21

User Interface

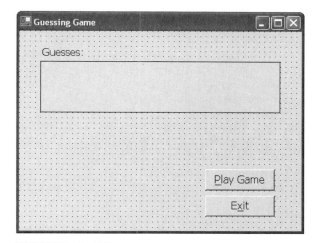

FIGURE 5.22

Pseudocode

btnPlay Click event procedure
1. clear the contents of the lblGuesses control
2. generate a random number from 1 through 100
3. repeat until the random number is guessed or the user makes 10 guesses
>   use the InputBox function to get a guess; assign to strGuess
>   if the user clicks the Cancel button
>   exit the loop
>   else if strGuess is numeric
>   assign strGuess to intGuess
>   end ifs
>   display the guess in lblGuesses
>   add 1 to the intNumberOfGuesses counter variable
>   if the guess is less than the random number
>   change the InputBox function's prompt to "Enter a higher number:"
>   else if the guess is greater than the random number
>   change the InputBox function's prompt to "Enter a lower number:"
>   else assign True to the blnNumberWasGuessed variable to indicate that
>   the number was guessed
>   end ifs
>   end repeat
4. if the random number was guessed
>   display the "Congratulations!" message
>   else
>   display the random number in a message
>   end if

btnExit Click event procedure
1. close the application

FIGURE 5.23

Activity

1. If necessary, start Visual Studio .NET.
2. Click **File** on the Visual Studio .NET menu bar, and then click **Open Solution**. The Open Solution dialog box opens.
3. Open the **VbDotNetLab\Chap05\Guessing Game Solution** folder, then click **Guessing Game Solution** (Guessing Game Solution.sln) in the list of filenames.
4. Click the **Open** button. The user interface shown in Figure 5.22 appears on the screen.

Now use the pseudocode shown in Figure 5.23 to code the application. The btnExit control's Click event procedure has already been coded for you, so you just need to code the btnPlay control's Click event procedure.

To code the btnPlay control's Click event procedure:

1. Open the Code Editor window.

2. Replace the `<enter your name and date here>` text with your name and the current date.

3. Scroll down to view the entire code template for the btnPlay control's Click event procedure, then position the insertion point as shown in Figure 5.24.

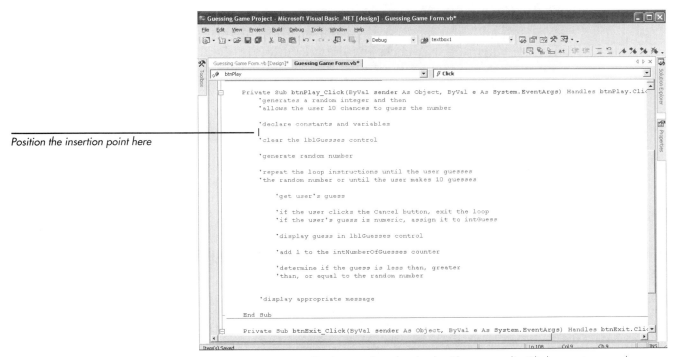

Position the insertion point here

FIGURE 5.24   Code template for the btnPlay control's Click event procedure

First, declare the procedure's constants and variables.

4. Enter the statements to declare three String constants named strFIRSTPROMPT, strHIGHERPROMPT, and strLOWERPROMPT. Assign the string "Enter a number from 1 through 100:" to the strFIRSTPROMPT constant, the string "Enter a higher number:" to the strHIGHERPROMPT constant, and the string "Enter a lower number:" to the strLOWERPROMPT constant.

5. Enter the statement to declare a Random object named rndGenerator. Recall that you learned how to create a Random object in Lab 4.4 in Chapter 4. The Random object will represent the pseudo-random number generator in the procedure.

6. Enter the statement to declare an Integer variable named intRandomNumber. The variable will store the random number produced by the random number generator.

7. Enter the statement to declare a String variable named strGuess. The variable will store the string returned by the InputBox function.

8. Enter the statement to declare an Integer variable named intGuess to store the user's guess after it has been converted to an Integer.

9. Enter the statement to declare an Integer variable named intNumberOfGuesses. The variable will be used as a counter variable to keep track of the number of guesses the user has made. Include the comment **'counter variable** at the end of the statement.

10. Enter the statement to declare a Boolean variable named blnNumberWasGuessed. The variable will be used to keep track of whether the user guessed the random number.

11. Enter the statement to declare a String variable named strPrompt. Initialize the variable using the strFIRSTPROMPT constant. The strPrompt variable will be used as the *prompt* argument in the InputBox function. Initially, the strPrompt variable will contain the string "Enter a number from 1 through 100:". Later in the procedure, the strHIGHERPROMPT and strLOWERPROMPT constants will be used to change the strPrompt variable's value to either "Enter a higher number:" or "Enter a lower number:".

12. Use the pseudocode shown in Figure 5.23, as well as the comments in the procedure, to finish coding the btnPlay Click event procedure. Recall that you learned how to generate a random number in Lab 4.4 in Chapter 4. Use the `Exit Do` statement to exit the Do...Loop structure when the user clicks the Cancel button in the InputBox function's dialog box. Display the user's guesses horizontally in the lblGuesses control; use two space characters to separate each guess. When coding Step 4 in the pseudocode, use the MessageBox.Show method to display the appropriate messages.

Now that you have finished coding the application, you can test the application to verify that the code is working correctly.

To test the application:

1. Save the solution, then start the application.

2. Click the **Play Game** button. The InputBox function in the btnPlay_Click procedure displays a dialog box similar to the one shown in Figure 5.25.

Dialog box

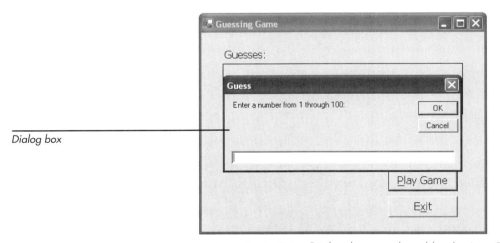

FIGURE 5.25 Dialog box produced by the InputBox function

3. Type **50** in the dialog box, and then click the **OK** button. The btnPlay_Click procedure displays the number 50 in the lblGuesses control. If you guessed the random number, the procedure also displays a message box that contains a "Congratulations!" message. However, if you did not guess the random number, the procedure displays a dialog box that contains one of two different messages, depending on whether the random number is (in this case) greater than 50 or less than 50. Figure 5.26 shows the message that appears when the random number is greater than the number 50. If your random number is less than 50, the message in the dialog box will say "Enter a lower number:".

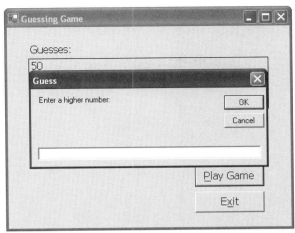

FIGURE 5.26   Message that appears when the random number is greater than the number 50

4. If you did not guess the random number, then continue guessing numbers until you either guess the random number or make 10 incorrect guesses. Figure 5.27 shows the message box that appears when you guess the random number. Figure 5.28 shows the message box that appears when you make 10 incorrect guesses.

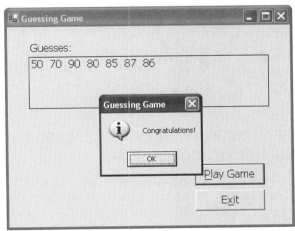

FIGURE 5.27   Message box that appears when you guess the random number

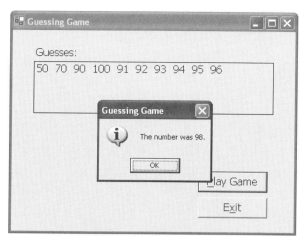

FIGURE 5.28   Message box that appears when you make 10 incorrect guesses

5. Click the **OK** button to close the message box.
6. Click the **Exit** button to end the application.
7. Close the Output window, then close the Code Editor window.

You are finished with the solution, so you can close it.

8. Close the solution. Temporarily display the Solution Explorer window to verify that the solution is closed.

 # BEYOND THE TEXT

LAB 5.4 SONHEIM MANUFACTURING COMPANY

Scenario   Sonheim Manufacturing Company wants an application that the accountant can use to calculate an asset's annual depreciation. The accountant will enter the asset's cost, useful life (in years), and salvage value (which is the value of the asset at the end of its useful life). The application should use the double-declining balance method to calculate the annual depreciation amounts, and then display the amounts in the interface.

In this lab, you learn how to use a text box control's Multiline, ScrollBars, and ReadOnly properties. The Multiline property allows you to display more than one line of text in a text box. The ScrollBars property allows you to display scroll bars on a text box, and the ReadOnly property allows you to prevent the user from changing the data stored in a text box.

In addition, you learn how to use the Financial.DDB function to calculate an asset's depreciation using the double-declining balance method. The syntax of the Financial.DDB function is **Financial.DDB**(*cost, salvage, life, period*). In the syntax, the *cost, salvage,* and *life* arguments are the asset's cost, salvage value, and useful life, respectively. The *period* argument is the period for which you want the depreciation amount calculated. The function returns the depreciation amount as a Double number. Figure 5.29 shows examples of using the Financial.DDB function to calculate depreciation amounts on an asset with a cost of $1000, a salvage value of $100, and a useful life of four years.

Examples

dblDepreciation = Financial.DDB(1000, 100, 4, 1)

calculates the depreciation amount for the first year of the asset's useful life, and then assigns the result (500) to the dblDepreciation variable

dblDepreciation = Financial.DDB(1000, 100, 4, 3)

calculates the depreciation amount for the third year of the asset's useful life, and then assigns the result (125) to the dblDepreciation variable

FIGURE 5.29 Examples of using the Financial.DDB function to calculate depreciation

Solution Discussion The Sonheim Manufacturing Company application needs to provide areas for the user to enter the asset's cost, salvage value, and useful life; you will use text boxes for this purpose. The application also needs to display the depreciation amounts for each of the years in the asset's useful life. The user should not be able to change the depreciation amounts after they have been displayed. In most applications, you use a label control to display information that you don't want the user to access. However, in this application, you will use a text box whose ReadOnly and Multiline properties are set to True. The ReadOnly and Multiline properties allow the text box to perform similarly to a label control. For example, when a text box's ReadOnly property is set to True, the user can view but not modify the contents of the text box. When a text box's Multiline property is set to True, the text box can display more than one line of text. The advantage of using a text box in this case is that, unlike a label control, a text box has a ScrollBars property that allows you to display a vertical scroll bar, a horizontal scroll bar, both horizontal and vertical scroll bars, or no scroll bars. Because you do not know how many depreciation amounts you will need to display at any one time, a text box with a vertical scroll bar is a better choice than a label control for displaying the information. The vertical scroll bar will allow the user to scroll the text box to view all of the depreciation amounts.

In addition, the interface will include two button controls: one for calculating and displaying the depreciation amounts, and the other for exiting the application.

TOE Chart

Task	Object	Event
1. Calculate the annual depreciation amounts 2. Display the annual depreciation amounts in the txtDepreciation control	btnDisplay	Click
End the application	btnExit	Click
Display the annual depreciation amounts (from btnDisplay)	txtDepreciation	None
Get and display the asset's cost	txtCost	None
Select the existing text		Enter
Get and display the asset's salvage value	txtSalvage	None
Select the existing text		Enter
Get and display the asset's useful life in years	txtLife	None
Select the existing text		Enter

FIGURE 5.30

User Interface

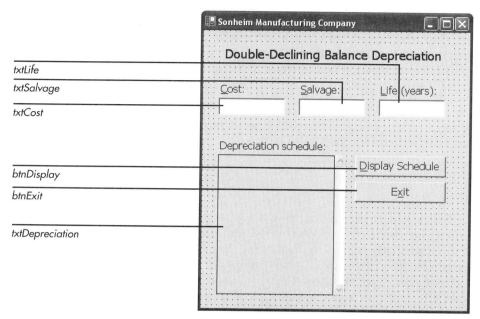

txtLife

txtSalvage

txtCost

btnDisplay

btnExit

txtDepreciation

FIGURE 5.31

Objects, Properties, and Settings

Object	Property	Setting
frmSonheim	Font Size StartPosition Text	Tahoma, 12pt 408, 464 CenterScreen Sonheim Manufacturing Company
Label1	AutoSize Font Text	True Tahoma, 14pt Double-Declining Balance Depreciation
Label2	AutoSize Text	True &Cost:
Label3	AutoSize Text	True &Salvage:
Label4	AutoSize Text	True &Life (years):
Label5	AutoSize Text	True Depreciation schedule:

(Figure is continued on next page)

Object	Property	Setting
TextBox1	Name	txtCost
	Text	(empty)
TextBox2	Name	txtSalvage
	Text	(empty)
TextBox3	Name	txtLife
	Text	(empty)
TextBox4	Name	txtDepreciation
	BorderStyle	FixedSingle
	Multiline	True
	ReadOnly	True
	ScrollBars	Vertical
	Size	192, 216
	Text	(empty)
Button1	Name	btnDisplay
	Text	&Display Schedule
Button2	Name	btnExit
	Text	E&xit

FIGURE 5.32

Tab Order

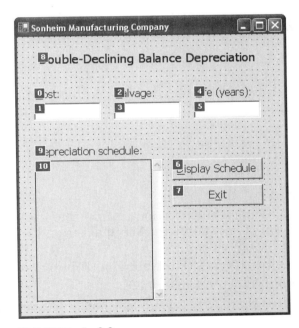

FIGURE 5.33

Pseudocode

btnDisplay Click event procedure
1. if the txtCost, txtSalvage, and txtLife controls contain data, and the data can be converted to a number

    assign the contents of each text box to a separate variable

    display the column headings "Year" and "Depreciation" in txtDepreciation

    repeat for years 1 through the asset's useful life

        use the Financial.DDB function to calculate the current year's depreciation

        display the current year's number and depreciation on a separate line in txtDepreciation

    end repeat

  else

    display a message requesting the user to re-enter the data

  end if

2. send the focus to the txtCost control

btnExit Click event procedure
1. close the application

txtCost Enter event procedure
1. select the application

txtSalvage Enter event procedure
1. select the application

txtLife Enter event procedure
1. select the application

FIGURE 5.34

Activity

1. If necessary, start Visual Studio .NET.
2. Create a new Visual Basic .NET Windows application. Name the solution **Sonheim Manufacturing Solution**. Name the project **Sonheim Manufacturing Project**. Save the application in the VbDotNetLab\Chap05 folder.
3. Change the form file object's name from Form1.vb to **Sonheim Manufacturing Form.vb**.
4. Change the form object's name from Form1 to **frmSonheim**.
5. Use the Sonheim Manufacturing Project Property Pages dialog box to set the Startup object to **frmSonheim**.

6. Add five label controls, four text boxes, and two buttons to the form.

7. Use the chart shown in Figure 5.32 to set the properties of the form and each control.

8. Position the controls as shown in Figure 5.31.

9. Lock the controls in place on the form.

10. Use Figure 5.33 to set the appropriate tab order.

11. Save the solution.

12. Use the pseudocode shown in Figure 5.34 to code the application. Use Double variables in the btnDisplay Click event procedure. Include meaningful comments in the application's code.

13. Save the solution, then start the application.

First, calculate the depreciation amounts for an asset with a cost of $1000, a salvage value of $100, and a useful life of four years. The depreciation amounts should be 500, 250, 125, and 25.

14. Type **1000** as the cost, **100** as the salvage value, and **4** as the life. Click the **Display Schedule** button. The btnDisplay_Click procedure displays the depreciation schedule shown in Figure 5.35.

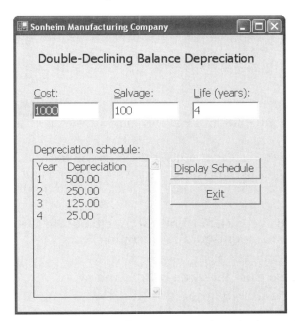

FIGURE 5.35   Depreciation schedule shown in the Sonheim Manufacturing Company application

Now observe what happens if you neglect to enter the cost before clicking the Display Schedule button.

15. Press **Delete** to remove the contents of the txtCost control, then click the **Display Schedule** button. A message box similar to the one shown in Figure 5.36 appears on the screen.

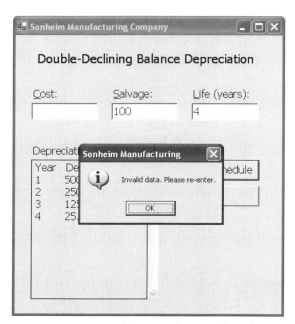

FIGURE 5.36 Message box resulting from invalid data entry

16. Click the **OK** button to close the message box.

Finally, calculate the depreciation amounts for an asset with a cost of $87000, a salvage value of $10000, and a useful life of 15 years.

17. Type **87000** as the cost, **10000** as the salvage value, and **15** as the life. Click the **Display Schedule** button. The btnDisplay_Click procedure displays the depreciation schedule in the txtDepreciation control. Notice that only the depreciation amounts for the first 10 years are visible in the control.

18. Use the vertical scroll bar on the txtDepreciation control to scroll down the text box. This allows you to view the depreciation amounts for the remaining years.

19. Click the **Exit** button to end the application.

20. Close the Output window, and then close the Code Editor window.

21. Close the solution, and then exit Visual Studio .NET.

String Manipulation

Labs included in this chapter:

LAB 6.1 SANDY COSMETICS

Scenario Sandy Hampton, the owner of Sandy Cosmetics, wants an application that she can use to calculate a salesperson's bonus amount, which is a percentage of the salesperson's sales. Ms. Hampton will enter the sales amount and the bonus rate. The application should display the bonus amount in the interface.

Solution Discussion The Sandy Cosmetics application needs to provide areas for the user to enter the sales amount and bonus rate; you will use text boxes for this purpose. The application also needs to display the bonus amount; you will use a label control for this purpose, because the user should not be able to change the amount after it has been displayed. You also will use a button control that allows the user to calculate and display the bonus amount, and a button control for exiting the application.

TOE Chart

Task	Object	Event
1. Calculate the bonus amount 2. Display the bonus amount in the lblBonus control	btnCalc	Click
End the application	btnExit	Click
Display the bonus amount (from btnCalc)	lblBonus	None
Get and display the sales amount	txtSales	None
Select the existing text		Enter
Get and display the bonus rate	txtRate	None
Select the existing text		Enter

FIGURE 6.1

User Interface

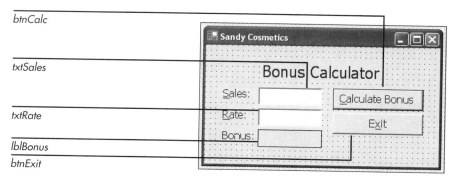

FIGURE 6.2

Objects, Properties, and Settings

Object	Property	Setting
Label1	AutoSize	True
	Font	Tahoma, 18pt
	Text	Bonus Calculator
Label2	AutoSize	True
	Text	&Sales:
Label3	AutoSize	True
	Text	&Rate:
Label4	AutoSize	True
	Text	Bonus:
Label5	Name	lblBonus
	BorderStyle	FixedSingle
	Text	(empty)
	TextAlign	MiddleCenter
TextBox1	Name	txtSales
	Text	(empty)
TextBox2	Name	txtRate
	Text	(empty)
Button1	Name	btnCalc
	Text	&Calculate Bonus
Button2	Name	btnExit
	Text	E&xit

FIGURE 6.3

Tab Order

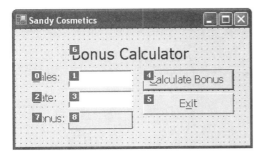

FIGURE 6.4

Pseudocode

btnCalc Click event procedure

1. assign the sales amount and bonus rate to String variables
2. remove any dollar signs or spaces from the sales amount
3. remove any percent signs from the bonus rate
4. if the String variables contain data, and the data can be converted to a number

> assign the sales amount to a Decimal variable
>
> if the bonus rate begins with a period
>
>> assign the bonus rate to a Decimal variable
>
> else
>
>> divide the bonus rate by 100, then assign the result to a Decimal variable
>
> end if
>
> calculate the bonus amount by multiplying the sales amount by the bonus rate
>
> display the bonus amount in the lblBonus control

> else
>
> > clear the contents of the lblBonus control
> >
> > display a message requesting the user to re-enter the data
>
> end if

5. send the focus to the txtSales control
6. select the existing text in the txtSales control

btnExit Click event procedure

1. close the application

txtSales Enter event procedure

1. select the existing text

txtRate Enter event procedure

1. select the existing text

FIGURE 6.5

Activity

1. Start Visual Studio .NET.
2. Click **File** on the Visual Studio .NET menu bar, point to **New**, and then click **Project**. The New Project dialog box opens.
3. If necessary, click **Visual Basic Projects** in the Project Types list box, and click **Windows Application** in the Templates list box.
4. Type **Sandy Cosmetics Project** in the Name text box.
5. Use the **Browse** button to open the **VbDotNetLab\Chap06** folder.
6. If necessary, click the **More** button.

7. If necessary, select the **Create directory for Solution** check box.

8. Type **Sandy Cosmetics Solution** in the New Solution Name text box.

9. Click the **OK** button to close the New Project dialog box.

Now set the appropriate properties of the form file object and form object.

To set the appropriate properties of the form file object and form object:

1. Right-click **Form1.vb** in the Solution Explorer window, then click **Rename**. Change the form file object's name from Form1.vb to **Sandy Cosmetics Form.vb**.

2. Click the **form**, then click **(Name)** in the Properties window. Change the form object's name from Form1 to **frmSandy**.

3. Right-click **Sandy Cosmetics Project** in the Solution Explorer window, then click **Properties**. Click the **Startup object** list arrow, and then click **frmSandy** in the list. Click the **OK** button.

4. Click the **form**, then change the values assigned to the following properties:

Font	**Tahoma, 12 pt**
Size	**360, 216**
StartPosition	**CenterScreen**
Text	**Sandy Cosmetics**

5. Save the solution by clicking **File** on the menu bar, and then clicking **Save All**.

Next, add the appropriate controls to the interface, and then set the values of some of their properties.

To add the appropriate controls, then set the values of some of their properties:

1. Use the Label tool to add five label controls to the form.

2. Use the TextBox tool to add two text boxes to the form.

3. Use the Button tool to add two buttons to the form.

4. Use the chart shown in Figure 6.3 to set the properties of each control.

5. Position the controls as shown in Figure 6.2.

6. Lock the controls in place on the form.

7. Use Figure 6.4 to set the appropriate tab order.

8. Make the Calculate Bonus button the default button by setting the form's AcceptButton property to **btnCalc**.

9. Save the solution.

Now that the interface is complete, you can begin coding the application. First you will enter the appropriate comments and Option statements.

To enter the appropriate comments and Option statements:

1. Right-click the **form**, and then click **View Code** to open the Code Editor window.

2. Type the comments shown in Figure 6.6, replacing `<enter your name and date here>` with your name and the current date. Also type the Option statements shown in the figure.

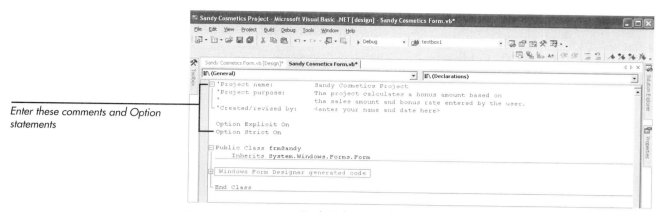

FIGURE 6.6 Code Editor window showing comments and Option statements

Now use the pseudocode shown earlier in Figure 6.5 to code the btnCalc control's Click event procedure.

To code the btnCalc control's Click event procedure:

1. Click the **Class Name** list arrow, and then click **btnCalc** in the list.
2. Click the **Method Name** list arrow, and then click **Click** in the list. The code template for the btnCalc_Click procedure appears in the Code Editor window.
3. Type '**calculates a bonus amount** and press **Enter** twice.

First, you will declare the procedure's variables.

4. Type '**declare variables** and press **Enter**.

You will use two String variables to store the sales amount and bonus rate entered by the user. After removing any unwanted characters from the String variables, you will store the results in two Decimal variables. You also will use a Decimal variable to store the bonus amount after it has been calculated. A variable is appropriate in each case because the amount will be different for each calculation.

5. Type **dim strSales as string** and press **Enter**.
6. Type **dim strRate as string** and press **Enter**.
7. Type **dim decSales as decimal** and press **Enter**.
8. Type **dim decRate as decimal** and press **Enter**.
9. Type **dim decBonus as decimal** and press **Enter** twice.

The first step in the pseudocode for the btnCalc Click event procedure is to assign to the String variables the sales amount and bonus rate entered by the user.

10. Type '**assign input to String variables** and press **Enter**.
11. Type **strsales = me.txtsales.text** and press **Enter**.
12. Type **strrate = me.txtrate.text** and press **Enter** twice.

The next step is to remove any dollar signs or spaces from the sales amount; you can use the Replace method to accomplish this step. Recall that the syntax of the Replace method is *string*.**Replace**(*oldValue*, *newValue*). In the syntax, *oldValue* is the sequence of characters that you want to replace in the *string*; in this case, *oldValue* is the dollar sign ("$") and also a space (" "). *NewValue* in the syntax is the replacement characters; in this case, *newValue* is the empty string (""). The Replace method returns a string with all occurrences of *oldValue* replaced with *newValue*.

13. Type '**remove any dollar signs or spaces from the sales amount** and press **Enter**.
14. Type **strsales = strsales.replace("$", "")** and press **Enter**.
15. Type **strsales = strsales.replace(" ", "")** and press **Enter** twice. (Be sure to include a space between the first set of quotation marks; but do not include any spaces between the second set.)

The next step is to remove any percent signs from the bonus rate. Here again, you can use the Replace method to accomplish this step.

16. Type '**remove any percent signs from the bonus rate** and press **Enter**.
17. Type **strrate = strrate.replace("%", "")** and press **Enter** twice.

The fourth step in the pseudocode is a selection structure that determines whether the strSales and strRate variables contain data, and whether the data can be converted to a number.

18. Type the comments and additional lines of code shown in Figure 6.7, and then position the insertion point as shown in the figure.

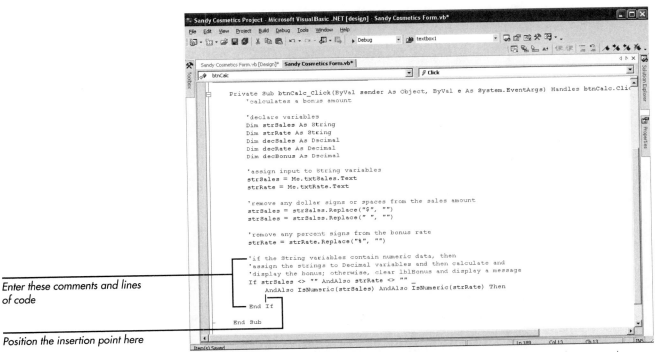

Enter these comments and lines of code

Position the insertion point here

FIGURE 6.7   Comments and additional lines of code shown in the procedure

According to the pseudocode, if the String variables contain data that can be converted to a number, the first instruction in the selection structure's true path should assign the sales amount to a Decimal variable—in this case, the decSales variable.

19. Type **decsales = convert.todecimal(strsales)** and press **Enter**.

The next instruction in the true path is a nested selection structure that determines whether the bonus rate begins with a period. You can use the StartsWith method to make this determination. Recall that the syntax of the StartsWith method is *string*.**StartsWith**(*subString*). In the syntax, *subString* is a string that represents the sequence of characters you want to search for at the beginning of the *string*. The StartsWith method returns the Boolean value True if *subString* is located at the beginning of *string*; otherwise, it returns the Boolean value False.

20. Type **if strrate.startswith(".") then** and press **Enter**.

If the first character in the bonus rate is a period, it means that the user entered the rate in decimal form; for example, he or she entered .05 rather than 5%. In that case, the true path in the nested selection structure should assign the bonus rate to the decRate variable.

21. Type **decrate = convert.todecimal(strrate)** and press **Enter**.

However, if the first character is not a period, it means that the user entered the rate as a whole number; for example, he or she entered 5 (or 5%) rather than .05. In that case, the nested selection structure's false path should divide the bonus rate by 100 and then assign the result to the decRate variable.

22. Type **else** and press **Enter**, then type **decrate = convert.todecimal(strrate) / 100d**.

After assigning the sales amount and bonus rate to Decimal variables, the outer selection structure's true path should calculate the bonus amount by multiplying the sales amount by the bonus rate. It then should display the bonus amount in the lblBonus control. You will display the bonus amount with a dollar sign and two decimal places.

23. Type the additional comments and lines of code indicated in Figure 6.8, and then position the insertion point as shown in the figure.

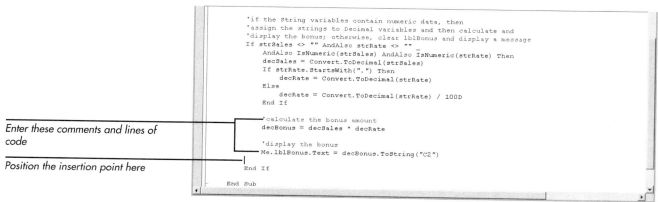

FIGURE 6.8   Completed true path for the outer selection structure

If the String variables do not contain data that can be converted to a number, the outer selection structure's false path should clear the contents of the lblBonus control, and then display an appropriate message.

24. Type the additional lines of code shown in Figure 6.9, then position the insertion point as shown in the figure.

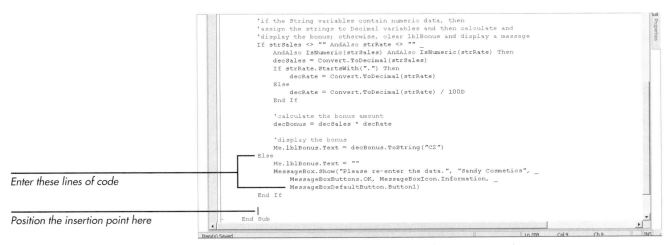

Enter these lines of code

Position the insertion point here

FIGURE 6.9   Completed false path for the outer selection structure

The last two steps in the btnCalc control's Click event procedure are to send the focus to the txtSales control, which is the control that the user most likely will access after making a calculation, and then select the existing text in the control.

25. Type '**set the focus, then select the existing text** and press **Enter**.

26. Type **me.txtsales.focus()** and press **Enter**.

27. Type **me.txtsales.selectall()** and press **Enter**.

TIP ••••⫶   In the Sandy Cosmetics application, the `Me.txtSales.SelectAll()` statement is necessary to select the text box control's existing text when the user presses Enter to select the default button. You learned this concept in Lab 4.1 in Chapter 4.

28. Save the solution by clicking **File** on the menu bar, and then clicking **Save All**.

Next, you will code the Click event procedure for the btnExit control, which is responsible for ending the application. You also will code the Enter event procedures for the txtSales and txtRate controls. The Enter event procedures are responsible for selecting the existing text in their respective text boxes when the text box receives the focus.

To code the btnExit_Click, txtSales_Enter, and txtRate_Enter procedures:

1. Display the code template for the btnExit control's Click event procedure.

2. Type '**ends the application** and press **Enter**.

3. Type **me.close()** and press **Enter**.

4. Display the code template for the txtSales control's Enter event procedure.

5. Type '**selects the existing text** and press **Enter**.

6. Type **me.txtsales.selectall()** and press **Enter**.

7. Display the code template for the txtRate control's Enter event procedure.

8. Type '**selects the existing text** and press **Enter**.

9. Type **me.txtrate.selectall()** and press **Enter**.

Now that you have finished coding the application, you can test the application to verify that the code is working correctly.

To test the application:

1. Save the solution.

2. Start the application by clicking **Debug** on the menu bar, and then clicking **Start**. The blinking insertion point indicates that the txtSales control has the focus.

First, calculate the bonus amount using a sales amount of $1,500 and a bonus rate of 10%. The bonus amount should be $150.00.

3. Type **$1,500** as the sales, and then type **10%** as the rate. Press **Enter** to select the Calculate Bonus button, which is the default button on the form. The btnCalc_Click procedure removes the dollar sign and comma from the sales amount. It also removes the percent sign from the bonus rate and divides the rate by 100. The procedure then calculates the bonus amount and displays the amount in the lblBonus control, as shown in Figure 6.10.

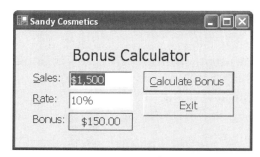

FIGURE 6.10   Sandy Cosmetics application

Now test the application using invalid data.

4. Type **p** in the txtSales control and then click the **Calculate Bonus** button. The btnCalc_Click procedure displays the message box shown in Figure 6.11.

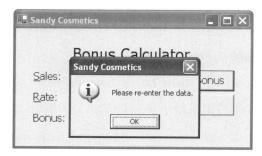

FIGURE 6.11   Message box resulting from invalid data entry

5. Click the **OK** button to close the message box.

6. Click the **Exit** button. The btnExit_Click procedure ends the application.

7. Close the Output window, and then close the Code Editor window.

You are finished with the solution, so you can close it.

8. Click **File** on the menu bar, and then click **Close Solution**.

LAB 6.2 CARRIE ANTIQUES

Scenario The manager of Carrie Antiques wants an application that he can use to calculate and display a 6% sales tax on a purchase amount. The application also should calculate and display the total amount due.

Solution Discussion The Carrie Antiques application needs to provide an area for the user to enter the purchase amount; you will use a text box for this purpose. The application also needs to display the sales tax and total amount due; you will use label controls for this purpose, because the user should not be able to change the amounts after they have been displayed. Additionally, you will use a button control for calculating the sales tax and total amount due, and a button control for exiting the application.

TOE Chart

Task	Object	Event
1. Calculate the sales tax 2. Calculate the total amount due 3. Display the sales tax in lblTax 4. Display the total amount due in lblTotal	btnCalc	Click
End the application	btnExit	Click
Display the sales tax (from btnCalc)	lblTax	None
Display the total amount due (from btnCalc)	lblTotal	None
Get and display the purchase amount	txtPurchase	None
Select the existing text		Enter

FIGURE 6.12

User Interface

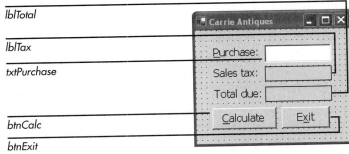

FIGURE 6.13

Pseudocode

btnCalc Click event procedure

1. if the user did not enter a purchase amount

    display an appropriate message

    else

    assign the purchase amount to a String variable

    repeat until each character in the String variable has been compared to a number or the current character is not a number

    if the current character is not a number

    assign True to the blnNonNumberFound variable to indicate that the character is not a number

    else

    add 1 to the counter variable that keeps track of the current character's position in the String variable

    end if

    end repeat

    if the purchase amount contains a character that is not a number

    display an appropriate message

    else

    assign the purchase amount to a Decimal variable

    calculate the sales tax by multiplying the purchase amount by the sales tax rate

    calculate the total amount due by adding the sales tax to the purchase amount

    display the sales tax in lblTax

    display the total amount due in lblTotal

    end if

2. send the focus to txtPurchase

btnExit Click event procedure

1. close the application

txtPurchase Enter event procedure

1. select the existing text

FIGURE 6.14

Activity

1. If necessary, start Visual Studio .NET.
2. Click **File** on the Visual Studio .NET menu bar, and then click **Open Solution**. The Open Solution dialog box opens.
3. Open the **VbDotNetLab\Chap06\Carrie Antiques Solution** folder. If necessary, click **Carrie Antiques Solution** (Carrie Antiques Solution.sln) in the list of filenames.
4. Click the **Open** button. The user interface shown in Figure 6.13 appears on the screen.

5. Open the Code Editor window.

6. Insert a blank line above the `Public Class frmCarrie` line. Type the following comments in the blank line, replacing *<enter your name and date here>* with your name and the current date. After typing the last comment, press **Enter** twice.

    'Project name: **Carrie Antiques Project**
    'Project purpose: **The project calculates the sales tax on a purchase.**
    '   **It also calculates the total amount due.**
    'Created/revised by: *<enter your name and date here>*

7. Type the Option statement that tells the computer to warn you if your code contains the name of an undeclared variable, and then press **Enter**.

8. Type the Option statement that tells the computer not to perform any implicit type conversions that might result in a loss of data, and then press **Enter**.

Now use the pseudocode shown in Figure 6.14 to code the btnCalc control's Click event procedure.

To code the btnCalc control's Click event procedure:

1. Display the code template for the btnCalc control's Click event procedure.

2. Type '**calculates the sales tax and total amount due** and press **Enter** twice.

First, you will declare the procedure's constant and variables. The procedure will use a constant for the sales tax rate, which is 6%. It also will use six variables named strPurchase, decPurchase, decTax, decTotalDue, intCount, and blnNonNumberFound.

3. Type '**declare constant and variables** and press **Enter**. Type the statement to declare a Decimal constant named **decTAXRATE** whose value is .06D.

4. Type the statement to declare a String variable named **strPurchase**, and then press **Enter**. The strPurchase variable will store the purchase amount entered by the user.

5. Type the statement to declare a Decimal variable named **decPurchase**, and then press **Enter**. The decPurchase variable also will store the purchase amount, but only after it is determined that the purchase amount contains only numbers.

6. Type the statement to declare a Decimal variable named **decTax**, and then press **Enter**. The decTax variable will store the sales tax amount.

7. Type the statement to declare a Decimal variable named **decTotalDue**, and then press **Enter**. The decTotalDue variable will store the total amount due.

8. Type the statement to declare an Integer variable named **intCount**, and then press **Tab**. Type '**counter** and press **Enter**. The intCount variable will be used as a counter variable in a loop that determines whether each character in the purchase amount is a number.

9. Type the statement to declare a Boolean variable named **blnNonNumberFound**, and then press **Enter** twice. The procedure will use the blnNonNumberFound variable to keep track of whether the purchase amount contains a character that is not a number.

The first step in the pseudocode for the btnCalc Click event procedure is a selection structure that determines whether the user entered a purchase amount. If he or she did not, the selection structure's true path should display an appropriate message.

10. Type '**if the user did not enter a purchase amount, then display a message** and press **Enter**.

11. Type '**otherwise, assign the purchase amount to strPurchase** and press **Enter**.

12. Type **if me.txtpurchase.text = "" then** and press **Enter**.

13. Enter the statement that will display (in a message box) a message that tells the user to enter the purchase amount.

However, if the user did enter a purchase amount, the selection structure's false path should assign the purchase amount to a String variable.

14. Type **else** and press **Enter**, then enter the statement to assign the contents of the txtPurchase control to the strPurchase variable.

After assigning the purchase amount to a String variable, the selection structure's false path should use a loop to determine whether each character in the purchase amount is a number. The loop should stop either after each character has been compared to a number or after finding a character that is not a number.

15. Enter the following comments.

    'determine whether each character in the purchase amount is a number
    'stop the loop either after comparing each character to a number
    'or after finding a character that is not a number

You can use the Length property to determine the number of characters contained in the purchase amount, which is stored in the strPurchase variable. Recall that the syntax of the Length property is *string*.**Length**. In this case, you want the loop to stop when the value stored in the intCount variable is equal to the value stored in the strPurchase variable's Length property.

16. Type **do until intcount = strpurchase.length** and press the **Spacebar** on your keyboard (but don't press Enter).

You also want the loop to stop if the purchase amount contains a character that is not a number.

17. Type **orelse blnnonnumberfound** and press **Enter**.

The first instruction in the loop is a nested selection structure that determines whether the current character in the strPurchase variable is not a number. You can use the Substring method to access the current character, and then use the Like operator to compare the character to the numbers zero through nine. Recall that the syntax of the Substring method is *string*.**Substring**(*startIndex*[, *count*]). In the syntax, *startIndex* is the index of the first character you want to access in the *string*; the first character in a string has an index of zero. The *count* argument, which is optional, specifies the number of characters you want to access. The Substring method returns *count* number of characters, beginning with the character whose index is *startIndex*. In this case, you will use the intCount counter variable as the *startIndex* argument. You will use the number one as the *count* argument, because you want the loop to look at only one character at a time.

18. Enter the following comments.

    'if the current character is not a number, assign True to
    'blnNonNumberFound; otherwise, add 1 to intCount

19. Type **if strpurchase.substring(intcount, 1)** and press the **Spacebar** on your keyboard (but don't press Enter).

Recall that the syntax of the Like operator is *string* **Like** *pattern*. In the syntax, both *string* and *pattern* must be String expressions; however, *pattern* can contain one or more pattern-matching characters. The Like operator evaluates to True if *string* matches *pattern*; otherwise, it evaluates to False. In this case, you will use `strPurchase.Substring(intCount, 1)` as the *string*, and "[!0-9]" as the *pattern*. (Recall that the exclamation point stands for "not".) The Like operator will evaluate to True if the current character in the strPurchase variable is *not* a number; otherwise, it will evaluate to False.

20. Type **like "[!0-9]"** and press **Enter**.

If the strPurchase variable contains a character that is not a number, the nested selection structure's true path should assign the Boolean value True to the blnNonNumberFound variable; otherwise, its false path should add one to the intCount variable.

21. Enter the appropriate statements in the nested selection structure's true and false paths.

After the loop ends, the btnCalc Click event procedure should use a nested selection structure to determine whether a character other than a number was found in the purchase amount.

22. Enter the following comments two lines below the Loop clause, but above the End Sub clause.

    'if the purchase amount contains a character that is not a number
    'display a message; otherwise, assign the purchase amount to a
    'Decimal variable and then calculate and display the sales tax
    'and total amount due

23. Type **if blnnonnumberfound then** and press **Enter**.

According to the pseudocode, if the purchase amount contains a character other than a number, the procedure should display an appropriate message.

24. In the nested selection structure's true path, enter the statement that will display (in a message box) a message telling the user that the purchase amount must contain numbers only.

However, if the purchase amount contains only numbers, the procedure should assign the purchase amount to a Decimal variable. It then should calculate the sales tax and total amount due, and display the results in the lblTax and lblTotal controls.

25. In the nested selection structure's false path, enter the statement to assign the purchase amount, which is stored in the strPurchase variable, to the decPurchase variable. Also enter the statements to calculate the sales tax and the total amount due, and then press **Enter** twice.

26. Now enter the statements to display the sales tax and total amount due in the lblTax and lblTotal controls. Display both amounts with two decimal places.

The last step in the pseudocode for the btnCalc Click event procedure is to send the focus to the txtPurchase control.

27. Type **'set the focus** two lines below the last End If clause, but above the End Sub clause, and press **Enter**.

28. Type the statement to send the focus to the txtPurchase control. You now have finished coding the btnCalc Click event procedure.

29. Save the solution.

Next, code the btnExit control's Click event procedure (which is responsible for ending the application) and the txtPurchase control's Enter event procedure (which is responsible for selecting the control's existing text).

To code the btnExit_Click and txtPurchase_Enter procedures:

1. Display the code template for the btnExit control's Click event procedure.

2. Type **'ends the application** and press **Enter**.

3. Type the statement that directs the computer to end the application, and then press **Enter**.

4. Display the code template for the txtPurchase control's Enter event procedure.

5. Type **'selects the existing text** and press **Enter**.

6. Type the statement that directs the computer to select the control's existing text when the control receives the focus, and then press **Enter**.

Now that you have finished coding the application, you can test the application to verify that the code is working correctly.

To test the application:

1. Save the solution, then start the application.

First, observe what happens when you click the Calculate button before entering a purchase amount.

2. Click the **Calculate** button. The btnCalc_Click procedure displays a message box similar to the one shown in Figure 6.15.

FIGURE 6.15   Message box that appears when the user does not enter a purchase amount

3. Click the **OK** button to close the message box.

Next, display the sales tax and total amount due for a purchase of $100. The sales tax should be $6 and the total amount due should be $106.

4. Type **100** as the purchase amount and then click the **Calculate** button. The btnCalc_Click procedure determines whether the purchase amount contains only numbers. In this case, because only numbers appear in the purchase amount, the procedure calculates and displays the sales tax and total amount due, as shown in Figure 6.16.

FIGURE 6.16   Carrie Antiques application

Now test the application using invalid data.

5. Type **7b6** as the purchase amount and then click the **Calculate** button. The procedure determines whether the purchase amount contains only numbers. In this case, because a letter appears in the purchase amount, the procedure displays a message box similar to the one shown in Figure 6.17.

FIGURE 6.17   Message box resulting from entering invalid data

6. Press **Enter** to select the OK button, which closes the message box.

7. Click the **Exit** button. The btnExit_Click procedure ends the application.

8. Close the Output window, then close the Code Editor window.

You are finished with the solution, so you can close it.

9. Close the solution. Temporarily display the Solution Explorer window to verify that the solution is closed.

LAB 6.3 MODIFIED CARRIE ANTIQUES

Scenario The manager of Carrie Antiques has asked you to modify the application that you coded in Lab 6.2. The application should now allow the user to enter a purchase amount that contains a dollar sign, a comma, and a period.

Solution Discussion The modified Carrie Antiques application will need to remove any dollar signs and commas from the purchase amount. Additionally, the application will need to allow the purchase amount to contain a period in addition to numbers.

Modified pseudocode

btnCalc Click event procedure (changes made to the original pseudocode are shaded in the figure)

1. if the user did not enter a purchase amount
        display an appropriate message
    else
        assign the purchase amount to a String variable
        remove any dollar signs and commas from the String variable
        repeat until each character in the String variable has been compared to a number and the period, or the current character is not a number or the period
            if the current character is not a number or the period
                assign True to blnNonNumberFound variable to indicate that the character is not a number or the period
            else
                add 1 to the counter variable that keeps track of the current character's position in the String variable
            end if
        end repeat

        if the purchase amount contains a character that is not a number or the period
            display an appropriate message
        else
            assign the purchase amount to a Decimal variable
            calculate the sales tax by multiplying the purchase amount by the sales tax rate
            calculate the total amount due by adding the sales tax to the purchase amount
            display the sales tax in lblTax
            display the total amount due in lblTotal
        end if
2. send the focus to txtPurchase

FIGURE 6.18

Activity

1. Use Windows to make a copy of the Carrie Antiques Solution folder, which is contained in the VbDotNetLab\Chap06 folder. Rename the copy Modified Carrie Antiques Solution.

2. If necessary, start Visual Studio .NET.

3. Open the Carrie Antiques Solution (Carrie Antiques Solution.sln) file contained in the VbDotNetLab\Chap06\Modified Carrie Antiques Solution folder.

4. Right-click **Carrie Antiques Form.vb** in the Solution Explorer window, then click **View Designer**. The user interface shown in Figure 6.13 in Lab 6.2 appears on the screen.

5. Start the application.

First, test the application using a purchase amount of $1,500.

6. Type **$1,500** as the purchase amount and then click the **Calculate** button. The application should display a message box similar to the one shown in Figure 6.17 in Lab 6.2.

7. Close the message box.

Now test the application using a purchase amount of 250.55.

8. Type **250.55** as the purchase amount and then click the **Calculate** button. The application should display a message box similar to the one shown in Figure 6.17 in Lab 6.2.

9. Close the message box.

10. Click the **Exit** button to end the application.

Now modify the btnCalc control's Click event procedure.

To modify the btnCalc control's Click event procedure, then test the procedure:

1. Open the Code Editor window.

2. Use the modified pseudocode shown in Figure 6.18 to make the appropriate changes to the btnCalc control's Click event procedure.

3. Save the solution, then start the application.

First, test the application using a purchase amount of $1,500. The sales tax should be $90 and the total amount due should be $1,590.

4. Type **$1,500** as the purchase amount and then click the **Calculate** button. The application displays the sales tax and total amount due, as shown in Figure 6.19.

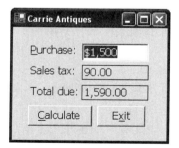

FIGURE 6.19   Modified Carrie Antiques application

Now test the application using a purchase amount of 250.55. The sales tax should be $15.03 and the total amount due should be $265.58.

5. Type **250.55** as the purchase amount and then click the **Calculate** button. The application displays the sales tax (15.03) and total amount due (265.58).

6. Click the **Exit** button to end the application.

7. Close the Output window, then close the Code Editor window.

You are finished with the solution, so you can close it.

8. Close the solution. Temporarily display the Solution Explorer window to verify that the solution is closed.

BEYOND THE TEXT

LAB 6.4 RACING ROCKETS GAME

Scenario In this lab, you learn how to use a label control to draw a line on a form. You also learn how to use the SetBounds method to change the location and/or size of a control while an application is running. The syntax of the SetBounds method is *control*.**SetBounds**(*x*, *y*, *width*, *height*, *specified*). In the syntax, *control* is the name of the control whose location and/or size you want to change. You change the control's location by setting the SetBounds method's *x* and *y* arguments. The *x* argument specifies the location of the left edge of the control on the form, and the *y* argument specifies the location of the top edge of the control. You change the control's size by setting the SetBounds method's *width* and *height* arguments. The *x*, *y*, *width*, and *height* arguments are measured in pixels. A pixel, which is short for "picture element", is one spot in a grid of thousands of such spots that form an image produced on the screen by a computer or printed on a page by a printer.

If you do not want to change the location of either the left or top edge of a control, or if you do not want to change the control's height or width, you simply set the appropriate argument to the number 0. For example, to keep the control's left border at its current location, you set the *x* argument to 0. Similarly, to keep the control at its current size, you set the *width* and *height* arguments to 0.

The *specified* argument in the SetBounds method is a constant that indicates the arguments that you are specifying in the method. For example, to indicate that you are specifying the *height* argument only, you use the constant `BoundsSpecified.Height`. To indicate that only the *y* argument is specified in the SetBounds method, you use the constant `BoundsSpecified.Y`. Finally, to indicate that you are specifying both the *x* and *width* arguments, you use the Or operator to combine two constants in the *specified* argument, like this: `BoundsSpecified.X Or BoundsSpecified.Width`. Figure 6.20 shows the constants that you can use in the *specified* argument and includes examples of using the SetBounds method.

specified argument constants	Meaning
BoundsSpecified.All	all arguments are specified
BoundsSpecified.Height	the *height* argument is specified
BoundsSpecified.Location	the *x* (left) and *y* (top) arguments are specified
BoundsSpecified.None	no arguments are specified
BoundsSpecified.Size	the *width* and *height* arguments are specified
BoundsSpecified.Width	the *width* argument is specified
BoundsSpecified.X	the *x* (left) argument is specified
BoundsSpecified.Y	the *y* (top) argument is specified

(Figure is continued on next page)

Examples

`Me.picCars.SetBounds(25, 50, 0, 0, BoundsSpecified.Location)`

positions the picture box at a location that is 25 pixels from the left edge of the form and 50 pixels from the top edge of the form; leaves the control at its current size

`Me.txtName.SetBounds(25, 50, 0, 0, BoundsSpecified.All)`

positions the text box at a location that is 25 pixels from the left edge of the form and 50 pixels from the top edge of the form; changes the width and height of the control to zero pixels

`Me.lblTotal.SetBounds(0, 0, 100, 0, BoundsSpecified.Width)`

leaves the label control at its current location and current height; changes the width of the control to 100 pixels

FIGURE 6.20   Constants used in and examples of the SetBounds method

Solution Discussion   The Racing Rockets game will use two picture boxes, each containing an image of a rocket ship. It also will include a label control that will represent the finish line. Additionally, the application will contain two button controls: one to start the game and the other to end the application.

TOE Chart

Task	Object	Event
1. Generate two random numbers from zero through 50 2. Use the random numbers to move the picRocket1 and picRocket2 controls from the bottom of the form to the finish line at the top of the form 3. If the picRocket1 and picRocket2 controls are at the finish line, display the "It's a tie!" message 4. If the picRocket1 control reaches the finish line before the picRocket2 control, display the "Rocket ship 1 wins!" message 5. If the picRocket2 control reaches the finish line before the picRocket1 control, display the "Rocket ship 2 wins!" message 6. Move the picRocket1 and picRocket2 controls to the bottom of the form	btnPlay	Click
End the application	btnExit	Click
Display the first rocket ship	picRocket1	None
Display the second rocket ship	picRocket2	None
Display the finish line	Label1	None

FIGURE 6.21

Pseudocode

btnPlay Click event procedure

1. repeat while neither picture box is at the finish line

    generate two random numbers from zero through 50

    subtract the first random number from the Y location of the picRocket1 control

    subtract the second random number from the Y location of the picRocket2 control

    if the picRocket1 control will be moved past the finish line

       use 10 (the location of the finish line) as the Y location for picRocket1

    end if

    if the picRocket2 control will be moved past the finish line

       use 10 (the location of the finish line) as the Y location for picRocket2

    end if

    move the picRocket1 and picRocket2 controls toward the finish line

   end repeat

2. if the picRocket1 and picRocket2 controls are at the finish line

    display the "It's a tie!" message

   else if the picRocket1 control is at the finish line

    display the "Rocket ship 1 wins!" message

   else

    display the "Rocket ship 2 wins!" message

   end ifs

3. move the picRocket1 and picRocket2 controls to the bottom of the form

btnExit Click event procedure

1. close the application

FIGURE 6.22

Activity

1. If necessary, start Visual Studio .NET.
2. Open the Racing Rockets Solution (Racing Rockets Solution.sln) file contained in the VbDotNetLab\Chap06\Racing Rockets Solution folder.

First, learn how to use a label control to draw a line on the form.

3. Use the toolbox to add a label control to the form.
4. Set the label control's BackColor property to **black** (use a black square on the Custom tab).
5. Set the label control's Location property to **40, 10**, then set its Size property to **625, 1**. A thin, black line appears at the top of the form, as shown in Figure 6.23.

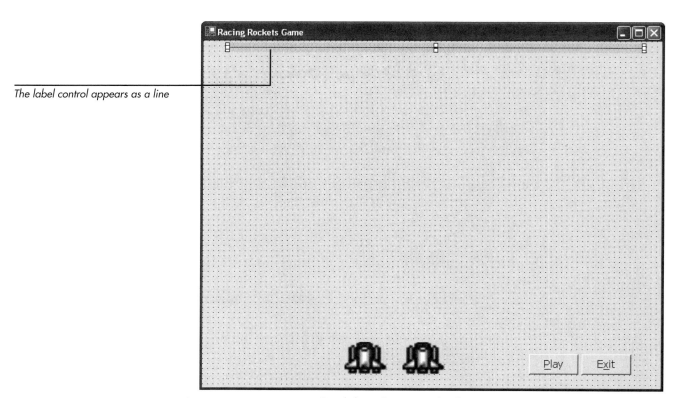

The label control appears as a line

FIGURE 6.23   Finish line shown on the form

6. Lock the controls in place on the form.

7. Open the Code Editor window. Notice that the btnExit_Click procedure has already been coded. Additionally, several comments appear in the btnPlay_Click procedure.

8. Replace the `<enter your name and date>` text with your name and the current date.

9. Enter the following statements below the `'declare constants and variables` comment.

    Const strTIE As String = "It's a tie!"
    Const strWINNER1 As String = "Rocket ship 1 wins!"
    Const strWINNER2 As String = "Rocket ship 2 wins!"
    Dim intNum1 As Integer
    Dim intNum2 As Integer
    Dim intYRocket1 As Integer
    Dim intYRocket2 As Integer
    Dim rndGenerator As New Random
    Dim strMessage As String

Now use the pseudocode shown in Figure 6.22 to code the application. The first step is a repetition structure that will repeat its instructions while neither picture box is at the finish line. A picture box is at the finish line when its top border is at the same location as the top border of the Label1 control. Recall that, in Step 5, you set the Label1 control's Location property to 40, 10. As you learned in Chapter 1, the first number in the Location property is the distance from the left border of the control to the left border of the form, and the second number is the distance from the top border of the control to the top border of the form. The first number is referenced in code using the Location.X property, and the second number is referred to using the Location.Y property. In other words, you can use a control's Location.X property to determine the location of its left border, and its Location.Y property to determine the location of its top border.

10. Position the insertion point below the `'perform the loop instructions while neither picture box is at the finish line` comment.

11. Type **do while me.picrocket1.location.y > 10 andalso me.picrocket2.location.y > 10** and press **Enter**. This clause tells the computer to stop the loop when either one or both picture boxes reach the finish line.

12. Delete the blank line below the `Do While` clause. Also delete the line containing the `Loop` clause.

13. Position the insertion point two lines below the `'move the picture boxes` comment, then type **loop** and press **Enter**.

14. Indent the comments that appear within the loop.

The first instruction in the loop is to generate two random numbers from zero through 50.

15. In the blank line below the `'generate two random numbers` comment, enter the appropriate statements to generate the random numbers. Assign the random numbers to the intNum1 and intNum2 variables.

The next two instructions in the loop are to subtract the random numbers from the Y location of the picture boxes.

16. In the blank line below the `'assign 10 as the Y location` comment, type the statement to subtract the contents of the intNum1 variable from the value stored in the picRocket1 control's Location.Y property. Assign the difference to the intYRocket1 variable. Press **Enter**.

17. Now enter the statement to subtract the contents of the intNum2 variable from the value stored in the picRocket2 control's Location.Y property. Assign the difference to the intYRocket2 variable.

Before changing the picRocket1 control's Location.Y property to the value stored in the intYRocket1 variable, you should determine whether the value will move the picRocket1 control past the finish line; if it will, you should use the number 10 as the Y location.

18. Type **if intyrocket1 < 10 then** and press **Enter**.

19. Type **intyrocket1 = 10.**

Similarly, before changing the picRocket2 control's Location.Y property to the value stored in the intYRocket2 variable, you should determine whether the value will move the picRocket2 control past the finish line; if it will, you should use the number 10 as the Y location.

20. If necessary, insert a blank line below the `End If` clause, then enter the appropriate selection structure.

The last instruction in the loop is to move the picRocket1 and picRocket2 controls toward the finish line. You can use the SetBounds method to accomplish this task.

21. In the blank line below the `'move the picture boxes` comment, type **me.picrocket1. setbounds(0, intyrocket1, 0, 0, boundsspecified.y)** and press **Enter**.

22. Now enter a similar statement to move the picRocket2 control toward the finish line.

The second step in the pseudocode is a selection structure that determines whether both picture box controls are at the finish line. If both controls are at the finish line, the procedure should display the "It's a tie!" message.

23. In the blank line below the `'determine the results of the race, then display the appropriate message` comment, type **if me.picrocket1.location.y = 10 andalso me.picrocket2.location.y = 10 then** and press **Enter**.

24. Enter the statement to assign the strTIE constant to the strMessage variable.

If both picture box controls are not at the finish line, then the procedure should use a nested selection to determine which of the two picture boxes finished first. (Recall that the loop in the procedure stops when either one or both picture boxes are at the finish line.) If the picRocket1 control is at the finish line, the procedure should display the "Rocket ship 1 wins!" message; otherwise, it should display the "Rocket ship 2 wins!" message.

25. Enter the appropriate nested selection structure.

26. If necessary, insert a blank line below the last End If clause. Type **messagebox. show(strmessage, "Racing Rockets Game", messageboxbuttons.ok, _** and press **Enter**.

27. Press **Tab**, then type **messageboxicon.information, messageboxdefaultbutton.button1)** and press **Enter**.

The last step in the pseudocode for the btnPlay control's Click event procedure is to move the picture box controls to the bottom of the form. Here again, you can use the SetBounds method to move the controls.

28. In the blank line below the 'reset the picture boxes for the next game comment, type the SetBounds method that will position the picRocket1 control so that its top border is at location 470. Press **Enter**.

29. Now enter the SetBounds method that will position the picRocket2 control so that its top border is at location 470.

30. Save the solution, then start the application.

31. Click the **Play** button. A message box similar to the one shown in Figure 6.24 appears on the screen. (The message that appears will depend on the results of your race.)

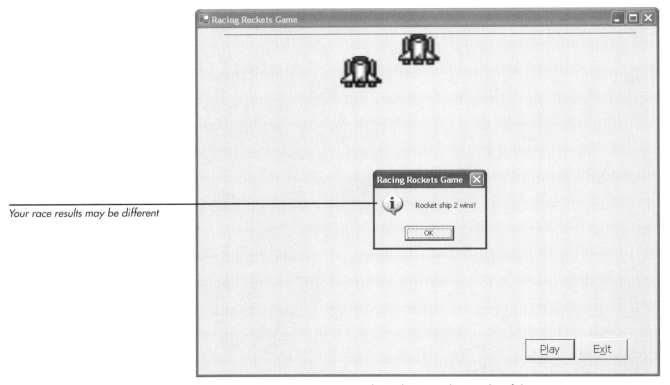

Your race results may be different

FIGURE 6.24   Message box showing the results of the race

32. Click the **OK** button to close the message box.

33. Click the **Exit** button to end the application.

34. Close the Output window, and then close the Code Editor window.

35. Close the solution, and then exit Visual Studio .NET.

Sub and Function Procedures

Labs included in this chapter:

LAB 7.1 TWO DOLLAR MANIA

Scenario Shane O'Brien, the manager of the Two Dollar Mania store, wants an application that calculates and displays the total amount a customer owes. Every item in the store costs $2. The store clerks will enter the number of items purchased and an optional coupon code. The coupon code entitles the customer to one of the following discounts:

Coupon code	Discount rate
H17	5%
H75	10%
H99	25%

Solution Discussion The Two Dollar Mania application needs to provide areas for the user to enter the number of items purchased and the coupon code; you will use text boxes for this purpose. To prevent the user from entering a coupon code that contains more than three characters, and also to ensure that the letter in the coupon code is uppercase, you will set one of the text box's MaxLength property to three and its CharacterCasing property to Upper.

The application also needs to display the total amount due; you will use a label control for this purpose, because the user should not be able to change the amount after it has been displayed. You also will use a button control that allows the user to calculate and display the total amount due, and a button control for exiting the application. Additionally, you will use a procedure named CalculateTotalDue to calculate the total due. In this lab, the CalculateTotalDue procedure will be a Sub procedure. You will change the procedure to a Function procedure in Lab 7.2.

TOE Chart

Task	Object	Event
1. Calculate the total amount due 2. Display the total amount due in the lblTotal control	btnCalc	Click
End the application	btnExit	Click
Display the total amount due (from btnCalc)	lblTotal	None
Get and display the quantity purchased	txtQuantity	None
Select the existing text		Enter
Get and display the coupon code	txtCode	None
Select the existing text		Enter

FIGURE 7.1

User Interface

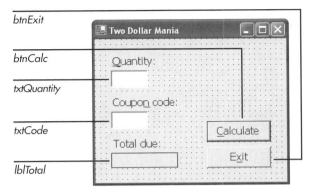

btnExit

btnCalc

txtQuantity

txtCode

lblTotal

FIGURE 7.2

Objects, Properties, and Settings

Object	Property	Setting
Label1	AutoSize Text	True &Quantity:
Label2	AutoSize Text	True Coupo&n code:
Label3	AutoSize Text	True Total due:
Label4	Name BorderStyle Text TextAlign	lblTotal FixedSingle (empty) MiddleCenter
TextBox1	Name Text	txtQuantity (empty)
TextBox2	Name CharacterCasing MaxLength Text	txtCode Upper 3 (empty)
Button1	Name Text	btnCalc &Calculate
Button2	Name Text	btnExit E&xit

FIGURE 7.3

Tab Order

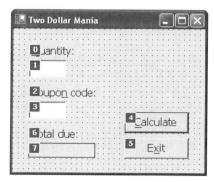

FIGURE 7.4

Pseudocode

---

btnCalc Click event procedure

1. assign the quantity purchased and coupon code to String variables
2. if the user entered a quantity purchased, and the quantity can be converted to a number

       assign the quantity purchased to an Integer variable

       call the CalculateTotalDue procedure to calculate the total due

       display the total due in the lblTotal control

     else

       display a message requesting the user to enter a valid quantity

     end if
3. send the focus to the txtQuantity control
4. select the existing text in the txtQuantity control

CalculateTotalDue procedure

1. assign the appropriate discount rate to a variable, as follows:

       coupon code value:

(empty)	assign 0 as the discount rate
H17	assign 5% as the discount rate
H75	assign 10% as the discount rate
H99	assign 25% as the discount rate
other	assign 0 as the discount rate
	display "Invalid coupon code." message

2. calculate the subtotal by multiplying the quantity purchased by the cost per item
3. calculate the discount by multiplying the subtotal by the discount rate
4. calculate the total due by subtracting the discount from the subtotal

(Figure is continued on next page)

> **btnExit Click event procedure**
> 1. close the application
>
> **txtQuantity Enter event procedure**
> 1. select the existing text
>
> **txtCode Enter event procedure**
> 1. select the existing text

FIGURE 7.5

Activity

1. Start Visual Studio .NET.
2. Click **File** on the Visual Studio .NET menu bar, point to **New**, and then click **Project**. The New Project dialog box opens.
3. If necessary, click **Visual Basic Projects** in the Project Types list box, and click **Windows Application** in the Templates list box.
4. Type **Two Dollar Mania Project** in the Name text box.
5. Use the **Browse** button to open the **VbDotNetLab\Chap07** folder.
6. If necessary, click the **More** button.
7. If necessary, select the **Create directory for Solution** check box.
8. Type **Two Dollar Mania Solution** in the New Solution Name text box.
9. Click the **OK** button to close the New Project dialog box.

Now set the appropriate properties of the form file object and form object.

To set the appropriate properties of the form file object and form object:
1. Right-click **Form1.vb** in the Solution Explorer window, then click **Rename**. Change the form file object's name from Form1.vb to **Two Dollar Mania Form.vb**.
2. Click the **form**, then click **(Name)** in the Properties window. Change the form object's name from Form1 to **frmDollar**.
3. Right-click **Two Dollar Mania Project** in the Solution Explorer window, then click **Properties**. Click the **Startup object** list arrow, and then click **frmDollar** in the list. Click the **OK** button.
4. Click the **form**, then change the values assigned to the following properties:

Font	**Tahoma, 12 pt**
Size	**296, 256**
StartPosition	**CenterScreen**
Text	**Two Dollar Mania**

5. Save the solution by clicking **File** on the menu bar, and then clicking **Save All**.

Next, add the appropriate controls to the interface, and then set the values of some of their properties.

To add the appropriate controls, then set the values of some of their properties:
1. Use the Label tool to add four label controls to the form.
2. Use the TextBox tool to add two text boxes to the form.

3. Use the Button tool to add two buttons to the form.

4. Use the chart shown in Figure 7.3 to set the properties of each control.

5. Position the controls as shown in Figure 7.2.

6. Lock the controls in place on the form.

7. Use Figure 7.4 to set the appropriate tab order.

8. Make the Calculate button the default button by setting the form's AcceptButton property to **btnCalc**.

9. Save the solution.

Now that the interface is complete, you can begin coding the application. First you will enter the appropriate comments and Option statements.

To enter the appropriate comments and Option statements:

1. Right-click the **form**, and then click **View Code** to open the Code Editor window.

2. Type the comments shown in Figure 7.6, replacing `<enter your name and date here>` with your name and the current date. Also type the Option statements shown in the figure.

Enter these comments and Option statements

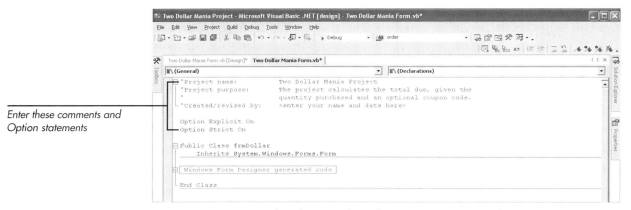

FIGURE 7.6 Code Editor window showing comments and Option statements

Now use the pseudocode shown earlier in Figure 7.5 to code the btnCalc control's Click event procedure.

To code the btnCalc control's Click event procedure:

1. Click the **Class Name** list arrow, and then click **btnCalc** in the list.

2. Click the **Method Name** list arrow, and then click **Click** in the list. The code template for the btnCalc_Click procedure appears in the Code Editor window.

3. Type **'calculates the total due** and press **Enter** twice.

First, you will declare the procedure's variables.

4. Type **'declare variables** and press **Enter**.

You will use two String variables to store the quantity ordered and coupon code entered by the user. If the user enters a quantity ordered, and the quantity can be converted to a number, you will store its numeric equivalent in an Integer variable. You will use a Decimal variable to store the total amount due. A variable is appropriate in each case because the amount will be different for each calculation.

5. Type **dim strCode as string** and press **Enter**.

6. Type **dim strQuantity as string** and press **Enter**.

7. Type **dim intQuantity as integer** and press **Enter**.

8. Type **dim decTotalDue as decimal** and press **Enter** twice.

The first step in the pseudocode for the btnCalc Click event procedure is to assign to the String variables the quantity purchased and coupon code entered by the user.

9. Type **'assign input to String variables** and press **Enter**.

10. Type **strcode= me.txtcode.text** and press **Enter**.

11. Type **strquantity = me.txtquantity.text** and press **Enter** twice.

The next step is a selection structure that determines whether the user entered a quantity purchased, and whether the quantity can be converted to a number. At this point, the quantity is stored in the strQuantity variable. If the strQuantity variable does not contain data, or if the data cannot be converted to a number, the selection structure's false path should display an appropriate message.

12. Type the comments and additional lines of code shown in Figure 7.7, and then position the insertion point as shown in the figure.

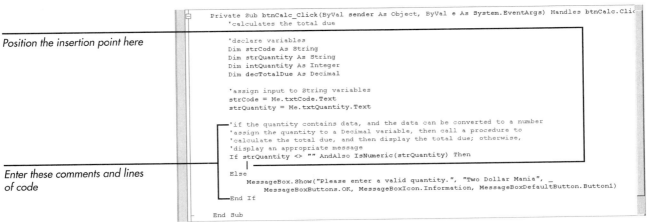

Position the insertion point here

Enter these comments and lines of code

```
Private Sub btnCalc_Click(ByVal sender As Object, ByVal e As System.EventArgs) Handles btnCalc.Cli
    'calculates the total due

    'declare variables
    Dim strCode As String
    Dim strQuantity As String
    Dim intQuantity As Integer
    Dim decTotalDue As Decimal

    'assign input to String variables
    strCode = Me.txtCode.Text
    strQuantity = Me.txtQuantity.Text

    'if the quantity contains data, and the data can be converted to a number
    'assign the quantity to a Decimal variable, then call a procedure to
    'calculate the total due, and then display the total due; otherwise,
    'display an appropriate message
    If strQuantity <> "" AndAlso IsNumeric(strQuantity) Then

    Else
        MessageBox.Show("Please enter a valid quantity.", "Two Dollar Mania", _
            MessageBoxButtons.OK, MessageBoxIcon.Information, MessageBoxDefaultButton.Button1)
    End If

End Sub
```

FIGURE 7.7 Comments and additional lines of code shown in the procedure

According to the pseudocode, if the user entered a quantity purchased that can be converted to a number, the first instruction in the selection structure's true path should assign the quantity to an Integer variable—in this case, the intQuantity variable.

13. Type **intquantity = convert.toint32(strquantity)** and press **Enter**.

The next instruction in the true path should call the CalculateTotalDue procedure to calculate the total due. In this lab, the CalculateTotalDue procedure will be a Sub procedure. Recall that you can use the Call statement, whose syntax is **Call** *procedurename*([*argumentlist*]), to call a Sub procedure. In the syntax, *procedurename* is the name of the procedure you are calling, and *argumentlist* (which is optional) is a comma-separated list of arguments you want passed to the procedure; most times, the arguments are variables. Recall that the arguments can be passed either *by value* or *by reference*. You pass an argument *by value* when the receiving procedure needs to know only the value stored in the variable. You pass an argument *by reference* when the receiving procedure needs to change the contents of the variable. The method you choose—*by value* or *by reference*—is specified in the receiving procedure's header.

For the CalculateTotalDue procedure to calculate the total due, it will need to know the quantity ordered and the coupon code; therefore, you will pass it the values stored in the intQuantity and strCode variables. The CalculateTotalDue procedure also will need a place to store the total amount due after it has been calculated; for this, you will pass it the address of the decTotalDue variable.

14. Type **call CalculateTotalDue(strcode, intquantity, dectotaldue)** and press **Enter**. (The squiggly line below the statement will go away when you enter the CalculateTotalDue procedure definition.)

The last instruction in the selection structure's true path should display the total due in the lblTotal control. You will display the total due with a dollar sign and two decimal places.

15. Type **me.lbltotal.text = dectotaldue.tostring("C2")**.

The last two steps in the btnCalc control's Click event procedure are to send the focus to the txtQuantity control, which is the control that the user most likely will access after making a calculation, and then select the existing text in the txtQuantity control.

16. Position the insertion point two lines below the `End If` clause, but above the `End Sub` clause. Type **'set the focus, then select the existing text** and press **Enter**.

17. Type **me.txtquantity.focus()** and press **Enter**.

18. Type **me.txtquantity.selectall()** and press **Enter**.

19. Save the solution.

Next, you will use the pseudocode shown earlier in Figure 7.5 to code the CalculateTotalDue procedure, which is responsible for calculating the total amount due.

To code the CalculateTotalDue procedure:

1. Position the insertion point in the blank line below the `Windows Form Designer generated code` entry, and then press **Enter**.

First, enter the procedure header and footer.

2. Type **private sub CalculateTotalDue()** and press **Enter**. Notice that the Code Editor enters the procedure footer (`End Sub`) for you.

When the CalculateTotalDue procedure is called, it will be passed the contents of the strCode and intQuantity variables along with the address of the decTotalDue variable. For the procedure to receive this information, you will need to enter three parameters in the procedure header. Two of the parameters will receive their respective information *by value*. The third parameter will receive its information *by reference*.

3. Enter the parameters shown in Figure 7.8, then position the insertion point as shown in the figure.

Enter these parameters

```
Public Class frmDollar
    Inherits System.Windows.Forms.Form

Windows Form Designer generated code

    Private Sub CalculateTotalDue(ByVal strCoupon As String, _
                          ByVal intNumber As Integer, _
                          ByRef decDue As Decimal)

    End Sub
```

Position the insertion point here

FIGURE 7.8 Parameters entered in the procedure header

TIP Notice that the number, data type, and sequence of the parameters in the procedure header match the number, data type, and sequence of the arguments in the Call statement entered in the btnCalc_Click procedure. Also notice that the names of the parameters do not need to be identical to the names of the arguments to which they correspond. Recall that, for clarity, it usually is better to use different names for the parameters and arguments.

TIP The variables in the CalculateTotalDue procedure header are procedure-level variables and can be used only by the CalculateTotalDue procedure.

4. Type **'calculates the total due** and press **Enter** twice.

First, declare a constant to represent the cost per item. Then declare the procedure's variables.

5. Type **'declare constant and variables** and press **Enter**.

6. Type **const decCOST as decimal = 2d** and press **Enter**.

The procedure will use three Decimal variables to store the discount rate, subtotal, and discount amount.

7. Type **dim decDiscountRate as decimal** and press **Enter**.

8. Type **dim decSubtotal as decimal** and press **Enter**.

9. Type **dim decDiscount as decimal** and press **Enter** twice.

The first step in the pseudocode for the CalculateTotalDue procedure is to assign the appropriate discount rate to a variable. The discount rate depends on the coupon code, which is passed to the CalculateTotalDue procedure by the Call statement in the btnCalc_Click procedure. For example, if the coupon code is H17, the discount rate is 5%. The CalculateTotalDue procedure stores the coupon code it receives in the strCoupon variable.

10. Type **'assign appropriate discount rate to variable** and press **Enter**.

11. Enter the Select Case statement shown in Figure 7.9, and then position the insertion point as shown in the figure.

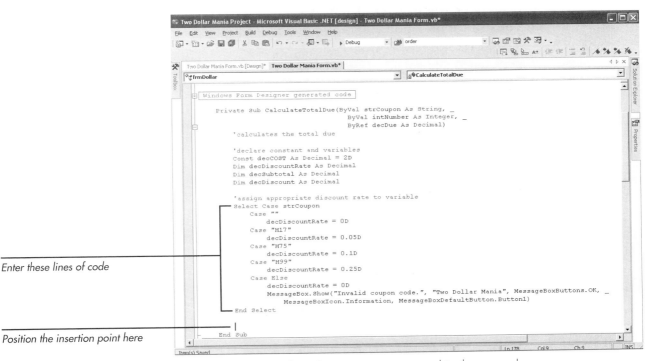

FIGURE 7.9 Select Case statement entered in the procedure

The second step in the pseudocode is to calculate the subtotal by multiplying the quantity purchased by the cost per item. The quantity purchased is passed to the CalculateTotalDue procedure by the Call statement in the btnCalc_Click procedure. The CalculateTotalDue procedure stores the value it receives in the intNumber variable. The cost per item is stored in the decCOST constant. You will store the result in the decSubtotal variable.

12. Type **'calculate subtotal, discount, and total due** and press **Enter**.

13. Type **decsubtotal = convert.todecimal(intnumber) * deccost** and press **Enter**.

The third step is to calculate the discount by multiplying the subtotal by the discount rate. The subtotal and discount rate are stored in the decSubtotal and decDiscountRate variables, respectively. You will store the result in the decDiscount variable.

14. Type **decdiscount = decsubtotal * decdiscountrate** and press **Enter**.

The last step in the pseudocode for the CalculateTotalDue procedure is to calculate the total due by subtracting the discount amount from the subtotal amount. You will assign the result to the decDue variable. Changing the contents of the decDue variable in the CalculateTotalDue procedure also changes the contents of the decTotalDue variable in the btnCalc_Click procedure. This is because the decTotalDue variable is passed *by reference* to the CalculateTotalDue procedure.

15. Type **decdue = decsubtotal – decdiscount** and press **Enter**.

Next, you will code the Click event procedure for the btnExit control, which is responsible for ending the application. You also will code the Enter event procedures for the txtQuantity and txtCode controls. The Enter event procedures are responsible for selecting the existing text in their respective text boxes when the text box receives the focus.

To code the btnExit_Click, txtQuantity_Enter, and txtCode_Enter procedures:

1. Display the code template for the btnExit control's Click event procedure.
2. Type **'ends the application** and press **Enter**.
3. Type **me.close()** and press **Enter**.
4. Display the code template for the txtQuantity control's Enter event procedure.
5. Type **'selects the existing text** and press **Enter**.
6. Type **me.txtquantity.selectall()** and press **Enter**.
7. Display the code template for the txtCode control's Enter event procedure.
8. Type **'selects the existing text** and press **Enter**.
9. Type **me.txtcode.selectall()** and press **Enter**.

Now that you have finished coding the application, you can test the application to verify that the code is working correctly.

To test the application:

1. Save the solution.
2. Start the application by clicking **Debug** on the menu bar, and then clicking **Start**. The blinking insertion point indicates that the txtQuantity control has the focus.

First, observe what happens when you click the Calculate button without entering a quantity.

3. Click the **Calculate** button. The message box shown in Figure 7.10 appears on the screen.

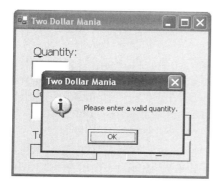

FIGURE 7.10   Message box resulting from invalid quantity entry

4. Press **Enter** to select the OK button, which closes the message box.

Now observe what happens when you enter a letter as the quantity.

5. Type **a** as the quantity and then press **Enter** to select the Calculate button, which is the default button. The message box shown in Figure 7.10 appears on the screen.

6. Close the message box.

Now display the total amount due for a customer purchasing 10 items. The total due should be $20.00.

7. Type **10** as the quantity and then press **Enter**. The btnCalc_Click procedure calls the CalculateTotalDue procedure to calculate the total amount due, and then displays the amount in the lblTotal control, as shown in Figure 7.11.

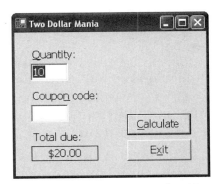

FIGURE 7.11 Two Dollar Mania application

Next, display the total amount due for a customer purchasing 5 items and using coupon code H17. The total due should be $9.50.

8. Type **5** as the quantity. Press **Tab**, and then type **h17** as the coupon code. Press **Enter**. The application calculates the total amount due and then displays the amount ($9.50) in the lblTotal control.

Now display the total amount due for a customer purchasing 20 items and using coupon code H75. The total due should be $36.00.

9. Type **20** as the quantity. Press **Tab**, and then type **h75** as the coupon code. Press **Enter**. The application calculates the total amount due and then displays the amount ($36.00) in the lblTotal control.

Next, display the total amount due for a customer purchasing 15 items and using coupon code H99. The total due should be $22.50.

10. Type **15** as the quantity. Press **Tab**, and then type **h99** as the coupon code. Press **Enter**. The application calculates the total amount due and then displays the amount ($22.50) in the lblTotal control.

Finally, observe what happens when you enter an incorrect coupon code.

11. Press **Tab** to move the focus to the txtCode control. Type **h12** as the coupon code and then press **Enter**. The CalculateTotalDue procedure displays the message box shown in Figure 7.12.

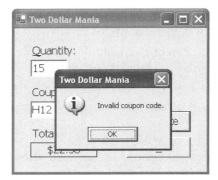

FIGURE 7.12 Message box resulting from invalid coupon code entry

12. Click the **OK** button to close the message box.

The CalculateTotalDue procedure calculates the total amount due without any discount; it then displays the amount in the lblTotal control. In this case, the total amount is $30.00, which is the number of items (15) multiplied by the cost per item ($2).

13. Click the **Exit** button. The btnExit_Click procedure ends the application.

14. Close the Output window, and then close the Code Editor window.

You are finished with the solution, so you can close it.

15. Click **File** on the menu bar, and then click **Close Solution**.

LAB 7.2 MODIFIED TWO DOLLAR MANIA

Scenario Shane O'Brien, the manager of the Two Dollar Mania store, has asked you to modify the application that you created in Lab 7.1. More specifically, he wants you to remove the total amount due when the user makes a change to the quantity or coupon code. This is because, when the user changes one or both of these values, the total amount due is no longer correct; to avoid confusion, the value should be removed from the lblTotal control. In addition, so that you can practice with Function procedures, you also will modify the application so that it uses a Function procedure rather than a Sub procedure.

Solution Discussion The application must remove the contents of the lblTotal control when the user changes the contents of either the txtQuantity control or the txtCode control. You can accomplish this task by coding each text box's TextChanged event. A control's TextChanged event occurs when a change is made to the control's Text property.

Activity

1. Use Windows to make a copy of the Two Dollar Mania Solution folder, which is contained in the VbDotNetLab\Chap07 folder. Rename the copy Modified Two Dollar Mania Solution.

2. If necessary, start Visual Studio .NET.

3. Open the **Two Dollar Mania Solution** (Two Dollar Mania Solution.sln) file contained in the **VbDotNetLab\Chap07\Modified Two Dollar Mania Solution** folder. The user interface shown in Figure 7.2 in Lab 7.1 appears on the screen.

First, you modify the application so that it clears the contents of the lblTotal control when the user changes the text in either text box. You can accomplish this task by entering the Me.lblTotal.Text = "" statement in each text box's TextChanged event, as shown in Example 1 in Figure 7.13. Or, you can enter the statement in an independent Sub procedure, and then use the Handles clause to associate both TextChanged events with the procedure, as shown in Example 2 in Figure 7.13. When either TextChanged event occurs, it automatically invokes the Sub procedure with which it is associated.

Example 1

```
Private Sub txtQuantity_TextChanged(ByVal sender As Object, ByVal e As System.EventArgs) _
    Handles txtQuantity.TextChanged
    'clears the total due
    Me.lblTotal.Text = ""
End Sub


Private Sub txtCode_TextChanged(ByVal sender As Object, ByVal e As System.EventArgs) _
    Handles txtCode.TextChanged
    'clears the total due
    Me.lblTotal.Text = ""
End Sub
```

Example 2

```
Private Sub ClearTotalDue(ByVal sender As Object, ByVal e As System.EventArgs) _
    Handles txtQuantity.TextChanged, txtCode.TextChanged
    'clears the total due
    Me.lblTotal.Text = ""
End Sub
```

FIGURE 7.13　　Examples of clearing the total due

To clear the contents of the lblTotal control when a change is made to a text box:

1. Open the Code Editor window. Position the insertion point in the blank line below the `Windows Form Designer generated code` entry, and then press **Enter**.

2. Enter the code shown in Example 2 in Figure 7.13.

3. Save the solution, then start the application.

First, display the total amount due for a customer purchasing 5 items.

4. Type **5** in the txtQuantity control, which causes the control's TextChanged event to occur. When the TextChanged event occurs, the computer processes the `Me.lblTotal.Text = ""` assignment statement in the ClearTotalDue procedure; this is because the Handles clause associates the event with the procedure. You do not see the effect of the assignment statement because the lblTotal control does not currently contain any text.

5. Press **Enter** to select the Calculate button. The application calculates the total amount due and then displays the amount ($10.00) in the lblTotal control.

Now display the total amount due for a customer purchasing 2 items.

6. Type **2** in the txtQuantity control. Here again, the txtQuantity control's TextChanged event occurs and the computer processes the assignment statement in the ClearTotalDue procedure; the assignment statement clears the contents of the lblTotal control.

7. Press **Enter** to select the Calculate button. The application calculates the total amount due and then displays the amount ($4.00) in the lblTotal control.

Now display the total amount due for a customer purchasing 2 items using coupon code H17.

8. Press **Tab** to move the focus to the txtCode control.

9. Type **h** in the txtCode control, which causes the control's TextChanged event to occur. When the TextChanged event occurs, the computer processes the `Me.lblTotal.Text = ""` assignment statement in the ClearTotalDue procedure; this is because the Handles clause associates the event with the procedure.

10. Type **17** and press **Enter**. The application calculates the total amount due and then displays the amount ($3.80) in the lblTotal control.

The txtCode control's TextChanged event occurs after you type the 1 and also after you type the 7.

11. Click the **Exit** button. The btnExit_Click procedure ends the application.

Finally, you modify the application so that it calculates the total amount due using a Function procedure rather than a Sub procedure.

To calculate the total amount due using a Function procedure rather than a Sub procedure:

1. Change the Call statement in the btnCalc_Click procedure to decTotalDue = CalculateTotalDue(strCode, intQuantity).

2. Make the appropriate modifications to the CalculateTotalDue procedure. The procedure should return the total amount due.

3. Save the solution, then start the application.

First, display the total amount due for a customer purchasing 5 items with a coupon code of H99.

4. Type **5** as the quantity. Press **Tab**, then type **h99** as the coupon code. Press **Enter**. The application calculates the total amount due and then displays the amount ($7.50) in the lblTotal control.

5. Click the **Exit** button.

6. Close the Output window, then close the Code Editor window.

You are finished with the solution, so you can close it.

7. Close the solution. Temporarily display the Solution Explorer window to verify that the solution is closed.

LAB 7.3 MONTHLY INCOME

Scenario In this lab, you modify an application that allows the user to enter four weekly income amounts. The application then calculates and displays the monthly income amount. You will modify the application so that it uses an independent Sub procedure to remove any dollar signs, commas, and spaces from the weekly amounts.

Solution Discussion The Monthly Income application uses four text boxes for entering the weekly income amounts, and a label control for displaying the monthly income amount. In addition, the application uses a button control for calculating and displaying the monthly income amount, and a button control for ending the application.

User Interface

FIGURE 7.14

Activity

1. If necessary, start Visual Studio .NET.

2. Open the Monthly Income Solution (Monthly Income Solution.sln) file contained in the VbDotNetLab\Chap07\Monthly Income Solution folder. The user interface shown in Figure 7.14 appears on the screen.

3. Open the Code Editor window. Most of the application's code has already been entered for you.

4. Replace the `<enter your name and date here>` text with your name and the current date.

5. Position the insertion point in the blank line below the `Windows Form Designer generated code` entry, and then press **Enter**.

6. Create a Sub procedure named RemoveCharacters. When the procedure is called, it will be passed the address of a String variable. The procedure should remove any dollar signs, commas, or spaces from the variable.

7. Study closely the code entered in the btnCalc_Click procedure.

8. Enter the appropriate Call statements in the blank line below the `'call a procedure to remove any dollar signs, commas, or spaces from the String variables` comment.

9. Save the solution, then start the application.

First, test the application using weekly income amounts of $50, 67.50, 1,230, and $24 35.

10. Type **$50** in the Week 1 box, **67.50** in the Week 2 box, **1,230** in the Week 3 box, and **$24 35** in the Week 4 box. (Be sure to include a space after the number 4.)

11. Click the **Calculate** button. The application displays the monthly income amount in the lblTotal control, as shown in Figure 7.15.

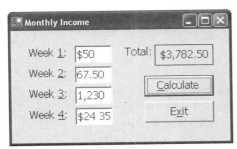

FIGURE 7.15 Monthly Income application

12. Click the **Exit** button to end the application.

13. Close the Output window, then close the Code Editor window.

You are finished with the solution, so you can close it.

14. Close the solution. Temporarily display the Solution Explorer window to verify that the solution is closed.

BEYOND THE TEXT

LAB 7.4 WAVER SWIMWEAR

Scenario The sales manager at Waver Swimwear wants an application that he can use to calculate a salesperson's bonus amount. The sales manager will enter the salesperson's sales amount. The application should calculate the bonus amount using rates of either 5% or 7%, and then display the bonus amount in the interface.

In this lab, you learn how to use a main menu control to include one or more menus in an application. Each menu contains a menu title, which appears on the menu bar at the top of a Windows form. When you click a menu title, its corresponding menu opens and displays a list of options, called menu items. The menu items can be commands (such as Open or Exit), separator bars, or submenu titles. As in all Windows applications, clicking a command on a menu executes the command, and clicking a submenu title opens an additional menu of options; each of the options on a submenu is referred to as a submenu item. The purpose of a separator bar is to visually group together the related items on a menu or submenu. Figure 7.16 identifies the location of these menu elements.

FIGURE 7.16 Location of menu elements

Each menu element is considered an object and has a set of properties associated with it. The most commonly used properties for a menu element are the Name and Text properties. The Name property is used by the programmer to refer to the menu element in code. The Text property, on the other hand, stores the menu element's caption, which is the text that the user sees when he or she is working with the menu. The caption indicates the purpose of the menu element. Examples of familiar captions for menu elements include Edit, Save As, Copy, and Exit.

Menu title captions should be one word only, with the first letter capitalized. Each menu title should have a unique access key. Menu item captions, on the other hand, can be from one to three words. Use book title capitalization for the menu item captions, and assign each menu item a unique access key. If a menu item requires additional information from the user, the Windows standard is to place an ellipsis (...) at the end of the caption. The ellipsis alerts the user that the menu item requires more information before it can perform its task.

When designing a menu, you must be sure to follow the standard conventions used in Windows applications. For example, the File menu is always the first menu on the menu bar, and typically contains commands for opening, saving, and printing files, as well as exiting the application. Cut, Copy, and Paste commands, on the other hand, are placed on an Edit menu. If an application contains an Edit menu, it typically is the second menu on the menu bar.

In addition to an access key, some menu items also have a shortcut key. Shortcut keys appear to the right of a menu item and allow you to select an item without opening the menu. For example, in Windows applications you can select the Save command when the File menu is closed by pressing Ctrl+S. You should assign shortcut keys only to commonly used menu items. The difference between a menu item's access key and its shortcut key is that the access key can be used only when the menu is open, whereas the shortcut key can be used only when the menu is closed.

Solution Discussion The Waver Swimwear application will use a text box for entering the sales amount, and a label control for displaying the bonus amount. It also will use a main menu control to display a File menu and a Calculate menu. The File menu will contain an Exit menu item that allows the user to end the application. The Calculate menu will contain two menu items that allow the user to calculate either a 5% bonus amount or a 7% bonus amount.

TOE Chart

Task	Object	Event
1. Calculate a 5% bonus amount 2. Display the bonus amount in the lblBonus control	mnuCalculate5	Click
1. Calculate a 7% bonus amount 2. Display the bonus amount in the lblBonus control	mnuCalculate7	Click
End the application	mnuFileExit	Click
Display the bonus amount (from either mnuCalculate5 or mnuCalculate7)	lblBonus	None
Get the sales amount	txtSales	None
Select the existing text		Enter

FIGURE 7.17

Pseudocode

txtSales Enter event procedure

1. select the existing text

mnuFileExit Click event procedure

1. close the application

mnuCalculate5 Click event procedure

1. Call the CalcAndShowBonus procedure; pass the bonus rate (5%) to the procedure

mnuCalculate7 Click event procedure

1. Call the CalcAndShowBonus procedure; pass the bonus rate (7%) to the procedure

CalcAndShowBonus procedure

1. assign the sales amount to a String variable
2. if the user entered a sales amount, and the sales amount can be converted to a number

   assign the sales amount to a Decimal variable

   calculate the bonus amount by multiplying the sales amount by the bonus rate, which is received from either mnuCalculate5_Click or mnuCalculate7_Click

   else

   assign 0 as the bonus amount

   display a message requesting the user to re-enter the sales amount

   end if
3. display the bonus amount in the lblBonus control
4. select the existing text in the txtSales control

FIGURE 7.18

Activity

1. If necessary, start Visual Studio .NET.
2. Open the Waver Swimwear Solution (Waver Swimwear Solution.sln) file contained in the VbDotNetLab\Chap07\Waver Swimwear Solution folder. The user interface appears on the screen.

First, learn how to use a main menu control to add a menu to the form.

3. Click the **MainMenu tool** in the toolbox, and then drag a main menu control to the form. When you release the mouse button, the main menu control appears in the component tray, and the words "Type Here" appear on the form's title bar, as shown in Figure 7.19. The component tray stores the objects that do not appear in the interface when an application is running.

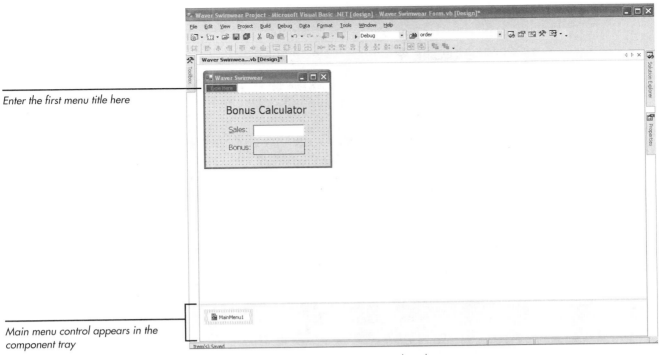

Enter the first menu title here

Main menu control appears in the component tray

FIGURE 7.19 Main menu control in the component tray

4. Use the Properties window to change the main menu control's name from MainMenu1 to **mnuMain**.

5. Click the **form**, then change the form's Menu property to **mnuMain**.

TIP ••••••

If you do not set the form's Menu property to the name of the main menu control, the menu will not appear on the form when the application is running. It also won't appear on the form during Design time, unless the main menu control is selected in the component tray.

First, create the File menu. As is customary in Windows applications, you use the letter F as the File menu's access key.

6. Click **Type Here** on the menu bar, then type **&File**. The words "Type Here" appear below the File menu title and also to the right of the File menu title, as shown in Figure 7.20. The "Type Here" that appears below the menu title allows you to add a menu item to the File menu. The "Type Here" that appears to the right of the menu title allows you to add another menu title to the menu bar.

Second menu title

First menu title

First menu item on the first menu

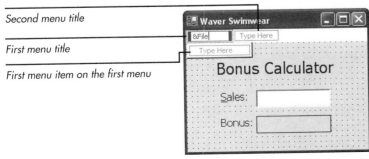

FIGURE 7.20 Menu title shown in the interface

Now change the menu title's name to mnuFile.

7. Use the Properties window to change the menu title's name from MenuItem1 to **mnuFile**.

Now include an Exit menu item on the File menu. The letter X is the standard access key for the Exit option.

8. Click the **Type Here** that appears below the File menu title, and then type **E&xit**. Use the Properties window to change the menu item's name to **mnuFileExit**.

Now create the Calculate menu.

9. Click the **Type Here** that appears to the right of the File menu title, and then type **&Calculate**. Use the Properties window to change the menu title's name to **mnuCalculate**.

10. Click the **Type Here** that appears below the Calculate menu title, and then type **&5% Bonus**. Use the Properties window to change the menu item's name to **mnuCalculate5**. Also change its Shortcut property to **F5**. When you start the application and open the Calculate menu, F5 will appear to the right of the 5% Bonus menu item. You verify that fact in the next set of steps.

11. Click the **Type Here** that appears below the 5% Bonus menu item, and then type **&7% Bonus**. Use the Properties window to change the menu item's name to **mnuCalculate7**. Also change its Shortcut property to **F7**. When you start the application and open the Calculate menu, F7 will appear to the right of the 7% Bonus menu item. The completed Calculate menu is shown in Figure 7.21.

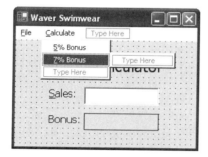

FIGURE 7.21   Completed Calculate menu

TIP ••••⁚ Shortcut keys do not appear when a menu is opened in Design mode. They appear only when the menu is opened while the application is running.

TIP ••••⁚ To insert a separator bar above a menu item, right-click the menu item, and then click Insert Separator.

Now that you have finished creating the File and Calculate menus, you can code the application and then test it to verify that it is working correctly.

To code the application, and then test it:

1. Open the Code Editor window.

2. Replace the `<enter your name and date here>` text with your name and the current date.

3. Display the code template for the txtSales control's Enter event procedure. Type **'selects the existing text** and press **Enter**, then type **me.txtsales.selectall()** and press **Enter**.

4. Display the code template for the mnuFileExit control's Click event procedure. Type **'ends the application** and press **Enter**, then type **me.close()** and press **Enter**.

5. Display the code template for the mnuCalculate5 control's Click event procedure. Type **'passes 5% to the CalcAndShowBonus procedure** and press **Enter**, then enter the appropriate Call statement.

6. Display the code template for the mnuCalculate7 control's Click event procedure. Type **'passes 7% to the CalcAndShowBonus procedure** and press **Enter**, then enter the appropriate Call statement.

7. Position the insertion point in the blank line below the `Windows Form Designer generated code` entry, and then press **Enter**.

8. Create a Sub procedure named CalcAndShowBonus. When the procedure is called, it will be passed a number of the Decimal data type.

9. Use the pseudocode shown earlier in Figure 7.18 to complete the CalcAndShowBonus procedure. Include meaningful comments in the procedure.

10. Save the solution, then start the application.

First, calculate a 5% bonus on sales of $1000. The bonus should be $50.00.

11. Type **1000** as the sales amount, then click **Calculate** on the menu bar. The Calculate menu opens and displays two options, as shown in Figure 7.22. Notice that the shortcut keys (F5 and F7) appear next to the menu items.

Shortcut keys

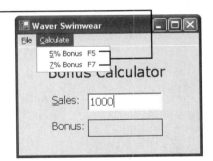

FIGURE 7.22 Calculate menu

12. Click **5% Bonus**. The mnuCalculate5_Click procedure passes the applicable bonus rate to the CalcAndShowBonus procedure, which calculates and displays the bonus amount, as shown in Figure 7.23.

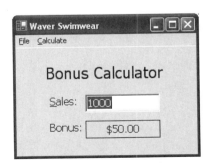

FIGURE 7.23 Monthly Income application

Now calculate a 7% bonus on sales of $1000. The bonus should be $70.00.

13. Press **F7** to select the 7% Bonus option on the Calculate menu. The mnuCalculate7_Click procedure passes the applicable bonus rate to the CalcAndShowBonus procedure, which calculates and displays the bonus amount—in this case, $70.00.

14. Click **File** on the menu bar, and then click **Exit**. The mnuFileExit_Click procedure ends the application.

15. Close the Output window, and then close the Code Editor window.

16. Close the solution, and then exit Visual Studio .NET.

Sequential Access Files and Error Handling

Labs included in this chapter:

- Lab 8.1 Micro Warehouse
- Lab 8.2 Modified Micro Warehouse
- Lab 8.3 Carlos Coffees
- Lab 8.4 Dialog Box Example

LAB 8.1 MICRO WAREHOUSE

Scenario Micro Warehouse sends mail-order catalogs to businesses in many U.S. cities. The company wants an application that will record the city names and corresponding ZIP codes in a sequential access file.

Solution Discussion The Micro Warehouse application needs to provide areas for the user to enter the ZIP code and city name; you will use text boxes for this purpose. You also will use a button control that allows the user to write the ZIP code and city name to a sequential access file, and a button control for exiting the application.

TOE Chart

Task	Object	Event
1. Open a sequential access file named zipcity.txt for append 2. Write the ZIP code and city name to the file 3. Close the file 4. Send the focus to the txtZip control 5. Select the existing text in the txtZip control	btnWrite	Click
End the application	btnExit	Click
Get and display the ZIP code	txtZip	None
Select the existing text		Enter
Get and display the city name	txtCity	None
Select the existing text		Enter

FIGURE 8.1

User Interface

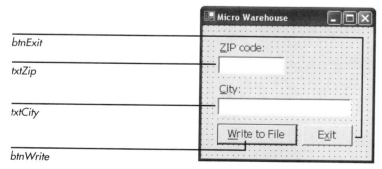

btnExit

txtZip

txtCity

btnWrite

FIGURE 8.2

Objects, Properties, and Settings

Object	Property	Setting
Label1	AutoSize Text	True &ZIP code:
Label2	AutoSize Text	True &City:
TextBox1	Name Text	txtZip (empty)
TextBox2	Name Text	txtCity (empty)
Button1	Name Text	btnWrite &Write to File
Button2	Name Text	btnExit E&xit

FIGURE 8.3

Tab Order

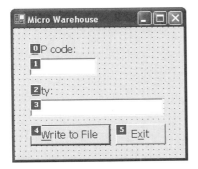

FIGURE 8.4

Pseudocode

btnWrite Click event procedure
1. assign the ZIP code and city name to variables
2. include the following in the Try section of a Try/Catch block:
    if the user entered a ZIP code and a city name
        open the zipcity.txt file for append
        write the ZIP code and city name to the file
        close the file
    else
        display a message prompting the user to enter the ZIP code and city name
    end if

    include the following in the Catch section of a Try/Catch block:
    use a general Catch statement to handle any errors
        if an error occurs, display a description of the error in a message box
3. send the focus to the txtZip control
4. select the existing text in the txtZip control

btnExit Click event procedure
1. close the application

txtCity Enter event procedure
1. select the existing text

txtZip Enter event procedure
1. select the existing text

FIGURE 8.5

Activity

1. Start Visual Studio .NET.
2. Click **File** on the Visual Studio .NET menu bar, point to **New**, and then click **Project**. The New Project dialog box opens.
3. If necessary, click **Visual Basic Projects** in the Project Types list box, and click **Windows Application** in the Templates list box.
4. Type **Micro Warehouse Project** in the Name text box.
5. Use the **Browse** button to open the **VbDotNetLab\Chap08** folder.
6. If necessary, click the **More** button.
7. If necessary, select the **Create directory for Solution** check box.
8. Type **Micro Warehouse Solution** in the New Solution Name text box.
9. Click the **OK** button to close the New Project dialog box.

Now set the appropriate properties of the form file object and form object.

To set the appropriate properties of the form file object and form object:

1. Right-click **Form1.vb** in the Solution Explorer window, then click **Rename**. Change the form file object's name from Form1.vb to **Micro Warehouse Form.vb**.

2. Click the **form**, then click **(Name)** in the Properties window. Change the form object's name from Form1 to **frmMicro**.

3. Right-click **Micro Warehouse Project** in the Solution Explorer window, then click **Properties**. Click the **Startup object** list arrow, and then click **frmMicro** in the list. Click the **OK** button.

4. Click the **form**, then change the values assigned to the following properties:

Font	**Tahoma, 12 pt**
Size	**264, 240**
StartPosition	**CenterScreen**
Text	**Micro Warehouse**

5. Save the solution by clicking **File** on the menu bar, and then clicking **Save All**.

Next, add the appropriate controls to the interface, and then set the values of some of their properties.

To add the appropriate controls, then set the values of some of their properties:

1. Use the Label tool to add two label controls to the form.

2. Use the TextBox tool to add two text boxes to the form.

3. Use the Button tool to add two buttons to the form.

4. Use the chart shown in Figure 8.3 to set the properties of each control.

5. Position the controls as shown in Figure 8.2.

6. Lock the controls in place on the form.

7. Use Figure 8.4 to set the appropriate tab order.

8. Make the Write to File button the default button by setting the form's AcceptButton property to **btnWrite**.

9. Save the solution.

Now that the interface is complete, you can begin coding the application. First you will enter the appropriate comments and Option statements.

To enter the appropriate comments and Option statements:

1. Right-click the **form**, and then click **View Code** to open the Code Editor window.

2. Type the comments shown in Figure 8.6, replacing <enter your name and date here> with your name and the current date. Also type the Option statements shown in the figure.

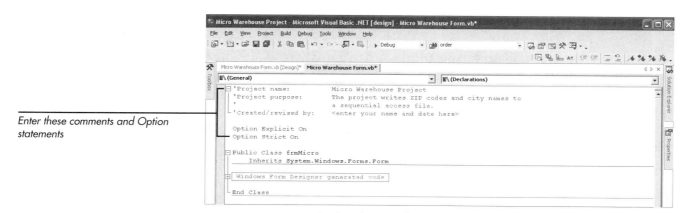

Enter these comments and Option statements

FIGURE 8.6   Code Editor window showing comments and Option statements

Now use the pseudocode shown earlier in Figure 8.5 to code the btnWrite control's Click event procedure.

To code the btnWrite control's Click event procedure:

1. Click the **Class Name** list arrow, and then click **btnWrite** in the list.

2. Click the **Method Name** list arrow, and then click **Click** in the list. The code template for the btnWrite_Click procedure appears in the Code Editor window.

3. Type **'writes information to a sequential access file** and press **Enter** twice.

First, you will declare the procedure's variables.

4. Type **'declare variables** and press **Enter**.

You will use two String variables to store the ZIP code and city name entered by the user. You also will use a StreamWriter variable to store the address of a StreamWriter object; the procedure will use the object to write the ZIP code and city name to a sequential access file.

5. Type **dim strZip as string** and press **Enter**.

6. Type **dim strCity as string** and press **Enter**.

7. Type **dim swrStreamWriter as io.streamwriter** and press **Enter** twice.

The first step in the pseudocode for the btnWrite Click event procedure is to assign to variables the ZIP code and city name entered by the user.

8. Type **'assign input to variables** and press **Enter**.

9. Type **strzip= me.txtzip.text** and press **Enter**.

10. Type **strcity = me.txtcity.text** and press **Enter** twice.

The next step is a Try/Catch block, which is a block of code that uses both the Try and Catch statements. Recall that you use the Try statement to catch (or trap) an exception when it occurs in a program. An exception is an error that occurs while a program is running. You use the Catch statement to have the computer take the appropriate action to resolve the exception.

11. Type **try** and press **Enter**. Notice that the Code Editor enters the `Catch ex As Exception` and `End Try` clauses for you.

According to the pseudocode, the Try section of the Try/Catch block should contain a selection structure that determines whether the user entered a ZIP code and a city name. If the user did not enter both items of data, the selection structure's false path should display an appropriate message.

12. Type the comments and additional lines of code shown in Figure 8.7, and then position the insertion point as shown in the figure.

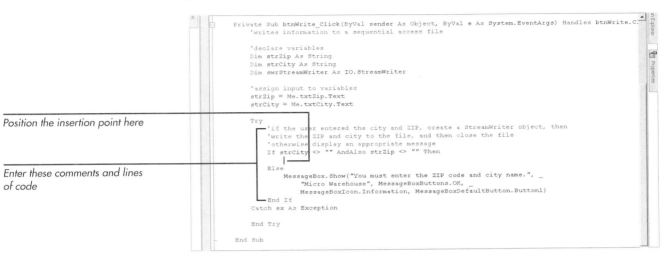

Position the insertion point here

Enter these comments and lines of code

FIGURE 8.7   Comments and additional lines of code shown in the procedure

If the user entered a ZIP code and a city name, the first instruction in the selection structure's true path should open a sequential access file named zipcity.txt for append. Opening a file for append allows you to write new data to the end of the existing data in the file. If the file does not exist, the file is created before data is written to it. Recall that the syntax for opening a sequential access file is *variablename* = **IO.File.***method*(*filename*). In the syntax, *variablename* is the name of either a StreamWriter or StreamReader variable, and *filename* is the name of the file you want to open. *Method* can be OpenText, CreateText, or AppendText.

13. Type **swrstreamwriter = io.file.appendtext("zipcity.txt")** and press **Enter**.

The next instruction in the true path should write the ZIP code and city name to the file. The ZIP code and city name are considered fields; together, they form a record.

TIP •••• A field is a single item of information about a person, place, or thing. A record is one or more related fields that contain all of the necessary data about a specific person, place, or thing.

You write a record to a sequential access file using the WriteLine method. The syntax of the WriteLine method is *variablename*.**WriteLine**(*data*), where *variablename* is the name of a StreamWriter variable, and *data* is the information you want written to the file associated with the variable. The WriteLine method writes the *data* and a line terminator character to the file. The line terminator character positions the file pointer at the beginning of the next line in the file. Recall that, when writing a multi-field record to a sequential access file, programmers separate each field with a special character, such as a comma or the number symbol (#); this is done to distinguish one field from the next when reading the record later.

14. Type **swrstreamwriter.writeline(strzip & "#" & strcity)** and press **Enter**.

The last instruction in the selection structure's true path should close the file. You close a sequential access file using the Close method. The syntax of the Close method is *variablename*.**Close**(), where *variablename* is the name of either a StreamReader or StreamWriter variable.

15. Type **swrstreamwriter.close()** and press **Enter**.

You have finished coding the Try section of the Try/Catch block; you now code the Catch section. According to the pseudocode, the Catch section should display a message indicating the error that occurred.

16. Type the comment and MessageBox.Show method shown in Figure 8.8, then position the insertion point as shown in the figure.

Enter this comment and code

Position the insertion point here

```
Catch ex As Exception
      'handles any errors
      MessageBox.Show(ex.Message, "Micro Warehouse", MessageBoxButtons.OK, _
                MessageBoxIcon.Information, MessageBoxDefaultButton.Button1)
End Try

End Sub
```

FIGURE 8.8   Comment and code entered in the Catch section

The last two steps in the pseudocode for the btnWrite Click event procedure are to send the focus to the txtZip control and also select the control's existing text.

17. Type **'set the focus and select the existing text** and press **Enter**.

18. Type **me.txtzip.focus()** and press **Enter**.

19. Type **me.txtzip.selectall()** and press **Enter**.

20. Save the solution.

Next, you will code the Click event procedure for the btnExit control, which is responsible for ending the application. You also will code the Enter event procedures for the txtCity and txtZip controls. The Enter event procedures are responsible for selecting the existing text in their respective text boxes when the text box receives the focus.

To code the btnExit_Click, txtCity_Enter, and txtZip_Enter procedures:

1. Display the code template for the btnExit control's Click event procedure.

2. Type **'ends the application** and press **Enter**.

3. Type **me.close()** and press **Enter**.

4. Display the code template for the txtCity control's Enter event procedure.

5. Type **'selects the existing text** and press **Enter**.

6. Type **me.txtcity.selectall()** and press **Enter**.

7. Display the code template for the txtZip control's Enter event procedure.

8. Type **'selects the existing text** and press **Enter**.

9. Type **me.txtzip.selectall()** and press **Enter**.

Now that you have finished coding the application, you can test the application to verify that the code is working correctly.

To test the application:

1. Save the solution.

2. Start the application by clicking **Debug** on the menu bar, and then clicking **Start**. The blinking insertion point indicates that the txtZip control has the focus.

First, observe what happens when you click the Write to File button without entering any data.

3. Click the **Write to File** button. The message box shown in Figure 8.9 appears on the screen.

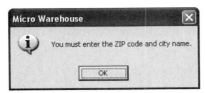

FIGURE 8.9   Message box that appears when the user does not enter the appropriate data

4. Press **Enter** to select the OK button, which closes the message box.

Now observe what happens when you enter a ZIP code but do not enter a city name.

5. Type **60101** as the ZIP code and then press **Enter** to select the Write to File button, which is the default button. The message box shown earlier in Figure 8.9 appears on the screen.

6. Close the message box.

Now observe what happens when you enter a city name but do not enter a ZIP code.

7. Press **Delete** to remove the contents of the txtZip control, then press **Tab** to move the focus to the txtCity control.

8. Type **Chicago** and press **Enter**. The message box shown earlier in Figure 8.9 appears on the screen.

9. Close the message box.

Now use the application to write a ZIP code and city name to the sequential access file.

10. Type **60101** as the ZIP code, and then press **Tab**. Type **Addison** as the city name, and then press **Enter**. The btnWrite_Click procedure opens the zipcity.txt file for append. It then writes the ZIP code and city name to the file, and then closes the file. Lastly, the procedure sends the focus to the txtZip control and also selects the control's existing text, as shown in Figure 8.10.

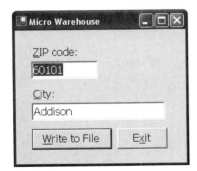

FIGURE 8.10   Micro Warehouse application

11. Enter the following five ZIP codes and city names to the file.

ZIP code	City name
60102	**Algonquin**
60103	**Bartlett**
61920	**Charleston**
60514	**Clarendon Hills**
60561	**Darien**

12. Click the **Exit** button. The btnExit_Click procedure ends the application.

13. Close the Output window, and then close the Code Editor window.

Now view the contents of the zipcity.txt file.

14. Click **File** on the menu bar. Point to **Open**, and then click **File**. The Open File dialog box opens.

15. Open the **bin** folder, which is located in the VbDotNetLab\Chap08\Micro Warehouse Solution\Micro Warehouse Project folder.

16. Click **zipcity.txt** in the list of filenames, and then click the **Open** button in the Open File dialog box. Six records appear in the file, as shown in Figure 8.11. Each record contains a ZIP code field followed by the number symbol and a city name field.

Close button

City name field

Number symbol

ZIP code field

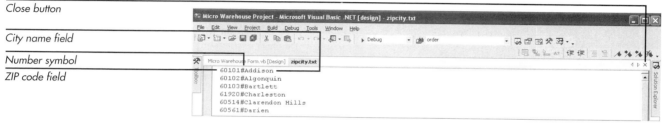

FIGURE 8.11 Contents of the zipcity.txt file

17. Close the zipcity.txt window by clicking its **Close** button.

You are finished with the solution, so you can close it.

18. Click **File** on the menu bar, and then click **Close Solution**.

LAB 8.2 MODIFIED MICRO WAREHOUSE

Scenario In this lab, you modify the application you created in Lab 8.1. The modified application will display the name of the city corresponding to the ZIP code entered by the user.

Solution Discussion In this application, the user will not enter the city name; rather, the application will display the city name. Therefore, you will replace the txtCity control with a label control named lblCity. Additionally, you will replace the Write to File button with a Display City button.

Pseudocode

btnDisplay Click event procedure
1. assign the ZIP code entered by the user to a variable
2. include the following in the Try section of a Try/Catch block:

    if the user entered a ZIP code

        open the zipcity.txt file for input

        repeat until there are no more characters to read or the ZIP code was found

            read a record from the file

            split the record into the ZIP code and city name fields

            if the ZIP code matches the ZIP code entered by the user

                display the city name in the lblCity control

                assign True to the blnZipFound variable

            end if

        end repeat

        close the file

        if the ZIP code was not found in the file

            display the "Unknown ZIP code." message

        end if

    else

        display a message prompting the user to enter the ZIP code

    end if

    include the following in the Catch section of a Try/Catch block:

    use a general Catch statement to handle any errors

        if an error occurs, display a description of the error in a message box
3. send the focus to the txtZip control
4. select the existing text in the txtZip control

btnExit Click event procedure
1. close the application

txtZip Enter event procedure
1. select the existing text

FIGURE 8.12

Activity

1. Use Windows to make a copy of the Micro Warehouse Solution folder, which is contained in the VbDotNetLab\Chap08 folder. Rename the copy Modified Micro Warehouse Solution.

2. If necessary, start Visual Studio .NET.

3. Open the Micro Warehouse Solution (Micro Warehouse Solution.sln) file contained in the VbDotNetLab\Chap08\Modified Micro Warehouse Solution folder.

4. Right-click **Micro Warehouse Form.vb** in the Solution Explorer window, and then click **View Designer**. The user interface shown in Figure 8.2 in Lab 8.1 appears on the screen.

5. Unlock the controls.

6. Delete the txtCity control from the interface.

7. Add a label control to the interface, then change the following properties of the control.

   Name   **lblCity**
   BorderStyle   **FixedSingle**
   Location   **24, 112**
   Size   **200, 25**
   Text   (empty)

8. Change the name of the Write to File button from btnWrite to **btnDisplay**.

9. Change the btnDisplay control's Text property to **&Display City**.

10. Lock the controls.

11. Change the tab order as follows:

    Label1   0
    txtZip   1
    btnDisplay   2
    btnExit   3
    Label2   4
    lblCity   5

12. Open the Code Editor window.

13. Change the project's purpose to **The project displays the city name corresponding to a ZIP code entered by the user.**

14. Delete the btnWrite_Click procedure.

15. Delete the txtCity_Enter procedure.

According to the pseudocode shown in Figure 8.12, only three event procedures need to be coded. The Code Editor window already contains the code for the btnExit control's Click event procedure and the txtZip control's Enter event procedure. You need to code only the btnDisplay control's Click event procedure.

To code the btnDisplay control's Click event procedure:

1. Display the code template for the btnDisplay control's Click event procedure.

2. Type **'displays the appropriate city name stored in a sequential access file** and press **Enter** twice.

First, you will declare seven variables for the procedure to use.

3. Type **'declare variables** and press **Enter**.

4. Type **dim strUserInput as string** and press **Enter**. This variable will store the ZIP code entered by the user.

5. Type **dim blnZipFound as boolean** and press **Enter**. This variable will keep track of whether the ZIP code entered by the user was located in the file.

6. Type **dim strRecord as string** and press **Enter**. This variable will store a record after it has been read from the file. The record consists of a ZIP code field, the number symbol (#), and a city name field.

7. Type **dim intIndex as integer** and press **Enter**. This variable will store the location of the number symbol in the record.

8. Type **dim strZip as string** and press **Enter**. This variable will store the contents of the ZIP code field in the record.

9. Type **dim strCity as string** and press **Enter**. This variable will store the contents of the city name field in the record.

10. Type **dim sreStreamReader as io.streamreader** and press **Enter** twice. This variable will store the address of a StreamReader object.

The first step in the pseudocode for this procedure is to assign the ZIP code entered by the user to a variable.

11. Type **'assign input to variable** and press **Enter**.

12. Type **struserinput = me.txtzip.text** and press **Enter** twice.

The next step is a Try/Catch block.

13. Type **try** and press **Enter**. Notice that the Code Editor enters the `Catch ex As Exception` and `End Try` clauses for you.

According to the pseudocode, the Try section of the Try/Catch block should contain a selection structure that determines whether the user entered a ZIP code. If the user did not enter a ZIP code, the selection structure's false path should display an appropriate message.

14. Type the comments and additional lines of code shown in Figure 8.13, and then position the insertion point as shown in the figure.

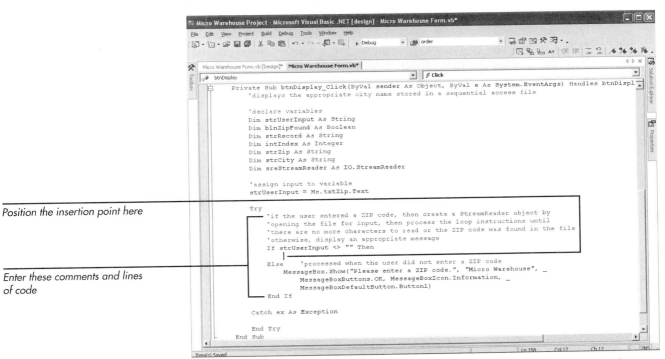

FIGURE 8.13 Comments and additional lines of code shown in the procedure

If the user entered a ZIP code, the first instruction in the selection structure's true path should open a sequential access file named zipcity.txt for input. Opening a file for input allows you to read the data in the file. (If the file does not exist, the Catch section, which you will code later, will display an appropriate message.)

15. Type **srestreamreader = io.file.opentext("zipcity.txt")** and press **Enter**.

The next instruction in the selection structure's true path should be a loop that repeats its instructions until either there are no more characters to read in the file or the ZIP code was found in the file. Recall that you can use the Peek method to determine whether a file contains another character to read. If the file contains another character, the Peek method returns the character; otherwise, it returns the number –1.

16. Type **do until srestreamreader.peek() = -1 orelse blnzipfound** and press **Enter**.

The first instruction in the loop should read a record from the file. You read a record from a sequential access file using the ReadLine method. The syntax of the ReadLine method is *variablename*.**ReadLine**(), where *variablename* is the name of a StreamReader variable. The ReadLine method reads a line of text (excluding the line terminator character) from the file.

17. Type **'read a record from the file** and press **Enter**.

18. Type the statement to read a record from the file and assign the record to the strRecord variable, then press **Enter** twice.

The second instruction in the loop should split the record into the ZIP code and city name fields.

19. Type **'search for #, then split the record into ZIP and city** and press **Enter**.

20. Enter the statement to search for the number symbol in the strRecord variable. Assign the location of the number symbol to the intIndex variable. (*Hint*: Use the IndexOf method.)

21. Enter the statement to assign the ZIP code from the record to the strZip variable. (*Hint*: Use the Substring method.)

22. Type the statement to assign the city name from the record to the strCity variable, then press **Enter** twice.

The third instruction in the loop is a nested selection structure that determines whether the ZIP code in the record matches the ZIP code entered by the user. If both ZIP codes are the same, the nested selection structure's true path should display the city name in the lblCity control and then assign True to the blnZipFound variable.

23. Type **'if the ZIP matches the user input, display the city name and** and press **Enter**.

24. Type **'set the blnZipFound variable to True** and press **Enter**.

25. Type **if strzip = struserinput then** and press **Enter**.

26. Type the statement to display the city name in the lblCity control, and then press **Enter**.

27. Type the statement to assign the value True to the blnZipFound variable.

The next instruction in the selection structure's true path is to close the file.

28. Position the insertion point two lines below the `Loop` clause, but above the `Else` clause.

29. Type **'close the file** and press **Enter**.

30. Type the statement to close the sequential access file, and then press **Enter** twice.

The last instruction in the selection structure's true path is a nested selection structure that determines whether the ZIP code was found in the file. If the ZIP code was not found, the nested selection structure's true path should display the message "Unknown ZIP code." in a message box.

31. Type **'if the ZIP was not in the file, display an appropriate message** and press **Enter**.

32. Enter the appropriate nested selection structure.

You have finished coding the Try section of the Try/Catch block; you now code the Catch section. According to the pseudocode, the Catch section should display a message indicating the error that occurred.

33. Type the MessageBox.Show method shown in Figure 8.14, then position the insertion point as shown in the figure.

Enter these lines of code

Position the insertion point here

FIGURE 8.14 Code entered in the Catch section

The last two steps in the pseudocode for the btnDisplay Click event procedure are to send the focus to the txtZip control and also to select the control's existing text.

34. Type '**set the focus and select the existing text** and press **Enter**.

35. Enter the statement to send the focus to the txtZip control.

36. Enter the statement to select the existing text in the txtZip control.

Now that you have finished coding the application, you can test it to verify that the code is working correctly.

To test the application's code:

1. Save the solution, then start the application.

First observe what happens when you click the Display City button without entering a ZIP code.

2. Click the **Display City** button. The btnDisplay_Click procedure displays the message box shown in Figure 8.15.

FIGURE 8.15 Message box requesting the user to enter a ZIP code

3. Press **Enter** to close the message box.

Now observe what happens when you enter a ZIP code that is not in the file.

4. Type **55555** as the ZIP code and press **Enter** to select the Display City button, which is the default button. The btnDisplay_Click procedure displays the message box shown in Figure 8.16.

FIGURE 8.16 Message box resulting from an invalid ZIP code entry

5. Press **Enter** to close the message box.

Finally, enter ZIP code 60514, which is in the file. The btnDisplay_Click procedure should display Clarendon Hills in the lblCity control.

6. Type **60514** and press **Enter**. The city name appears in the lblCity control, as shown in Figure 8.17.

FIGURE 8.17 Modified Micro Warehouse application

7. Click the **Exit** button.

8. Close the Output window, then close the Code Editor window.

You are finished with the solution, so you can close it.

9. Close the solution. Temporarily display the Solution Explorer window to verify that the solution is closed.

LAB 8.3 CARLOS COFFEES

Scenario The sales manager at Carlos Coffees wants an application that she can use to keep track of the number of pounds of each flavored coffee sold. She wants to record the information in a sequential access file named coffee.txt. A sample of the file is shown in Figure 8.18.

FIGURE 8.18 Sample of the coffee.txt file

Solution Discussion The Carlos Coffees application uses two text boxes for entering the name of the flavored coffee and the number of pounds sold. In addition, the application uses a button control for saving the coffee name and number of pounds sold to a sequential access file, and a button control for ending the application.

User Interface

FIGURE 8.19

Activity

1. If necessary, start Visual Studio .NET.
2. Open the Carlos Coffees Solution (Carlos Coffees Solution.sln) file contained in the VbDotNetLab\Chap08\Carlos Coffees Solution folder. The user interface shown in Figure 8.19 appears on the screen.
3. Open the Code Editor window. Some of the application's code has already been entered for you.
4. Replace the <enter your name and date here> text with your name and the current date.
5. Finish coding the btnSave_Click procedure, using the comments entered in the procedure as your guide.
6. Save the solution, then start the application.
7. Save the data shown earlier in Figure 8.18 to the coffee.txt file.
8. Click the **Exit** button to end the application.
9. Close the Output window, then close the Code Editor window.
10. Open the coffee.txt file contained in the VbDotNetLab\Chap08\Carlos Coffees Solution\ Carlos Coffees Project\bin folder. The file should look similar to the one shown in Figure 8.18.
11. Close the coffee.txt window.

You are finished with the solution, so you can close it.

12. Close the solution. Temporarily display the Solution Explorer window to verify that the solution is closed.

BEYOND THE TEXT

LAB 8.4 DIALOG BOX EXAMPLE

Scenario The Windows Forms tab on the Toolbox window provides several tools that allow you to display standard dialog boxes for operations such as opening, saving, and printing files, as well as selecting colors and fonts. In this lab, you learn how to use the SaveFileDialog tool to display the Save As dialog box used in many Windows applications. A sample Save As dialog box is shown in Figure 8.20.

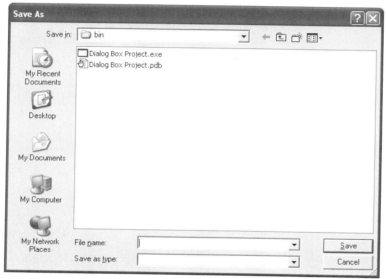

FIGURE 8.20 Sample Save As dialog box

Solution Discussion The Dialog Box Example application uses a text box for entering text. The text box's Multiline property is set to true to allow the user to enter more than one line of text. Its ScrollBars property is set to Vertical, which provides a vertical scroll bar that the user can use to scroll through the text. The application uses a button control for saving the contents of the text box to a sequential access file, and a button control for ending the application. In addition, the application will use a SaveFileDialog control that allows the user to enter the name of the sequential access file.

Activity

1. If necessary, start Visual Studio .NET.
2. Open the Dialog Box Solution (Dialog Box Solution.sln) file contained in the VbDotNetLab\ Chap08\Dialog Box Solution folder. The user interface appears on the screen.

First, add a SaveFileDialog control to the interface.

3. Scroll the Toolbox window until you see the SaveFileDialog tool. As you scroll, notice the other dialog box tools listed in the toolbox, such as the OpenFileDialog and FontDialog tools.

4. Click the **SaveFileDialog tool** in the toolbox, and then drag a SaveFileDialog control to the form. When you release the mouse button, the control appears in the component tray, as shown in Figure 8.21.

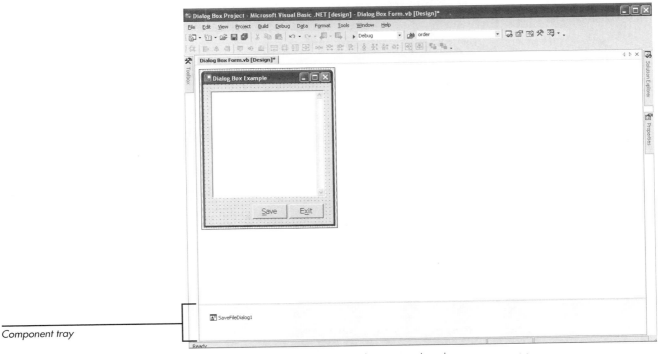

Component tray

FIGURE 8.21 SaveFileDialog control in the component tray

5. Use the Properties window to change the control's name from SaveFileDialog1 to **dlgSave**.

Now that you have finished creating the interface, you can code the application and then test it to verify that it is working correctly.

To code the application, and then test it:

1. Open the Code Editor window. Most of the application has already been coded for you.

2. Replace the `<enter your name and date here>` text with your name and the current date.

Now finish coding the btnSave_Click procedure. The procedure will use two variables.

3. Position the insertion point below the `'declare variables` comment.

4. Type **dim strFilename as string** and press **Enter**. The procedure will use this variable to store the filename entered by the user.

5. Type **dim swrStreamWriter as io.streamwriter** and press **Enter**. The procedure will use this variable to store the address of a StreamWriter object.

You use the ShowDialog method to display a dialog box created using one of the dialog box tools in the toolbox.

6. Position the insertion point below the `'show Save As dialog box` comment.

7. Type **me.dlgsave.showdialog()** and press **Enter**.

When the user clicks the Save button in the Save As dialog box, the filename entered in the File name text box is stored in the dialog box's Filename property. However, when the user clicks either the Cancel button or the Close button, a zero-length string is stored in the Filename property.

8. Position the insertion point below the `'assign filename to strFilename variable` comment.

9. Type **strfilename = me.dlgsave.filename** and press **Enter**.

You want to save the contents of the text box only when the user enters a filename.

10. Position the insertion point below the `'if the user entered a filename` comment.

11. Type the additional comments and code shown in Figure 8.22.

```
Private Sub btnSave_Click(ByVal sender As Object, ByVal e As System.EventArgs) Handles btnSave.Clic
    'saves the contents of the txtNotes control to a sequential access file

    'declare variables
    Dim strFilename As String
    Dim swrStreamWriter As IO.StreamWriter

    'show Save As dialog box
    Me.dlgSave.ShowDialog()

    'assign filename to strFilename variable
    strFilename = Me.dlgSave.FileName

    'if the user entered a filename
    If strFilename <> "" Then
        'open the file for output
        swrStreamWriter = IO.File.CreateText(strFilename)
        'write the contents of the text box to the file
        swrStreamWriter.WriteLine(Me.txtNotes.Text)
        'close the file
        swrStreamWriter.Close()
    End If
End Sub
```

Enter these comments and lines of code

FIGURE 8.22   Completed btnSave_Click procedure

12. Save the solution, then start the application.

13. In the text box, type **This project uses a SaveFileDialog control to display the Save As dialog box.** and press **Enter**.

14. Click the **Save** button. The btnSave_Click procedure displays the Save As dialog box.

15. If necessary, open the bin folder contained in the VbDotNetLab\Chap08\Dialog Box Solution\Dialog Box Project folder.

16. Type **notes.txt** in the File name box, as shown in Figure 8.23.

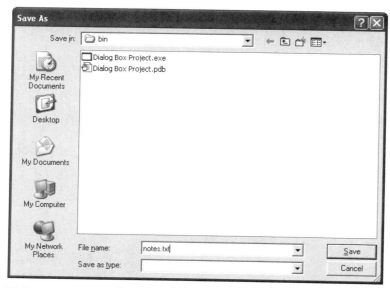

FIGURE 8.23   Save As dialog box

First, observe what happens when you click the Cancel button in the dialog box.

17. Click the **Cancel** button in the Save As dialog box. The dialog box closes and the btnSave_Click procedure ends without saving the contents of the text box.

Now save the contents of the text box to a file.

18. Click the **Save** button in the interface.

19. Type **notes.txt** in the File name box, and then click the **Save** button in the Save As dialog box. The dialog box closes and the btnSave_Click procedure ends after saving the contents of the text box.

20. Click the **Exit** button. The btnExit_Click procedure ends the application.

Now verify that the contents of the text box were saved to the notes.txt file.

21. Click **File** on the menu bar. Point to **Open**, and then click **File**.

22. Open the bin folder contained in the VbDotNetLab\Chap08\Dialog Box Solution\Dialog Box Project folder.

23. Click **notes.txt** in the list of filenames, and then click the **Open** button. Figure 8.24 shows the contents of the file.

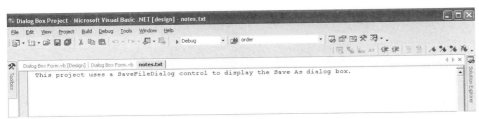

FIGURE 8.24   Contents of the notes.txt file

24. Close the notes.txt window.

25. Close the Output window, and then close the Code Editor window.

26. Close the solution, and then exit Visual Studio .NET.

Arrays

Labs included in this chapter:

- Lab 9.1 Laury Cosmetics
- Lab 9.2 Modified Laury Cosmetics
- Lab 9.3 Lottery
- Lab 9.4 Previewing/Printing Example

LAB 9.1 LAURY COSMETICS

Scenario Mr. Laury, the owner of Laury Cosmetics, wants an application that allows an employee to enter the number of items ordered by a customer, and then display the appropriate shipping charge. The shipping charge is based on the number of items ordered, as shown in the following shipping rate chart.

Minimum order	Maximum order	Shipping charge
1	10	15
11	50	10
51	100	5
101	99999	0

Solution Discussion The Laury Cosmetics application will use a text box for entering the quantity ordered, and a label control for displaying the shipping charge. It also will use two button controls: one that allows the user to display the shipping charge and the other for exiting the application.

The application will use two parallel one-dimensional Integer arrays named intOrder and intShipping. The intOrder array will contain the values entered in the Maximum order column in the shipping rate chart shown above, and the intShipping array will contain the corresponding shipping charges.

TOE Chart

Task	Object	Event
1. Search the intOrder array for the quantity ordered 2. Display (in lblShipping) the shipping charge from the intShipping array 3. Send the focus to the txtOrdered control 4. Select the existing text in the txtOrdered control	btnDisplay	Click
End the application	btnExit	Click
Get and display the quantity ordered	txtOrdered	None
Select the existing text		Enter
Clear the shipping charge from lblShipping		TextChanged
Display the shipping charge (from btnDisplay)	lblShipping	None

FIGURE 9.1

User Interface

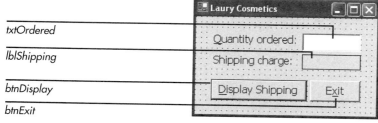

txtOrdered

lblShipping

btnDisplay

btnExit

FIGURE 9.2

Objects, Properties, and Settings

Object	Property	Setting
Label1	AutoSize	True
	Text	&Quantity ordered:
Label2	AutoSize	True
	Text	Shipping charge:
Label3	Name	lblShipping
	BorderStyle	FixedSingle
	Text	(empty)
	TextAlign	MiddleCenter
TextBox1	Name	txtOrdered
	Text	(empty)
Button1	Name	btnDisplay
	Text	&Display Shipping
Button2	Name	btnExit
	Text	E&xit

FIGURE 9.3

Tab Order

FIGURE 9.4

Pseudocode

btnDisplay Click event procedure
1. include the following in the Try section of a Try/Catch block:

    assign the quantity ordered to an Integer variable

    repeat until each element in the intOrder array has been searched or the quantity ordered is less than or equal to the quantity in the current array element

    > add 1 to the contents of the intSubscript variable to continue the search in the next element in the array

    end repeat

    if the array subscript is valid

    > display (in lblShipping) the shipping charge from the intShipping array

    else

    > display the message "The quantity must be less than 100,000." in a message box

    end if

    include the following in the Catch section of a Try/Catch block:

    use a FormatException Catch statement to handle the error that occurs when the quantity ordered cannot be converted to an integer

    > if an error occurs, display the message "The quantity must be a number." in a message box

    use a general Catch statement to handle any other errors

    > if an error occurs, display a description of the error in a message box
2. send the focus to the txtOrdered control
3. select the existing text in the txtOrdered control

btnExit Click event procedure
1. close the application

txtOrdered Enter event procedure
1. select the existing text

txtOrdered TextChanged event procedure
1. clear the shipping charge from lblShipping

FIGURE 9.5

Activity

1. Start Visual Studio .NET.
2. Click **File** on the Visual Studio .NET menu bar, point to **New**, and then click **Project**. The New Project dialog box opens.
3. If necessary, click **Visual Basic Projects** in the Project Types list box, and click **Windows Application** in the Templates list box.
4. Type **Laury Project** in the Name text box.
5. Use the **Browse** button to open the **VbDotNetLab\Chap09** folder.
6. If necessary, click the **More** button.

7. If necessary, select the **Create directory for Solution** check box.

8. Type **Laury Solution** in the New Solution Name text box.

9. Click the **OK** button to close the New Project dialog box.

Now set the appropriate properties of the form file object and form object.

To set the appropriate properties of the form file object and form object:

1. Right-click **Form1.vb** in the Solution Explorer window, then click **Rename**. Change the form file object's name from Form1.vb to **Laury Form.vb**.

2. Click the **form**, then click **(Name)** in the Properties window. Change the form object's name from Form1 to **frmLaury**.

3. Right-click **Laury Project** in the Solution Explorer window, then click **Properties**. Click the **Startup object** list arrow, and then click **frmLaury** in the list. Click the **OK** button.

4. Click the **form**, then change the values assigned to the following properties:

Font	**Tahoma, 12 pt**
Size	**280, 184**
StartPosition	**CenterScreen**
Text	**Laury Cosmetics**

5. Save the solution by clicking **File** on the menu bar, and then clicking **Save All**.

Next, add the appropriate controls to the interface, and then set the values of some of their properties.

To add the appropriate controls, then set the values of some of their properties:

1. Use the Label tool to add three label controls to the form.

2. Use the TextBox tool to add one text box to the form.

3. Use the Button tool to add two buttons to the form.

4. Use the chart shown in Figure 9.3 to set the properties of each control.

5. Position the controls as shown in Figure 9.2.

6. Lock the controls in place on the form.

7. Use Figure 9.4 to set the appropriate tab order.

8. Make the Display Shipping button the default button by setting the form's AcceptButton property to **btnDisplay**.

9. Save the solution.

Now that the interface is complete, you can begin coding the application. First you will enter the appropriate comments and Option statements.

To enter the appropriate comments and Option statements:

1. Right-click the **form**, and then click **View Code** to open the Code Editor window.

2. Type the comments shown in Figure 9.6, replacing `<enter your name and date here>` with your name and the current date. Also type the Option statements shown in the figure.

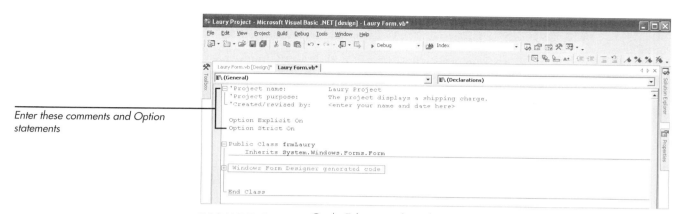

Enter these comments and Option statements

FIGURE 9.6   Code Editor window showing comments and Option statements

Now use the pseudocode shown earlier in Figure 9.5 to code the btnDisplay control's Click event procedure.

To code the btnDisplay control's Click event procedure:

1. Click the **Class Name** list arrow, and then click **btnDisplay** in the list.
2. Click the **Method Name** list arrow, and then click **Click** in the list. The code template for the btnDisplay_Click procedure appears in the Code Editor window.
3. Type '**displays a shipping charge that is based on the quantity ordered** and press **Enter** twice.

First, you will declare the procedure's variables.

4. Type '**declare variables** and press **Enter**.
5. Type **dim intOrdered as integer** and press **Enter**. This variable will store the quantity ordered entered by the user.
6. Type **dim intSubscript as integer** and press **Enter** twice. This variable will keep track of the subscripts in both arrays.

Next, you will declare and fill the intOrder and intShipping arrays. In the intOrder array, you will store the values listed in the Maximum order column in the shipping rate chart, which was shown earlier. In the intShipping array, you will store the corresponding shipping charges.

7. Type '**declare and fill arrays** and press **Enter**.
8. Type **dim intOrder() as integer = {10, 50, 100, 99999}** and press **Enter**.
9. Type **dim intShipping() as integer = {15, 10, 5, 0}** and press **Enter** twice.

The first step in the pseudocode for the btnDisplay Click event procedure is a Try/Catch block, which is a block of code that uses both the Try and Catch statements. Recall that you use the Try statement to catch an exception (error) when it occurs in a program. You use the Catch statement to have the computer take the appropriate action to resolve the exception.

10. Type **try** and press **Enter**. Notice that the Code Editor enters the `Catch ex As Exception` and `End Try` clauses for you.

According to the pseudocode, the first instruction in the Try section should assign the quantity ordered to an Integer variable.

11. Type '**assign input to variable** and press **Enter**.
12. Type **intordered = convert.toint32(me.txtordered.text)** and press **Enter** twice.

The next instruction is a loop that adds the number one to the intSubscript variable either until each element in the intOrder array has been searched or until the quantity ordered is less than or equal to the quantity in the current array element.

13. Type the comments and repetition structure shown in Figure 9.7, and then position the insertion point as shown in the figure.

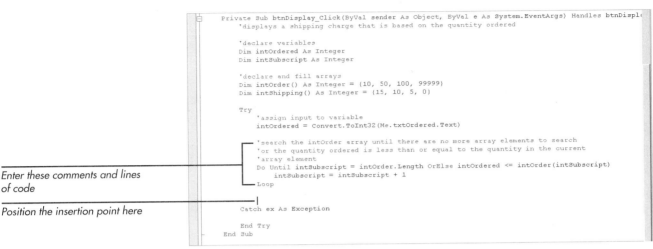

Enter these comments and lines of code

Position the insertion point here

```
Private Sub btnDisplay_Click(ByVal sender As Object, ByVal e As System.EventArgs) Handles btnDispla
    'displays a shipping charge that is based on the quantity ordered

    'declare variables
    Dim intOrdered As Integer
    Dim intSubscript As Integer

    'declare and fill arrays
    Dim intOrder() As Integer = {10, 50, 100, 99999}
    Dim intShipping() As Integer = {15, 10, 5, 0}

    Try
        'assign input to variable
        intOrdered = Convert.ToInt32(Me.txtOrdered.Text)

        'search the intOrder array until there are no more array elements to search
        'or the quantity ordered is less than or equal to the quantity in the current
        'array element
        Do Until intSubscript = intOrder.Length OrElse intOrdered <= intOrder(intSubscript)
            intSubscript = intSubscript + 1
        Loop

    Catch ex As Exception

    End Try
End Sub
```

FIGURE 9.7   Comments and repetition structure shown in the procedure

The next instruction is a selection structure that determines whether the array subscript stored in the intSubscript variable is valid. To be valid, the subscript must be less than the number of elements in the intOrdered array. If the subscript is valid, the selection structure's true path should use the subscript to display the appropriate shipping charge from the intShipping array. If the subscript is not valid, the selection structure's false path should display a message informing the user that the quantity must be less than 100,000.

TIP • • • • Recall that the first subscript in a one-dimensional array is the number zero. Also recall that the number of elements in a one-dimensional array is stored in the array's Length property and is one number more than the highest subscript in the array.

14. Type the comments and selection structure shown in Figure 9.8, and then position the insertion point as shown in the figure.

Enter these comments and lines of code

Position the insertion point here

```
        'search the intOrder array until there are no more array elements to search
        'or the quantity ordered is less than or equal to the quantity in the current
        'array element
        Do Until intSubscript = intOrder.Length OrElse intOrdered <= intOrder(intSubscript)
            intSubscript = intSubscript + 1
        Loop

        'if the array subscript is valid, display the shipping charge from the
        'intShipping array; otherwise, display an appropriate message
        If intSubscript < intOrder.Length Then
            Me.lblShipping.Text = intShipping(intSubscript).ToString("C2")
        Else
            MessageBox.Show("The quantity must be less than 100,000.", "Laury Cosmetics", _
                MessageBoxButtons.OK, MessageBoxIcon.Information, MessageBoxDefaultButton.Button1)
        End If

    Catch ex As Exception

    End Try
End Sub
```

FIGURE 9.8   Comments and selection structure shown in the procedure

You have finished coding the Try section of the Try/Catch block; you now code the Catch section. According to the pseudocode, the Catch section will contain two Catch statements. The first Catch statement will be processed when the quantity ordered cannot be converted to a number; this error results in a FormatException. The second Catch statement will be processed when any other error occurs.

15. Type the Catch statements shown in Figure 9.9, and then position the insertion point as shown in the figure.

Enter these lines of code

Position the insertion point here

```
        Catch exFormat As FormatException
            MessageBox.Show("The quantity must be a number.", "Laury Cosmetics", _
                MessageBoxButtons.OK, MessageBoxIcon.Information, MessageBoxDefaultButton.Button1)
        Catch ex As Exception
            MessageBox.Show(ex.Message, "Laury Cosmetics", _
                MessageBoxButtons.OK, MessageBoxIcon.Information, MessageBoxDefaultButton.Button1)
        End Try

    End Sub
```

FIGURE 9.9   Catch statements shown in the procedure

The last two steps in the pseudocode for the btnDisplay Click event procedure are to send the focus to the txtOrdered control and also select the control's existing text.

16. Type '**set the focus and select the existing text** and press **Enter**.

17. Type **me.txtordered.focus()** and press **Enter**.

18. Type **me.txtordered.selectall()** and press **Enter**.

19. Save the solution.

Next, you will code the Click event procedure for the btnExit control, which is responsible for ending the application. You also will code the Enter event procedure for the txtOrdered control. The Enter event procedure is responsible for selecting the txtOrdered control's existing text when the control receives the focus. In addition, you will code the txtOrdered control's TextChanged event, which is responsible for clearing the shipping charge from the lblShipping control. The TextChanged event occurs when the contents of the text box are changed.

To code the btnExit_Click, txtOrdered_Enter, and txtOrdered_TextChanged procedures:

1. Display the code template for the btnExit control's Click event procedure.

2. Type '**ends the application** and press **Enter**.

3. Type **me.close()** and press **Enter**.

4. Display the code template for the txtOrdered control's Enter event procedure.

5. Type '**selects the existing text** and press **Enter**.

6. Type **me.txtordered.selectall()** and press **Enter**.

7. Display the code template for the txtOrdered control's TextChanged event procedure.

8. Type '**clears the shipping charge** and press **Enter**.

9. Type **me.lblshipping.text = ""** and press **Enter**.

Now that you have finished coding the application, you can test the application to verify that the code is working correctly.

To test the application:

1. Save the solution.

2. Start the application by clicking **Debug** on the menu bar, and then clicking **Start**. The blinking insertion point indicates that the txtOrdered control has the focus.

First, observe what happens when you click the Display Shipping button without entering the quantity ordered.

3. Click the **Display Shipping** button. The message box shown in Figure 9.10 appears on the screen.

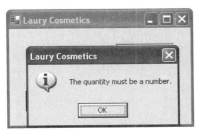

FIGURE 9.10 Message box that appears when the user does not enter the appropriate data

4. Press **Enter** to select the OK button, which closes the message box.

Now observe what happens when you enter a letter as the quantity ordered.

5. Type **a** as the quantity ordered and then press **Enter** to select the Display Shipping button, which is the default button. The message box shown earlier in Figure 9.10 appears on the screen.

6. Close the message box.

Now use the application to display the shipping charge for six items. The shipping charge should be $15.00.

7. Type **6** as the quantity ordered, and then press **Enter**. The btnDisplay_Click procedure searches the intOrdered array for the first value that is greater than or equal to the number six. In this case, the search stops with the first value in the intOrdered array, which is 10. The procedure then displays the corresponding value from the intShipping array, as shown in Figure 9.11.

FIGURE 9.11 Laury Cosmetics application

Now display the shipping charge for 50 items. The shipping charge should be $10.00.

8. Type **50** as the quantity ordered. Notice that, when you type a new value into the txtOrdered control, the instruction in the control's TextChanged event removes the shipping charge from the lblShipping control.

9. Press **Enter**. The btnDisplay_Click procedure searches the intOrdered array for the first value that is greater than or equal to the number 50. In this case, the search stops with the second value in the intOrdered array, which is 50. The procedure then displays $10.00, which is the corresponding value from the intShipping array.

Next, display the shipping charge for 51 items. The shipping charge should be $5.00.

10. Type **51** as the quantity ordered and press **Enter**. The btnDisplay_Click procedure searches the intOrdered array for the first value that is greater than or equal to the number 51. In this case, the search stops with the third value in the intOrdered array, which is 100. The procedure then displays $5.00, which is the corresponding value from the intShipping array.

Now display the shipping charge for 150 items. The shipping charge should be $0.00.

11. Type **150** as the quantity ordered and press **Enter**. The btnDisplay_Click procedure searches the intOrdered array for the first value that is greater than or equal to the number 150. In this case, the search stops with the last value in the intOrdered array, which is 99999. The procedure then displays $0.00, which is the corresponding value from the intShipping array.

Finally, observe what happens when you enter a quantity that is greater than 99,999.

12. Type **101500** as the quantity ordered and press **Enter**. The btnDisplay_Click procedure searches the intOrdered array for the first value that is greater than or equal to the number 101,500. The procedure displays the message box shown in Figure 9.12, because the intOrdered array does not contain a value that is greater than or equal to 101,500.

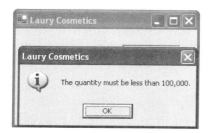

FIGURE 9.12   Message box that appears when the user enters an invalid number

13 Press **Enter** to close the message box.

14. Click the **Exit** button. The btnExit_Click procedure ends the application.

15. Close the Output window, and then close the Code Editor window.

You are finished with the solution, so you can close it.

16. Click **File** on the menu bar, and then click **Close Solution**.

LAB 9.2 MODIFIED LAURY COSMETICS

Scenario   In this lab, you modify the Laury Cosmetics application that you created in Lab 9.1. The modified application will use a two-dimensional array, rather than two parallel one-dimensional arrays, to store the shipping rate information.

Solution Discussion   In Lab 9.1, you used a four-element one-dimensional array named intOrder to store the values entered in the Maximum order column in the shipping chart. You also used a four-element one-dimensional array named intShipping to store the corresponding shipping charges. In this lab, you replace both one-dimensional arrays with a two-dimensional array named intShippingInfo. The intShippingInfo array will contain four rows and two columns. You will store the Maximum order values in the first column, and store the shipping charges in the second column.

In addition, you will use the GetUpperBound method to determine the highest row subscript and highest column subscript in the two-dimensional array. The syntax of the GetUpperBound method is *array*.**GetUpperBound**(*dimension*). In the syntax, *array* is the name of the array, and *dimension* (in the case of a two-dimensional array) is either 0 for the row subscript or 1 for the column subscript.

Modified Pseudocode

btnDisplay Click event procedure (changes made to the original pseudocode are shaded in the figure)

1. include the following in the Try section of a Try/Catch block:

    assign the quantity ordered to an Integer variable

    repeat until each element in the first column in the intShippingInfo array has been searched or the quantity ordered is less than or equal to the quantity in the current array element

       add 1 to the contents of the intSubscript variable to continue the search in the next element in the array

    end repeat

    if the row array subscript is valid
       display (in lblShipping) the shipping charge from the second column in the intShippingInfo array

    else
       display the message "The quantity must be less than 100,000." in a message box
    end if

    include the following in the Catch section of a Try/Catch block:

    use a FormatException Catch statement to handle the error that occurs when the quantity ordered cannot be converted to an integer

       if an error occurs, display the message "The quantity must be a number." in a message box

    use a general Catch statement to handle any other errors

       if an error occurs, display a description of the error in a message box

2. send the focus to the txtOrdered control
3. select the existing text in the txtOrdered control

FIGURE 9.13

Activity

1. Use Windows to make a copy of the Laury Solution folder, which is contained in the VbDotNetLab\Chap09 folder. Rename the copy Modified Laury Solution.
2. If necessary, start Visual Studio .NET.
3. Open the Laury Solution (Laury Solution.sln) file contained in the VbDotNetLab\Chap09\ Modified Laury Solution folder.
4. Right-click **Laury Form.vb** in the Solution Explorer window, then click **View Designer**. The user interface shown in Figure 9.2 in Lab 9.1 appears on the screen.

Now use the pseudocode shown in Figure 9.13 to modify the btnDisplay_Click event procedure.

To modify the btnDisplay_Click event procedure:

1. Open the Code Editor window.
2. In the btnDisplay_Click procedure, change the `'declare and fill arrays` comment to **'declare and fill two-dimensional array**.

3. Replace the two statements that declare the one-dimensional arrays with a statement that declares a two-dimensional array, as shown in Figure 9.14.

```
Private Sub btnDisplay_Click(ByVal sender As Object, ByVal e As System.EventArgs) Handles btnDispla
    'displays a shipping charge that is based on the quantity ordered

    'declare variables
    Dim intOrdered As Integer
    Dim intSubscript As Integer

    'declare and fill two-dimensional array
    Dim intShippingInfo(,) As Integer = {{10, 15}, _
                                         {50, 10}, _
                                         {100, 5}, _
                                         {99999, 0}}
```

Replace the two array declaration statements with this statement

FIGURE 9.14   Two-dimensional array declaration statement shown in the procedure

According to the modified pseudocode shown in Figure 9.13, you will need to change the loop that searches for the quantity ordered. In this case, the loop should repeat its instructions either until each element in the first column in the intShippingInfo array has been searched or until the quantity ordered is less than or equal to the quantity in the current array element. To search each element in the first column, you need to know the highest row subscript in the intShippingInfo array. You can determine the highest row subscript using the code `intShipingInfo.GetUpperBound(0)`.

4. Modify the comments and `Do Until` clause, as shown in Figure 9.15.

```
Try
    'assign input to variable
    intOrdered = Convert.ToInt32(Me.txtOrdered.Text)

    'search the first column in the intShippingInfo array until there are no more
    'array elements to search or the quantity ordered is less than or equal to the
    'quantity in the current array element
    Do Until intSubscript > intShippingInfo.GetUpperBound(0) _
        OrElse intOrdered <= intShippingInfo(intSubscript, 0)
        intSubscript = intSubscript + 1
    Loop
```

Modify these comments and Do Until *clause*

FIGURE 9.15   Modified comments and `Do Until` clause shown in the procedure

You also need to modify the selection structure that determines whether the subscript—in this case, the row subscript—is valid. The row subscript is valid if it is less than or equal to the highest row subscript in the array.

5. Modify the comments above the selection structure as follows:

    'if the row array subscript is valid, display the shipping charge from the

    'second column in the intShippingInfo array; otherwise, display an appropriate message

6. Modify the If clause appropriately.

If the row subscript is valid, the selection structure's true path should use the row subscript to display the shipping charge from the second column in the intShippingInfo array.

7. Modify the instruction in the selection structure's true path.

Now test the application to verify that it is working correctly.

To test the application:

1. Save the solution, then start the application.
2. Click the **Display Shipping** button. The message box shown earlier in Figure 9.10 in Lab 9.1 appears on the screen.
3. Close the message box.

4. Type **a** as the quantity ordered and then press **Enter**. The message box shown earlier in Figure 9.10 in Lab 9.1 appears on the screen.

5. Close the message box.

6. Type **6** as the quantity ordered, and then press **Enter**. The btnDisplay_Click procedure searches the first column in the intShippingInfo array for the first value that is greater than or equal to the number six. In this case, the search stops with the first value, which is 10. The procedure then displays the corresponding value from the second column in the intShippingInfo array (formatted using the C2 style): $15.00.

7. Type **50** as the quantity ordered, and then press **Enter**. The btnDisplay_Click procedure searches the first column in the intShippingInfo array for the first value that is greater than or equal to the number 50. In this case, the search stops with the second value, which is 50. The procedure then displays $10.00, which is the corresponding value from the second column in the intShippingInfo array.

8. Type **51** as the quantity ordered and press **Enter**. The btnDisplay_Click procedure searches the first column in the intShippingInfo array for the first value that is greater than or equal to the number 51. In this case, the search stops with the third value, which is 100. The procedure then displays $5.00, which is the corresponding value from the second column in the intShippingInfo array.

9. Type **150** as the quantity ordered and press **Enter**. The btnDisplay_Click procedure searches the first column in the intShippingInfo array for the first value that is greater than or equal to the number 150. In this case, the search stops with the last value, which is 99999. The procedure then displays $0.00, which is the corresponding value from the second column in the intShippingInfo array.

10. Type **101500** as the quantity ordered and press **Enter**. The btnDisplay_Click procedure searches the first column in the intShippingInfo array for the first value that is greater than or equal to the number 101,500. The procedure displays the message box shown earlier in Figure 9.12 in Lab 9.1, because the first column of the array does not contain a value that is greater than or equal to 101,500.

11. Press **Enter** to close the message box.

12. Click the **Exit** button to end the application.

13. Close the Output window, then close the Code Editor window.

You are finished with the solution, so you can close it.

14. Close the solution. Temporarily display the Solution Explorer window to verify that the solution is closed.

LAB 9.3 LOTTERY

Scenario Jacques Cousard has been playing the lottery for four years and has yet to win any money. He wants an application that will select the six lottery numbers for him. Each lottery number can range from 1 through 54 only.

Solution Discussion The lottery application will use the Visual Studio .NET random number generator to generate random numbers from 1 through 54. Each lottery number will need to be unique; to accomplish this, you will use a one-dimensional array to store only the first six unique numbers produced by the generator. The application will use a label control to display the six lottery numbers. It also will use two button controls: one that allows the user to display the lottery numbers and the other for exiting the application.

User Interface

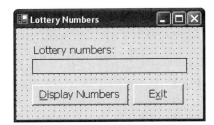

Pseudocode

btnDisplay Click event procedure
1. generate first random number, assign to first position in intNumbers array
2. fill remaining array elements with random numbers as follows:

    assign 1 to intSubscript

    repeat until intSubscript is greater than the highest subscript in the array

        generate another random number

        search the array to determine whether it contains the random number, as follows:

            assign 0 to intSearchSubscript to begin the search with the first element

            assign False to blnNumberFound

            repeat until there are no more elements to search or the random number is found

                if the value in the current array element is equal to the random number

                    assign True to blnNumberFound

                else

                    add 1 to intSearchSubscript to continue the search in the next element

                end if

            end repeat

        if the random number was not found in the array

            assign the random number to the current array element

            add 1 to intSubscript to continue filling array elements

        end if

    end repeat
3. display the contents of the intNumbers array in lblNumbers

btnExit Click event procedure
1. close the application

Activity

1. If necessary, start Visual Studio .NET.

2. Open the Lottery Solution (Lottery Solution.sln) file, which is contained in the VbDotNetLab\Chap09\Lottery Solution folder. The user interface shown earlier in Figure 9.16 appears on the screen.

3. Open the Code Editor window. Notice that the btnExit_Click procedure has already been coded for you.

4. Replace the `<enter your name and date here>` text with your name and the current date.

Now use the pseudocode shown in Figure 9.17 to code the btnDisplay control's Click event procedure.

To code the btnDisplay control's Click event procedure:

1. Display the code template for the btnDisplay control's Click event procedure.

2. Type '**displays six unique random lottery numbers from 1 through 54** and press **Enter** twice.

First, declare a Random object to represent the random number generator.

3. Type '**declare Random object to represent the random number generator** and press **Enter**.

4. Type **dim rndGenerator as new random** and press **Enter** twice.

Next, declare four variables for the procedure to use.

5. Type '**declare variables** and press **Enter**.

6. Type **dim intRandomNumber as integer** and press **Enter**. This variable will store a number generated by the random number generator.

7. Type **dim intSubscript as integer** and press **Tab** three times, then type '**used to fill and display the array** and press **Enter**. The intSubscript variable will keep track of the array subscript while the array is being filled and also while it is being displayed.

8. Type **dim intSearchSubscript as integer** and press **Tab**, then type '**used to search the array** and press **Enter**. The intSearchSubscript variable will keep track of the array subscript while the array is being searched.

9. Type **dim blnNumberFound as boolean** and press **Enter** twice. This variable will keep track of whether the current random number is already in the array.

Now declare a one-dimensional array to store the six unique random numbers.

10. Type '**declare six-element one-dimensional array** and press **Enter**.

11. Type the statement to declare a six-element one-dimensional Integer array named intNumbers, and then press **Enter** twice.

The first step in the pseudocode for this procedure is to generate the first random number and assign it to the first position in the intNumbers array.

12. Type '**generate first random number and store it in the first array element** and press **Enter**.

13. Type **intnumbers(0) = rndgenerator.next(1, 55)** and press **Enter** twice.

The second step is to fill the remaining array elements—in this case, the elements with subscripts from one through five. You begin by assigning the number one to the intSubscript variable.

14. Type '**fill remaining array elements with unique random numbers** and press **Enter**.

15. Type the statement to assign the number one to the intSubscript variable, and then press **Enter**.

Next, you need to enter a loop that repeats its instructions until the value in the intSubscript variable is greater than the highest subscript in the array. The highest subscript is always one number less than the number of elements in the array. The number of elements is stored in the array's Length property.

16. Type **do until intsubscript > intnumbers.length – 1** and press **Enter**.

According to the pseudocode, the first instruction in the loop should generate another random number.

17. Type **'generate another random number** and press **Enter**.

18. Type the statement to generate the next random number and assign the number to the intRandomNumber variable, and then press **Enter** twice.

Next, the loop instructions should search the intNumbers array to determine whether it contains the random number. You begin by assigning the number zero to the intSearchSubscript variable to ensure that the search begins with the first array element. You also assign the Boolean value False to the blnNumberFound variable because, before the search begins, the loop should assume that the number is not in the array.

19. Type **'search the array to determine whether it contains the random number** and press **Enter**.

20. Type **'stop the search when there are no more array elements or when** and press **Enter**.

21. Type **'the random number is found in the array** and press **Enter**.

22. Type **intsearchsubscript = 0** and press **Enter**.

23. Type **blnnumberfound = false** and press **Enter**.

Now enter a nested loop that repeats its instructions either until there are no more elements to search or until the random number is found in the array. There are no more elements to search when the value in the intSearchSubscript variable is greater than the value in the intSubscript variable.

24. Type **do until intsearchsubscript > intsubscript orelse blnnumberfound** and press **Enter**.

The nested loop contains a selection structure that determines whether the value in the current array element is equal to the random number. If both numbers are the same, the selection structure's true path should assign the Boolean value True to the blnNumberFound variable to indicate that the random number is a duplicate. If both numbers are not the same, however, the selection structure's false path should add the number one to the intSearchSubscript variable; this allows the nested loop to continue the search in the next array element.

25. Type **'if the random number is in the array, assign True to blnNumberFound** and press **Enter**.

26. Type **'otherwise, search the next element in the array** and press **Enter**.

27. Type the appropriate selection structure, including the instructions in the true and false paths.

After the nested loop completes its processing, the next instruction in the outer loop is a selection structure that determines whether the random number was found in the array. If the random number was not found in the array, the selection structure's true path should assign the random number to the current array element. It then should add the number one to the intSubscript variable to allow the procedure to fill the next array element.

28. Position the insertion point two lines below the first Loop clause, but above the second Loop clause.

29. Type **'if the array does not contain the random number** and press **Enter**.

30. Type **'assign the random number to the array, then move to the next array element** and press **Enter**.

31. Type the appropriate selection structure, including the instructions in the true path.

The last step in the btnDisplay Click event procedure is to display the contents of the intNumbers array in the lblNumbers control.

32. Position the insertion point two lines below the second `Loop` clause, but above the `End Sub` clause.

33. Type '**display the contents of the array in lblNumbers** and press **Enter**.

First, clear the contents of the lblNumbers control.

34. Type the statement to clear the contents of the lblNumbers control, and then press **Enter**.

35. Enter the code to display the contents of the intNumbers array in the lblNumbers control. Use the For...Next statement. Display the six numbers on the same line in the lblNumbers control, but use two space characters to separate each number from the next number.

Now that you have finished coding the application, you can test it to verify that the code is working correctly.

To test the application's code:

1. Save the solution, then start the application.

2. Click the **Display Numbers** button. The btnDisplay_Click procedure generates a series of random numbers, storing the first six unique numbers in the intNumbers array. The procedure then displays the contents of the intNumbers array in the lblNumbers control, as shown in Figure 9.18. (Because the numbers generated by the procedure are random, the numbers appearing on your screen might be different from the ones shown in the figure.)

Your lottery numbers might be different

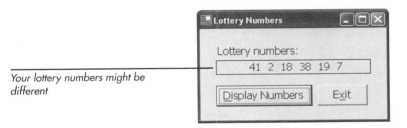

FIGURE 9.18 Lottery application

3. Click the **Display Numbers** button several times to verify that, in each case, the six numbers are unique.

4. Click the **Exit** button. The btnExit_Click procedure ends the application.

5. Close the Output window, then close the Code Editor window.

You are finished with the solution, so you can close it.

6. Close the solution. Temporarily display the Solution Explorer window to verify that the solution is closed.

BEYOND THE TEXT

LAB 9.4 PREVIEWING/PRINTING EXAMPLE

Scenario In this lab, you learn how to preview and then print a document from within a Windows application. The document will contain the first and last names stored in a two-dimensional array named strNames.

Solution Discussion The Previewing/Printing Example application will use two button controls: one for indicating that the user wants to preview (and possibly print) a document, and the other for exiting the application.

Before you can preview or print a document from within a Windows application, you need to add a PrintDocument control to the interface. You then can use the PrintPreviewDialog control to preview the document before printing. The PrintPreviewDialog control also allows you to print the document.

TOE Chart

Task	Object	Event
Use the prtPreviewDialog control to preview and (optionally) print the document	btnPreviewPrint	Click
End the application	btnExit	Click
Set up the document for previewing/printing	prtDocument	PrintPage
Preview the document and allow the user to print	prtPreviewDialog	None

FIGURE 9.19

Pseudocode

btnPreviewPrint Click event procedure

1. assign the prtDocument control to the Document property of the prtPreviewDialog control
2. display the dialog box generated by the prtPreviewDialog control

prtDocument PrintPage event procedure

1. repeat for each row in the strNames array

    print the first name, a space character, and the last name in the prtPreviewDialog control

    advance to the next line before displaying the next name

    end repeat

btnExit Click event procedure

1. close the application

FIGURE 9.20

Activity

1. If necessary, start Visual Studio .NET.

2. Open the Print Solution (Print Solution.sln) file contained in the VbDotNetLab\ Chap09\Print Solution folder. The user interface appears on the screen.

First, add both a PrintDocument control and a PrintPreviewDialog control to the interface.

3. Scroll down the Toolbox window until you see the PrintDocument tool. Click the **PrintDocument tool** in the toolbox, and then drag a PrintDocument control to the form. When you release the mouse button, the control appears in the component tray.

4. Use the Properties window to change the control's name from PrintDocument1 to **prtDocument**.

5. Scroll down the Toolbox window until you see the PrintPreviewDialog tool. Click the **PrintPreviewDialog tool** in the toolbox, and then drag a PrintPreviewDialog control to the component tray.

6. Use the Properties window to change the control's name from PrintPreviewDialog1 to **prtPreviewDialog**. Figure 9.21 shows the prtDocument and prtPreviewDialog controls in the component tray.

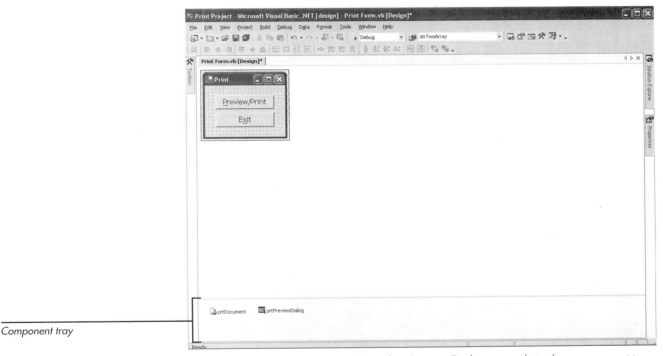

Component tray

FIGURE 9.21 prtDocument and prtPreviewDialog controls in the component tray

7. Save the solution.

Now that you have finished creating the interface, you can begin coding the application. First, code the btnPreviewPrint control's Click event procedure.

To code the btnPreviewPrint control's Click event procedure:

1. Open the Code Editor window. Notice that the btnExit_Click procedure has already been coded for you.

2. Replace the <enter your name and date here> text with your name and the current date.

3. Display the code template for the btnPreviewPrint control's Click event procedure.

4. Type **'previews and allows the user to print a document** and press **Enter** twice.

According to the pseudocode, the first step in the procedure is to assign the prtDocument control to the Document property of the prtPreviewDialog control.

5. Type **me.prtpreviewdialog.document = me.prtdocument** and press **Enter**.

The next step is to display the dialog box generated by the prtPreviewDialog control. As you learned in Lab 8.4 in Chapter 8, you use the ShowDialog method to display a dialog box created using one of the dialog box tools in the toolbox.

6. Type **me.prtpreviewdialog.showdialog()** and press **Enter**.

Next, code the prtDocument control's PrintPage event procedure. In the procedure, you indicate the information you want to preview, as well as how you want the information to appear.

To code the prtDocument control's PrintPage event procedure:

1. Display the code template for the prtDocument control's PrintPage event procedure.

2. Type **'sets up the preview page** and press **Enter** twice.

First, declare the variables. The procedure will use two Integer variables: one to keep track of the vertical location of the lines on the preview page, and the other to keep track of the row subscript in the array. (The vertical location is the location of the text from the top edge of the page.)

3. Type **'declare variables** and press **Enter**.

4. Type **dim intY as integer** and press **Tab** twice, then type **'keeps track of the vertical location on the preview page** and press **Enter**.

5. Type **dim intRow as integer** and press **Tab**, then type **'keeps track of the row subscript in the array** and press **Enter** twice.

Now declare a two-dimensional array named strNames. Fill the first column of the array with the first names of four people, and fill the second column with the corresponding last names.

6. Type the comments and array declaration statement shown in Figure 9.22, then position the insertion point as shown in the figure.

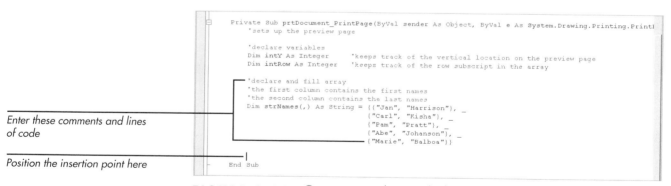

Enter these comments and lines of code

Position the insertion point here

FIGURE 9.22   Comments and array declaration statement shown in the procedure

Next, create a Font object that specifies the name and size of the font to use for previewing and printing. You can create a Font object using the syntax **Dim** *variablename* **As New Font**(*fontName, fontSize*). In this case, you will use the 14-point Courier New font.

7. Type **'create Font object** and press **Enter**.

8. Type **dim fntPrint as new font("courier new", 14)** and press **Enter** twice.

According to the pseudocode, the prtDocument_PrintPage procedure uses a loop that repeats its instructions for each row in the strNames array.

9. Type '**display the first name, a space, and the last name, then advance to the next line** and press **Enter**.

10. Type **for introw = 0 to strnames.getupperbound(0)** and press **Enter**.

The first instruction in the loop should print the first name, a space character, and the last name in the print preview dialog control. The first name is stored in the first column of the strNames array, and the last name is stored in the second column of the array. You use the e.Graphics.DrawString method to print text either in a print preview control or on the printer. The method's syntax is **e.Graphics.DrawString(**_string_, _font_, **Brushes.Black,** _horizontalPosition_, _verticalPosition_**)**. In the syntax, _string_ is the text to print, and _font_ is the name and size of the print font. The _horizontalPosition_ argument determines the location of the text from the left edge of the print page, and the _verticalPosition_ argument controls the location of the text from the top edge of the print page. In this case, the information for the _font_ and _verticalPosition_ arguments are stored in the fntPrint object and intY variable, respectively.

11. Type **e.graphics.drawstring(strnames(introw, 0) & " " & strnames(introw, 1),** _ and press **Enter**.

12. Press **Tab**, then type **fntPrint, Brushes.Black, 10, intY)** and press **Enter**.

The last instruction in the loop should advance to the next line in the print preview dialog control.

13. Type the additional instruction indicated in Figure 9.23. Also change the Next clause to **Next intRow**, as shown in the figure.

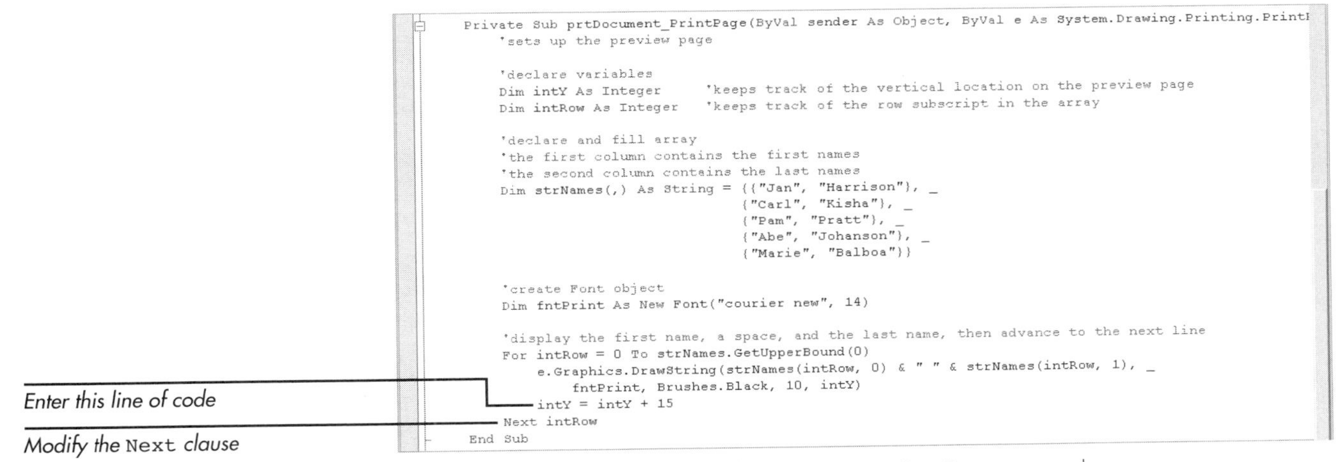

```
Private Sub prtDocument_PrintPage(ByVal sender As Object, ByVal e As System.Drawing.Printing.PrintP
    'sets up the preview page

    'declare variables
    Dim intY As Integer        'keeps track of the vertical location on the preview page
    Dim intRow As Integer      'keeps track of the row subscript in the array

    'declare and fill array
    'the first column contains the first names
    'the second column contains the last names
    Dim strNames(,) As String = {("Jan", "Harrison"), _
                                 ("Carl", "Kisha"), _
                                 ("Pam", "Pratt"), _
                                 ("Abe", "Johanson"), _
                                 ("Marie", "Balboa")}

    'create Font object
    Dim fntPrint As New Font("courier new", 14)

    'display the first name, a space, and the last name, then advance to the next line
    For intRow = 0 To strNames.GetUpperBound(0)
        e.Graphics.DrawString(strNames(intRow, 0) & " " & strNames(intRow, 1), _
            fntPrint, Brushes.Black, 10, intY)
        intY = intY + 15
    Next intRow
End Sub
```

Enter this line of code

Modify the Next clause

FIGURE 9.23   Completed prtDocument_PrintPage procedure

Now that you have finished coding the application, you can test it to verify that it is working correctly.

To test the application:

1. Close the Code Editor window.

2. Save the solution, then start the application.

3. Click the **Preview/Print** button. The Print preview window appears on the screen.

4. Click the **down arrow** that appears to the right of the magnifying glass in the Print preview window's toolbar, then click **100%** in the list. See Figure 9.24.

Down arrow next to the magnifying glass

Print button

Close button

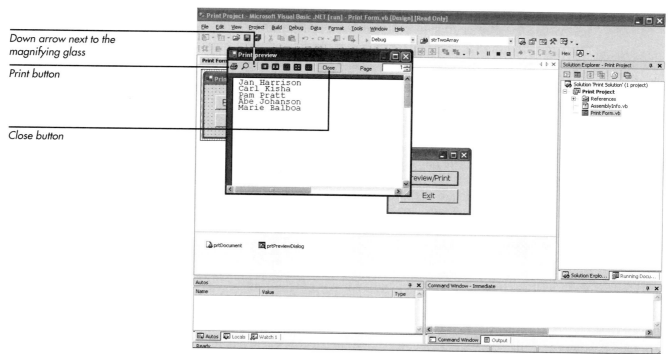

FIGURE 9.24   Print preview window

You can use the Print button in the Print preview window's toolbar to print the contents of the window.

5. If your computer is connected to a printer, click the **Print** button on the Print preview window's toolbar.

6. Click the **Close** button in the Print preview window to close the window.

7. Click the **Exit** button. The btnExit_Click procedure ends the application.

8. Close the Output window.

9. Close the solution, and then exit Visual Studio .NET.

Structures and More Controls

Labs included in this chapter:

LAB 10.1 VENUS MOTORS

Scenario The manager of Venus Motors wants an application that allows a salesperson to display the base price of a car. The car models and base prices are shown in the following chart.

Car model	Base price
Comet JS	10,500
Moonbeam	21,000
Orbit J10	15,500
Planet XL	9,000
Starfire	25,000
Star XL	23,000

Solution Discussion The Venus Motors application will use a list box to display the names of the car models. Using a list box for this purpose has several advantages. First, most users prefer to select a value rather than type it. Second, typing errors are eliminated when using a list box. Third, because the list box displays only valid values, the programmer does not have to be concerned with data validation on this input.

The Venus Motors application will display in a label control the base price corresponding to the name of the model selected in the list box. The application also will use a button control for exiting the application.

In addition, the application will use a structure named Car that contains the name and base price of a car model. It will store six Car structure variables, each corresponding to a car model, in a one-dimensional array.

TOE Chart

Task	Object	Event
1. Fill mcarInfo array with model names and base prices 2. Fill the lstModel control with model names 3. Select the first item in the lstModel control	frmVenus	Load
End the application	btnExit	Click
Get and display the model names	lstModel	None
Display the base price in lblPrice		SelectedIndexChanged
Display the base price (from lstModel)	lblPrice	None

FIGURE 10.1

User Interface

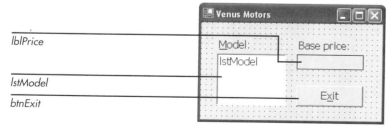

FIGURE 10.2

Objects, Properties, and Settings

Object	Property	Setting
Label1	AutoSize Text	True &Model:
Label2	AutoSize Text	True Base price:
Label3	Name BorderStyle Text TextAlign	lblPrice FixedSingle (empty) MiddleCenter
ListBox1	Name Size	lstModel 104, 80
Button1	Name Text	btnExit E&xit

FIGURE 10.3

Tab Order

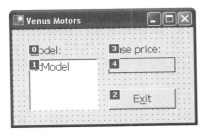

FIGURE 10.4

Pseudocode

frmVenus Load event procedure
1. assign the model names and base prices to the mcarInfo array
2. repeat for array subscripts of 0 through 5
   add the model name from the mcarInfo array to the lstModel control
   end repeat
3. select the first item in the lstModel control

lstModel SelectedIndexChanged event procedure
1. display (in lblPrice) the base price from the mcarInfo array

btnExit Click event procedure
1. close the application

FIGURE 10.5

Activity

1. Start Visual Studio .NET.
2. Click **File** on the Visual Studio .NET menu bar, point to **New**, and then click **Project**. The New Project dialog box opens.
3. If necessary, click **Visual Basic Projects** in the Project Types list box, and click **Windows Application** in the Templates list box.
4. Type **Venus Motors Project** in the Name text box.
5. Use the **Browse** button to open the **VbDotNetLab\Chap10** folder.
6. If necessary, click the **More** button.
7. If necessary, select the **Create directory for Solution** check box.
8. Type **Venus Motors Solution** in the New Solution Name text box.
9. Click the **OK** button to close the New Project dialog box.

Now set the appropriate properties of the form file object and form object.

To set the appropriate properties of the form file object and form object:

1. Right-click **Form1.vb** in the Solution Explorer window, then click **Rename**. Change the form file object's name from Form1.vb to **Venus Motors Form.vb**.
2. Click the **form**, then click (**Name**) in the Properties window. Change the form object's name from Form1 to **frmVenus**.
3. Right-click **Venus Motors Project** in the Solution Explorer window, then click **Properties**. Click the **Startup object** list arrow, and then click **frmVenus** in the list. Click the **OK** button.
4. Click the **form**, then change the values assigned to the following properties:

Font	**Tahoma, 12 pt**
Size	**280, 184**
StartPosition	**CenterScreen**
Text	**Venus Motors**

5. Save the solution by clicking **File** on the menu bar, and then clicking **Save All**.

Next, add the appropriate controls to the interface, and then set the values of some of their properties.

To add the appropriate controls, then set the values of some of their properties:

1. Use the Label tool to add three label controls to the form.
2. Use the ListBox tool to add one list box to the form.
3. Use the Button tool to add one button to the form.
4. Use the chart shown in Figure 10.3 to set the properties of each control.
5. Position the controls as shown in Figure 10.2.
6. Lock the controls in place on the form.
7. Use Figure 10.4 to set the appropriate tab order.
8. Save the solution.

Now that the interface is complete, you can begin coding the application. First, you will enter the appropriate comments and Option statements.

To enter the appropriate comments and Option statements:

1. Right-click the **form**, and then click **View Code** to open the Code Editor window.
2. Type the comments shown in Figure 10.6, replacing `<enter your name and date here>` with your name and the current date. Also type the Option statements shown in the figure.

Enter these comments and Option statements

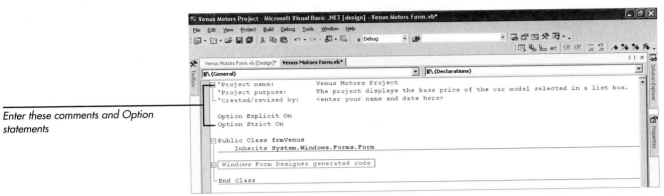

FIGURE 10.6   Code Editor window showing comments and Option statements

Next, you will define a structure (user-defined data type) named Car that contains two member variables: one to store the model name and the other to store the base price. You then will use the Car structure to declare a six-element one-dimensional array.

To define a structure and also declare an array of structure variables:

1. Position the insertion point in the blank line below the `Windows Form Designer generated code` entry, and then press **Enter**.
2. Type `'define structure` and press **Enter**.

Recall that you use the Structure statement to define a structure.

3. Type the following Structure statement, and then press **Enter** twice.

> **Structure Car**
> **Public strModel As String**
> **Public intPrice As Integer**
> **End Structure**

Now use the Car structure to declare a module-level one-dimensional array that has six elements. A module-level array is appropriate in this case because the array will be used by more than one procedure in the application. In this case, the array will be used by the frmVenus_Load procedure (which will fill the array with data) and by the lstModel_SelectedIndexChanged procedure (which will use the array to display the base price).

4. Type `'declare module-level array of structure variables` and press **Enter**.
5. Type `private mcarInfo(5) as car` and press **Enter**.

Next, you will use the pseudocode shown earlier in Figure 10.5 to code the frmVenus Load event procedure.

To code the frmVenus Load event procedure:

1. Click the **Class Name** list arrow, and then click **(frmVenus Events)** in the list.
2. Click the **Method Name** list arrow, and then click **Load** in the list. The code template for the frmVenus_Load procedure appears in the Code Editor window.

3. Type '**fills the mcarInfo array and lstModel control with data** and press **Enter** twice.

First, declare a variable that the procedure can use to keep track of each subscript in the mcarInfo array.

4. Type '**declare variable** and press **Enter**.

5. Type **dim intSubscript as integer** and press **Enter** twice.

The first step in the pseudocode for this procedure is to assign the model names and base prices to the mcarInfo array. Each element in the mcarInfo array is a Car structure variable that contains two member variables: a String variable named strModel and an Integer variable named intPrice. You will assign the model names to the strModel member variables in the array, and assign the base prices to the intPrice member variables. Recall that you refer to a member variable in an array element using the syntax *arrayname*(*subscript*).*memberVariableName*. For example, to assign the first model name (Comet JS) to the strModel member variable in the first array element, you use the statement mcarInfo(0).strModel = "Comet JS". Similarly, you use the statement mcarInfo(0).intPrice = 10500 to assign the corresponding base price to the intPrice member variable in the first array element.

6. Type the comment and additional lines of code shown in Figure 10.7, and then position the insertion point as shown in the figure.

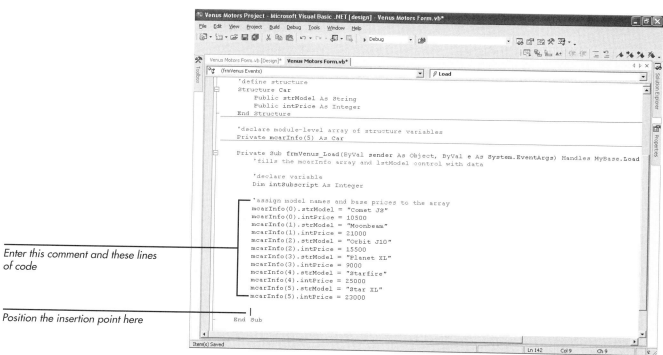

FIGURE 10.7   Comment and additional lines of code shown in the procedure

The next step is a loop that repeats its instruction for array subscripts of zero through five; in other words, it repeats its instruction for each element in the mcarInfo array.

7. Type '**fill the lstModel control with data** and press **Enter**.

8. Type **for intsubscript = 0 to 5** and press **Enter**.

The loop instruction should add to the lstModel control the model name from the current element in the mcarInfo array. You add an item to a list box using the Add method, whose syntax is *object*.**Items.Add**(*item*). In the syntax, *object* is the name of the control to which you want the item added, and *item* is the text you want displayed in the control. In this case, *object* is Me.lstModel and *item* is mcarInfo(intSubscript).strModel.

9. Type **me.lstmodel.items.add(mcarinfo(intsubscript).strmodel)**. The first time the instruction is processed, the intSubscript variable will contain the number zero; therefore, the instruction will add Comet JS, which is the model name stored in the first array element, to the lstModel control. The next time the instruction is processed, the intSubscript variable will contain the number one and the statement will add Moonbeam, which is the model name stored in the second array element, to the lstModel control, and so on. Because the list box's Sorted property is set to False, the model names will appear in the list box in the same order they are entered, which is the same order they appear in the array. The importance of this fact will become apparent when you code the lstModel control's SelectedIndexChanged event.

10. Change the `Next` clause to **Next intSubscript**, and then press **Enter** twice.

The last step in the pseudocode for the frmVenus Load event procedure is to select the first item in the lstModel control. You can use the SelectedIndex property to select a list box item from code. Recall that the first item in a list box has a SelectedIndex value of zero.

11. Type '**select the first item in the list** and press **Enter**.

12. Type **me.lstmodel.selectedindex = 0** and press **Enter**.

13. Save the solution.

Next, you will code the SelectedIndexChanged event procedure for the lstModel control. The procedure is responsible for displaying in the lblPrice control the base price from the mcarInfo array. Recall that the SelectedIndexChanged event occurs each time you select a different item in the list box.

To code the lstModel_SelectedIndexChanged procedure:

1. Display the code template for the lstModel control's SelectedIndexChanged event procedure.

2. Type '**displays the base price of the model selected in the list box** and press **Enter** twice.

First, declare a variable that the procedure can use to store the base price.

3. Type '**declare variable** and press **Enter**.

4. Type **dim intBase as integer** and press **Enter** twice.

Next, assign the appropriate base price to the intBase variable.

5. Type '**assign base price to variable** and press **Enter**.

As mentioned earlier, the model names appear in the same order in both the list box and the array. For example, Comet JS is the first item in the list box as well as the first model name in the array. Likewise, Moonbeam is the second item in the list box as well as the second model name in the array, and so on. Looking at it another way, each model name's index in the list box is the same as its subscript in the array. For instance, Comet JS has an index of zero in the list box and a subscript of zero in the array. Moonbeam has an index of one in the list box and a subscript of one in the array, and so on. Because each model name's index is the same as its subscript, you can use the index of the item selected in the list box to access the appropriate array element. You can determine the index of the selected item using the SelectedIndex property, like this: `Me.lstModel.SelectedIndex`. To access the corresponding array element, you use the code `mcarInfo(Me.lstModel.SelectedIndex)`. However, in this case, you need to access the base price from the array element. You can do so using the code `mcarInfo(Me.lstModel.SelectedIndex).intPrice`.

6. Type **intbase = mcarinfo(me.lstmodel.selectedindex).intprice** and press **Enter** twice.

Now display the base price in the lblPrice control.

7. Type '**display base price in lblPrice** and press **Enter**.

8. Type **me.lblprice.text = intbase.tostring("C0")** and press **Enter**.

Lastly, you code the Click event procedure for the btnExit control, which is responsible for ending the application.

To code the btnExit_Click procedure:

1. Display the code template for the btnExit control's Click event procedure.
2. Type **'ends the application** and press **Enter**.
3. Type **me.close()** and press **Enter**.

Now that you have finished coding the application, you can test the application to verify that the code is working correctly.

To test the application:

1. Save the solution.
2. Start the application by clicking **Debug** on the menu bar, and then clicking **Start**.

The form's Load event procedure fills the array with model names and base prices, and then fills the list box with the model names from the array. The procedure then selects the first model name (Comet JS) in the list box. Selecting the model name causes the lstModel control's SelectedIndexChanged event to occur, which invokes the lstModel_SelectedIndexChanged procedure. The instruction in the procedure displays the appropriate base price in the lblPrice control, as shown in Figure 10.8.

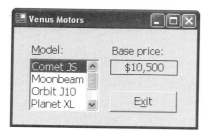

FIGURE 10.8　　Venus Motors application

3. Press the **down arrow** key on your keyboard to select Moonbeam in the list box. $21,000 appears in the lblPrice control.
4. Scroll down the list box and then click **Star XL** in the list. $23,000 appears in the lblPrice control.
5. On your own, verify that when you select each of the remaining model names in the list box, the appropriate base price appears in the lblPrice control.
6. Click the **Exit** button. The btnExit_Click procedure ends the application.
7. Close the Output window, and then close the Code Editor window.

You are finished with the solution, so you can close it.

8. Click **File** on the menu bar, and then click **Close Solution**.

LAB 10.2 PAULA'S PORCELAIN DOLLS

Scenario Paula Harrison, the owner of Paula's Porcelain Dolls, wants an application that allows the sales clerk to enter the price of an item and a shipping method—either Standard, Overnight, or Express 2-day. The application should calculate and display the shipping charge, which is based on the item's price and shipping method. The application also should calculate and display the total price. The Standard shipping charges are listed in the following chart. Overnight shipping is $15 more than the Standard charge, and Express 2-day shipping is $9 more than the Standard charge.

Item price	Standard shipping charge ($)
1 – 100.99	7
101 – 300.99	6
301 – 500.99	5
501 and up	0

Solution Discussion The Paula's Porcelain Dolls application will provide a text box for entering the item's price, and three radio buttons for entering the shipping method. Using radio buttons rather than a text box for the shipping method has several advantages. First, most users prefer to select a value rather than type it. Second, selecting a value from a group of radio buttons eliminates typing errors. Third, the programmer does not have to validate the shipping method entered by the user, because the radio buttons display only valid values for this input.

The application will use a button control that allows the user to calculate and display the shipping charge and total price; the amounts will be displayed in two label controls. It also will use a button control for exiting the application.

TOE Chart

Task	Object	Event
Get and display the price	txtPrice	None
Select the existing text		Enter
Clear the contents of lblShipping and lblTotal		TextChanged
Get and display the shipping method	radStandard, radOvernight, radExpress	None
Clear the contents of lblShipping and lblTotal		Click
1. Calculate the shipping charge 2. Calculate the total price 3. Display the shipping charge in lblShipping 4. Display the total price in lblTotal 5. Send the focus to txtPrice	btnCalc	Click
End the application	btnExit	Click
Display the shipping charge (from btnCalc)	lblShipping	None
Display the total price (from btnCalc)	lblTotal	None

FIGURE 10.9

User Interface

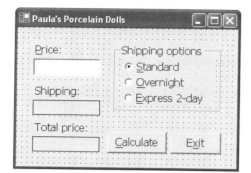

FIGURE 10.10

Tab Order

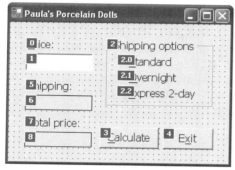

FIGURE 10.11

Pseudocode

btnCalc Click event procedure

1. include the following in the Try section of a Try/Catch block:

   assign the price to a String variable

   remove any dollar signs or spaces from the price

   assign the price to a Decimal variable

   assign the standard shipping charge to a variable, as follows:

price:	
1 – 100.99	assign 7
101 – 300.99	assign 6
301 – 500.99	assign 5
501 and up	assign 0

   if the Overnight radio button is selected

       add 15 to the standard shipping charge

   else if the Express 2-day radio button is selected

       add 9 to the standard shipping charge

   end ifs

   calculate the total price by adding together the price and shipping charge

   display the shipping charge in lblShipping

   display the total price in lblTotal

   include the following in the Catch section of a Try/Catch block:

   use a FormatException Catch statement to handle the error that occurs when the price cannot be converted to Decimal

       if an error occurs, display the message "Please re-enter the price." in a message box

   use a general Catch statement to handle any other errors

       if an error occurs, display a description of the error in a message box

2. send the focus to the txtPrice control

radStandard Click event procedure, radOvernight Click event procedure, radExpress Click event procedure, txtPrice TextChanged event procedure

1. clear the contents of the lblShipping control
2. clear the contents of the lblTotal control

btnExit Click event procedure

1. close the application

txtPrice Enter event procedure

1. select the existing text

FIGURE 10.12

Activity

1. If necessary, start Visual Studio .NET.
2. Open the Paula Solution (Paula Solution.sln) file contained in the VbDotNetLab\Chap10\ Paula Solution folder. The partially completed interface appears on the screen.
3. Use the GroupBox tool in the toolbox to add a group box control to the form. Change the values assigned to the following properties:

Location	**144, 24**
Size	**160, 104**
Text	**Shipping options**

4. Use the RadioButton tool in the toolbox to add three radio buttons to the group box, as shown earlier in Figure 10.10.
5. Change the values assigned to the following properties of the RadioButton1 control:

Name	**radStandard**
Location	**16, 24**
Size	**136, 24**
Text	**&Standard**

6. Change the radStandard control's Checked property to **True**. This will make the control the default radio button in the interface.
7. Change the values assigned to the following properties of the RadioButton2 control:

Name	**radOvernight**
Location	**16, 48**
Size	**136, 24**
Text	**&Overnight**

8. Change the values assigned to the following properties of the RadioButton3 control:

Name	**radExpress**
Location	**16, 72**
Size	**136, 24**
Text	**&Express 2-day**

9. Lock the controls in place on the form.
10. Use Figure 10.11 to set the appropriate tab order.
11. Open the Code Editor window. Notice that the btnExit_Click and txtPrice_Enter procedures have been coded for you.
12. Replace the <enter your name and date here> text with your name and the current date.
13. Save the solution.

Now use the pseudocode shown in Figure 10.12 to code the btnCalc control's Click event procedure.

To code the btnCalc control's Click event procedure:

1. Display the code template for the btnCalc control's Click event procedure.
2. Type '**calculates the shipping charge and total price** and press **Enter** twice.

First, declare four variables for the procedure to use.

3. Type '**declare variables** and press **Enter**.
4. Type **dim strPrice as string** and press **Enter**. This variable will store the price entered by the user.
5. Type **dim decPrice as decimal** and press **Enter**. This variable will store the price after any dollar signs and spaces have been removed.

6. Type **dim decShipping as decimal** and press **Enter**. This variable will store the shipping charge.

7. Type **dim decTotal as decimal** and press **Enter** twice. This variable will store the total price.

The first step in the pseudocode for this procedure is a Try/Catch block.

8. Type **try** and press **Enter**.

The first instruction in the Try section should assign to a String variable the price entered by the user.

9. Type **'assign price to String variable** and press **Enter**.

10. Type **strprice = me.txtprice.text** and press **Enter** twice.

Now remove any dollar signs or spaces from the price; you can use the Replace method to accomplish this step. Recall that the syntax of the Replace method is *string*.**Replace**(*oldValue*, *newValue*). The Replace method returns a string with all occurrences of *oldValue* replaced with *newValue*.

11. Type **'remove any dollar signs and spaces from the price** and press **Enter**.

12. Type **strprice = strprice.replace("$", "")** and press **Enter**.

13. Type **strprice = strprice.replace(" ", "")** and press **Enter** twice. (Be sure to include a space character between the first set of quotation marks; but do not include any space characters between the second set.)

Next, assign the price to a Decimal variable.

14. Type **'assign price to Decimal variable** and press **Enter**.

15. Type **decprice = convert.todecimal(strprice)** and press **Enter** twice.

The next instruction in the Try section is to assign the standard shipping charge, which depends on the item's price, to a variable. You will use a selection structure to determine the appropriate charge to assign.

16. Type the comment and selection structure shown in Figure 10.13, then position the insertion point as shown in the figure.

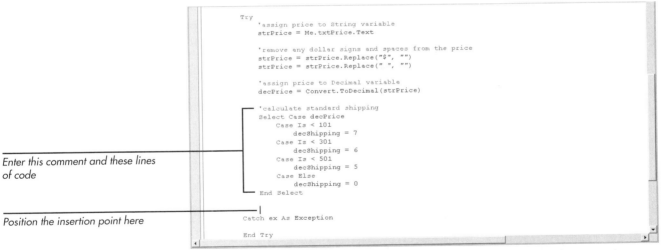

FIGURE 10.13   Comment and selection structure shown in the procedure

The next instruction in the Try section is a selection structure that determines whether the Overnight radio button is selected. If the Overnight radio button is selected, the selection structure's true path should add $15 to the standard shipping charge. If the Overnight radio button is not selected, the selection structure's false path should use a nested selection structure to determine whether the Express 2-day radio button is selected. If the Express 2-day radio button is selected, the nested selection structure's true path should add $9 to the standard shipping charge.

17. Type '**if necessary, add either overnight or express charges** and press **Enter**.
18. Use the If...Then...Else statement to code the appropriate If/ElseIf/Else selection structure.
19. Position the insertion point two lines below the `End  If` clause, but above the `Catch` clause.

The next instruction in the Try section should calculate the total price by adding together the price and the shipping charge.

20. Type '**calculate the total price** and press **Enter**.
21. Type the statement to calculate the total price and assign the result to the decTotal variable, then press **Enter** twice.

The last two instructions in the Try section are to display the shipping charge and total price in the lblShipping and lblTotal controls, respectively.

22. Type '**display shipping charge and total price** and press **Enter**.
23. Type the statement to display the shipping charge in the lblShipping control, then press **Enter**. Display the shipping charge using the "N2" format style.
24. Type the statement to display the total price in the lblTotal control, then press **Enter**. Display the total price using the "N2" format style.

Now that you have finished coding the Try section, you can code the Catch section. According to the pseudocode, the Catch section will need to contain two Catch statements.

25. Enter the Catch statement that will handle the error that occurs when the price cannot be converted to the Decimal data type. When the error occurs, display the message "Please re-enter the price." in a message box.
26. Enter a general Catch statement that will handle any other errors. When an error occurs, display a description of the error in a message box.

The last step in the btnCalc Click event procedure is to send the focus to the txtPrice control, which is the control the user most likely will access after making a calculation.

27. Position the insertion point two lines below the `End  Try` clause, but above the `End  Sub` clause.
28. Type '**set the focus** and press **Enter**.
29. Type the statement to send the focus to the txtPrice control, and then press **Enter**. You now have finished coding the btnCalc_Click procedure.
30. Save the solution.

Next, you will code the Click event procedures for the three radio buttons, as well as the TextChanged event procedure for the txtPrice control.

To code the Click event procedures for the radio buttons, and the TextChanged event procedure for the text box:

1. Display the code template for the radStandard control's Click event procedure.
2. Type '**clears the shipping charge and total price** and press **Enter** twice.
3. Type the statement to clear the contents of the lblShipping control, and then press **Enter**.
4. Type the statement to clear the contents of the lblTotal control, and then press **Enter**.
5. Display the code template for the radOvernight control's Click event procedure.

6. Copy the comment and two statements from the radStandard_Click procedure to the radOvernight_Click procedure.

7. Display the code template for the radExpress control's Click event procedure.

8. Copy the comment and two statements from the radStandard_Click procedure to the radExpress_Click procedure.

9. Display the code template for the txtPrice control's TextChanged event procedure.

10. Copy the comment and two statements from the radStandard_Click procedure to the txtPrice_TextChanged procedure.

Now test the application to verify that it is working correctly.

To test the application:

1. Save the solution, then start the application. Notice that the Standard radio button is the default radio button; you can tell that because it is already selected in the interface. The blinking insertion point indicates that the txtPrice control has the focus.

First, display the standard shipping charge and total price for an item with a price of $90. The shipping charge and total price should be $7 and $97, respectively.

2. Type **$90** and then click the **Calculate** button. The btnCalc_Click procedure removes the dollar sign from the price before calculating and displaying the shipping charge and total price. It then sends the focus to the txtPrice control, as shown in Figure 10.14.

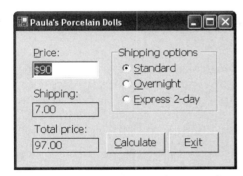

FIGURE 10.14   Paula's Porcelain Dolls application

Next, display the overnight shipping charge and total price for an item with a price of $200.

3. Type **2** in the txtPrice control. The action invokes the txtPrice_TextChanged procedure, which removes the shipping charge and total price from the label controls. Complete the price by typing **00**.

4. Click the **Overnight** radio button, and then click the **Calculate** button. The btnCalc_Click procedure displays the shipping charge (21.00) and total due (221.00) in the label controls.

Now display the express shipping charge and total price for an item with a price of $200.

5. Click the **Express 2-day** radio button. The action invokes the radExpress_Click procedure, which removes the shipping charge and total price from the label controls.

6. Click the **Calculate** button. The btnCalc_Click procedure displays the shipping charge (15.00) and total due (215.00) in the label controls.

Finally, observe what happens when the user enters a letter as the price.

7. Type **7s** as the price, and then click the **Calculate** button. A message box similar to the one shown in Figure 10.15 appears on the screen.

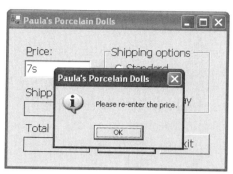

FIGURE 10.15   Message box resulting from an invalid price entry

8. Close the message box.

9. Test the application several more times to verify that it is working correctly.

10. Click the **Exit** button to end the application.

11. Close the Output window, then close the Code Editor window.

You are finished with the solution, so you can close it.

12. Close the solution. Temporarily display the Solution Explorer window to verify that the solution is closed.

LAB 10.3 MODIFIED PAULA'S PORCELAIN DOLLS

Scenario In this lab, you modify the Paula's Porcelain Dolls application that you created in Lab 10.2. The modified application will prevent the txtPrice control from accepting an inappropriate character. In this case, an inappropriate character is one that is not a number, the period, or the Backspace key. Additionally, the application will use one procedure (rather than four procedures) to clear the contents of the lblShipping and lblTotal controls.

Solution Discussion You will use the txtPrice control's KeyPress event to prevent the control from accepting an inappropriate character, such as a letter, a space, or a dollar sign. Recall that the KeyPress event occurs when the user presses a key while the control has the focus. You also will modify the btnCalc control's Click event procedure by deleting the code that removes any dollar signs or spaces from the price. This code is no longer needed, because the KeyPress event prevents the user from entering a dollar sign or space character.

Currently, the code to clear the contents of the lblShipping and lblTotal controls appears in four event procedures: radStandard_Click, radOvernight_Click, radExpress_Click, and txtPrice_TextChanged. You will place the code in one procedure, and then associate the procedure with the four events.

Activity

1. Use Windows to make a copy of the Paula Solution folder, which is contained in the VbDotNetLab\Chap10 folder. Rename the copy **Modified Paula Solution**.

2. If necessary, start Visual Studio .NET.

3. Open the Paula Solution (Paula Solution.sln) file contained in the VbDotNetLab\Chap10\Modified Paula Solution folder.

4. Right-click **Paula Form.vb** in the Solution Explorer window, then click **View Designer**. The user interface shown in Figure 10.10 in Lab 10.2 appears on the screen.

First you will code and then test the txtPrice control's KeyPress event procedure.

To code and then test the txtPrice control's KeyPress event procedure:

1. Open the Code Editor window.
2. Display the code template for the txtPrice control's KeyPress event procedure.

When the KeyPress event occurs, a character corresponding to the key that was pressed is sent to the KeyPress event's e parameter, which appears in the procedure header. To prevent a text box from accepting an inappropriate character, you first use the e parameter's KeyChar property to determine the key that the user pressed. In this case, an inappropriate character is one that is not a number, the period, or the Backspace key.

3. Type **'allows the text box to accept only numbers, the period, and the Backspace key** and press **Enter** twice.
4. Type **if (e.keychar < "0" orelse e.keychar > "9") _** and press **Enter**.
5. Press **Tab**, then type **andalso e.keychar <> "." andalso e.keychar <> controlchars.back then** and press **Enter**.

You then use the e parameter's Handled property to cancel the key if it is an inappropriate one.

6. Type the statement to assign the Boolean value **True** to the e parameter's Handled property.
7. Save the solution, then start the application.
8. Try typing a dollar sign into the txtPrice control; you won't be able to.
9. Try typing a letter into the txtPrice control; you won't be able to.
10. Try typing a comma into the txtPrice control; you won't be able to.
11. Press the **Spacebar** on your keyboard to try typing a space character into the txtPrice control; you won't be able to.
12. Type **7.56** into the txtPrice control, and then use the **Backspace** key to remove the number. Notice that the text box accepts numbers, the period, and the Backspace key.
13. Click the **Exit** button to end the application.

Next, you will modify the btnCalc_Click procedure.

To modify the btnCalc_Click procedure:

1. Locate the btnCalc_Click procedure in the Code Editor window.

The txtPrice_KeyPress procedure does not allow the text box to accept a dollar sign or the space character, so you can delete the code that removes these characters from the price.

2. Delete the line containing the `'remove any dollar signs and spaces from the price` comment.
3. Delete the line containing the `strPrice = strPrice.Replace("$", "")` statement.
4. Delete the line containing the `strPrice = strPrice.Replace(" ", "")` statement. Also delete the blank line below the statement.
5. Save the solution.

Next, you will delete three of the four event procedures that clear the contents of the lblShipping and lblTotal controls. You then will rename the remaining procedure and associate it with the four events.

To delete three procedures, then rename a procedure, and then associate the procedure with four events:

1. Delete the entire radOvernight_Click procedure from the Code Editor window.
2. Delete the entire radExpress_Click procedure from the Code Editor window.

3. Delete the entire txtPrice_TextChanged procedure from the Code Editor window.

Now change the name of the radStandard_Click procedure to ClearLabels.

4. Locate the radStandard control's Click event procedure in the Code Editor window. Change `radStandard_Click` in the procedure header to **ClearLabels**.

Now associate the ClearLabels procedure with the Click events for the three radio buttons and the TextChanged event for the txtPrice control. To associate a procedure with more than one event, you list each event, separated by commas, in the Handles section of the procedure header. A procedure is automatically invoked when one of the events listed in its Handles section occurs.

5. Make the additional modifications to the procedure header, as shown in Figure 10.16.

Line continuation character

Modify the Handles clause

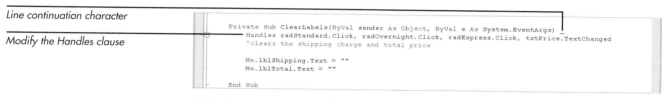

```
Private Sub ClearLabels(ByVal sender As Object, ByVal e As System.EventArgs) _
    Handles radStandard.Click, radOvernight.Click, radExpress.Click, txtPrice.TextChanged
    'clears the shipping charge and total price

    Me.lblShipping.Text = ""
    Me.lblTotal.Text = ""

End Sub
```

FIGURE 10.16   ClearLabels procedure

6. Save the solution.

Now that you have finished modifying the application, you can test it to verify that the code is working correctly.

To test the application:

1. Start the application.

First, display the standard shipping charge and total price for an item with a price of $9.

2. Type **9** in the txtPrice control. The action causes the txtPrice control's TextChanged event to occur. The event is associated with the ClearLabels procedure, which is processed and removes the shipping charge and total price from the label controls. You cannot observe the result of the ClearLabels procedure because the label controls are currently empty.

3. Click the **Calculate** button. The btnCalc_Click procedure displays the shipping charge (7.00) and total due (16.00) in the label controls.

Next, display the overnight shipping charge and total price for an item with a price of $9.

4. Click the **Overnight** radio button. The action causes the radOvernight control's Click event to occur. The event is associated with the ClearLabels procedure, which is processed and removes the shipping charge and total price from the label controls.

5. Click the **Calculate** button. The btnCalc_Click procedure displays the shipping charge (22.00) and total due (31.00) in the label controls.

Now display the express shipping charge and total price for an item with a price of $700.

6. Type **700** as the price, and then click the **Express 2-day** radio button.

7. Click the **Calculate** button. The btnCalc_Click procedure displays the shipping charge (9.00) and total due (709.00) in the label controls.

8. Test the application several more times to verify that it is working correctly.

9. Click the **Exit** button to end the application.

10. Close the Output window, then close the Code Editor window.

You are finished with the solution, so you can close it.

11. Close the solution. Temporarily display the Solution Explorer window to verify that the solution is closed.

BEYOND THE TEXT

LAB 10.4 DOLLAR HAVEN

Scenario In this lab, you learn how to use the ToolTip tool. You also learn how to code a form's Closing event procedure.

Solution Discussion You use the ToolTip tool to create a tool tip, which is a small box that appears when you hover the mouse pointer over an object while an application is running; the box contains a description of the object. In the Dollar Haven application, you will use tool tips to identify the purpose of the two picture boxes in the interface.

A form's Closing event occurs when the computer processes the `Me.Close()` statement. It also occurs when the user clicks the Close button on the form's title bar. When a form's Closing event occurs, any code in the Closing event procedure is processed before the form is removed from the screen and from the computer's memory. The Closing event procedure also allows you to cancel the removal of the form. In the Dollar Haven application, you will use the Closing event procedure to verify that the user wants to exit the application, and then take the appropriate action depending on the answer.

Activity

1. If necessary, start Visual Studio .NET.
2. Open the Dollar Haven Solution (Dollar Haven Solution.sln) file, which is contained in the VbDotNetLab\Chap10\Dollar Haven Solution folder. The user interface appears on the screen.

First, add a ToolTip control to the interface.

3. Scroll down the Toolbox window until you see the ToolTip tool. Click the **ToolTip tool** in the toolbox, and then drag a **ToolTip** control to the form. When you release the mouse button, the control appears in the component tray, as shown in Figure 10.17.

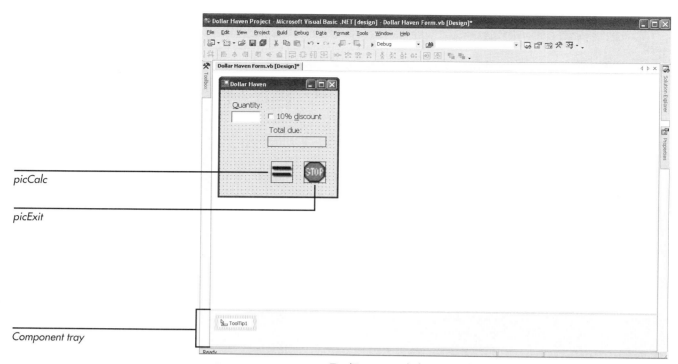

picCalc

picExit

Component tray

FIGURE 10.17   ToolTip control shown in the component tray

The ToolTip control allows you to add a tool tip to one or more objects in the interface. You specify the text for the tool tip by setting the object's ToolTip on ToolTip1 property.

4. Click the **picCalc** control in the interface, then click **ToolTip on ToolTip1** in the Properties list. Type **Calculates the total due.** and press **Enter**.

5. Click the **picExit** control in the interface, and then enter an appropriate tool tip.

6. Save the solution, then start the application.

7. Place your mouse pointer on the picCalc control, which contains an image of an equal sign. The tool tip shown in Figure 10.18 appears. The tool tip identifies the purpose of the control. (Depending on where you placed your mouse pointer, your tool tip may appear in a location that is slightly different from the one shown in the figure.)

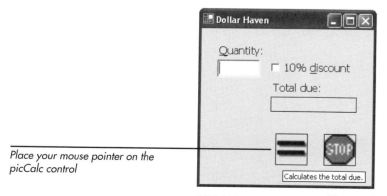

Place your mouse pointer on the picCalc control

FIGURE 10.18   The picCalc control's tool tip

8. Now place your mouse pointer on the picExit control, which contains an image of a stop sign. The tool tip for the picExit control appears.

Use the application to calculate the total due for 10 items. The total due should be $10, because each item in the store costs $1.

9. Type **10** as the quantity, and then click the **picCalc** control. The picCalc_Click procedure, which has already been coded for you, displays $10.00 in the lblTotalDue control.

Now calculate the total due for 10 items, but with a 10% discount.

10. Click the **10% discount** check box. The action causes the chkDiscount control's CheckedChanged event to occur. The event is associated with the ClearTotalDue procedure, which is processed and removes the total due from the lblTotalDue control. (The ClearTotalDue procedure has already been coded for you.)

11. Click the **picCalc** control. The picCalc_Click procedure displays $9.00 in the lblTotalDue control.

12. Click the **picExit** control to end the application. (The picExit_Click procedure has already been coded for you.)

Next, you code and then test the form's Closing event procedure.

To code and then test the form's Closing event procedure:

1. Open the Code Editor window. All of the application's code, except the code for the Closing event procedure, has already been entered for you.

2. Replace the `<enter your name and date here>` text with your name and the current date.

3. Click the **Class Name** list arrow, and then click (**frmDollar Events**) in the list.

4. Click the **Method Name** list arrow, and then click **Closing** in the list. The code template for the frmDollar_Closing procedure appears in the Code Editor window.

In the procedure, you will use the MessageBox.Show method to display a dialog box that asks the user if he or she wants to exit the application.

5. Type '**verifies that the user wants to exit the application** and press **Enter** twice.

First, declare a variable that the procedure can use to store the value returned by the MessageBox.Show method. Recall that the method returns an integer that indicates which button the user chose in the dialog box.

6. Type '**declare variable** and press **Enter**.

7. Type **dim intButton as integer** and press **Enter** twice.

Now display a dialog box that contains the "Do you want to exit?" message, as well as Yes and No buttons.

8. Type the comment and MessageBox.Show method shown in Figure 10.19, and then position the insertion point as shown in the figure.

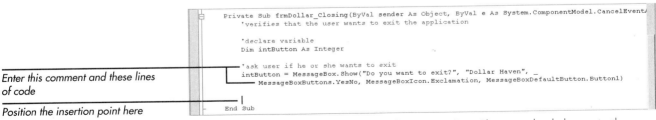

Enter this comment and these lines of code

Position the insertion point here

FIGURE 10.19   Comment and MessageBox.Show method shown in the procedure

If the user selects the Yes button in the dialog box, then the procedure should allow the form to be removed from the screen and from memory. However, if the user selects the No button, the procedure should prevent the form from being removed. You can prevent the form's removal by setting the e parameter's Cancel argument to the Boolean value True.

9. Type '**if the user chose the No button, cancel the exit** and press **Enter**.

10. Type **if intbutton = dialogresult.no then** and press **Enter**.

11. Type the statement to assign the Boolean value True to the **e** parameter's Cancel argument.

12. Save the solution, then start the application.

13. Click the **picExit** control (the stop sign). The dialog box shown in Figure 10.20 appears on the screen.

FIGURE 10.20   Dialog box displayed by the MessageBox.Show method

14. Click the **No** button in the dialog box. The form remains on the screen and in memory.

15. Click the **picExit** control again. This time, click the **Yes** button in the dialog box. The form is removed from the screen and from the computer's memory.

A user also can close a form by clicking the Close button on the title bar.

16. Start the application. Click the **Close** button on the form's title bar. The same dialog box shown in Figure 10.20 appears on the screen.

17. Click the **Yes** button in the dialog box to remove the form from the screen and from memory.

18. Close the Output window, and then close the Code Editor window.

19. Close the solution, and then exit Visual Studio .NET.

11 Creating Classes and Objects

Labs included in this chapter:

- Lab 11.1 Cornwall Calendars
- Lab 11.2 Mayflower College
- Lab 11.3 Modified Mayflower College
- Lab 11.4 Modified Cornwall Calendars

LAB 11.1 CORNWALL CALENDARS

Scenario Jesse Washington, the manager of the Accounts Payable department at Cornwall Calendars, wants an application that he can use to keep track of the checks written by his department. More specifically, he wants to record (in a sequential access file) the check number, date, payee, and amount of each check.

Solution Discussion The Cornwall Calendars application will provide text boxes for entering the check number, date, payee, and amount of each check. The application will use the KeyPress event to prevent the user from entering a check number, date, and amount that contains an inappropriate character. The application also will provide a button control for saving the information to a sequential access file, and a button control for exiting the application.

In this lab, you will create a class named Check that contains four properties and two methods. The application will use the Check class to create a Check object. It will store the user input in the object's properties, and use the object's methods to initialize the Private variables and save the check information to a sequential access file.

TOE Chart

Task	Object	Event
Get and display the check amount	txtAmount	None
Select the existing text		Enter
Allow the text box to accept numbers, the period, and the Backspace key		KeyPress
Get and display the check date	txtDate	None
Select the existing text		Enter
Allow the text box to accept numbers, the slash, and the Backspace key		KeyPress
Get and display the check number	txtNumber	None
Select the existing text		Enter
Allow the text box to accept numbers and the Backspace key		KeyPress
Get and display the payee	txtPayee	None
Select the existing text		Enter
End the application	btnExit	Click
Save the check information to a sequential access file	btnSave	Click

FIGURE 11.1

User Interface

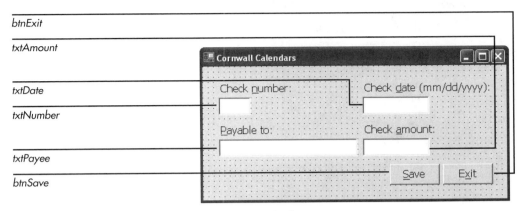

btnExit

txtAmount

txtDate

txtNumber

txtPayee

btnSave

FIGURE 11.2

Objects, Properties, and Settings

Object	Property	Setting
Label1	AutoSize Text	True Check &number:
Label2	AutoSize Text	True Check &date (mm/dd/yyyy):
Label3	AutoSize Text	True &Payable to:
Label4	AutoSize Text	True Check &amount:
TextBox1	Name Text	txtNumber (empty)
TextBox2	Name Text	txtDate (empty)
TextBox3	Name Text	txtPayee (empty)
TextBox4	Name Text	txtAmount (empty)
Button1	Name Text	btnSave &Save
Button2	Name Text	btnExit E&xit

FIGURE 11.3

Tab Order

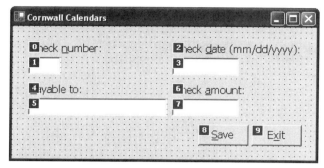

FIGURE 11.4

Pseudocode

New method (default constructor) – Check class
1. initialize the mstrNumber, mstrDate, mstrPayee variables to the empty string
2. initialize the mdecAmount variable to zero

SaveRecord method – Check class
1. include the following in the Try section of a Try/Catch block:
   open for append the sequential access file whose name is passed to the procedure
   write the contents of the Private variables to the sequential access file
   close the sequential access file

   include the following in the Catch section of a Try/Catch block:
   use a general Catch statement to handle any errors
       if an error occurs, display a description of the error in a message box

btnSave Click event procedure
1. use the Check class to create a Check object
2. if the user entered the check number, date, payee, and amount
       assign the check number to the Number property of the Check object
       assign the date to the CheckDate property of the Check object
       assign the payee to the Payee property of the Check object
       assign the amount to the Amount property of the Check object
       call the Check object's SaveRecord method to write the check information to a sequential access file named checks.txt
   else
       display an appropriate message in a message box
   end if
3. send the focus to the txtNumber control

(Figure is continued on next page)

---

txtAmount, txtDate, txtNumber, txtPayee Enter event procedures

1. select the existing text

txtAmount KeyPress event procedure

1. allow the text box to accept only numbers, the period, and the Backspace key

txtNumber KeyPress event procedure

1. allow the text box to accept only numbers and the Backspace key

txtDate KeyPress event procedure

1. allow the text box to accept only numbers, the slash, and the Backspace key

btnExit Click event procedure

1. close the application

FIGURE 11.5

Activity

1. Start Visual Studio .NET.
2. Click **File** on the Visual Studio .NET menu bar, point to **New**, and then click **Project**. The New Project dialog box opens.
3. If necessary, click **Visual Basic Projects** in the Project Types list box, and click **Windows Application** in the Templates list box.
4. Type **Cornwall Calendars Project** in the Name text box.
5. Use the **Browse** button to open the **VbDotNetLab\Chap11** folder.
6. If necessary, click the **More** button.
7. If necessary, select the **Create directory for Solution** check box.
8. Type **Cornwall Calendars Solution** in the New Solution Name text box.
9. Click the **OK** button to close the New Project dialog box.

Now set the appropriate properties of the form file object and form object.

To set the appropriate properties of the form file object and form object:

1. Right-click **Form1.vb** in the Solution Explorer window, then click **Rename**. Change the form file object's name from Form1.vb to **Cornwall Form.vb**.
2. Click the **form**, then click **(Name)** in the Properties window. Change the form object's name from Form1 to **frmCornwall**.
3. Right-click **Cornwall Calendars Project** in the Solution Explorer window, then click **Properties**. Click the **Startup object** list arrow, and then click **frmCornwall** in the list. Click the **OK** button.
4. Click the **form**, then change the values assigned to the following properties:

Font	**Tahoma, 12 pt**
Size	**464, 240**
StartPosition	**CenterScreen**
Text	**Cornwall Calendars**

5. Save the solution by clicking **File** on the menu bar, and then clicking **Save All**.

Next, add the appropriate controls to the interface, and then set the values of some of their properties.

To add the appropriate controls, then set the values of some of their properties:

1. Use the Label tool to add four label controls to the form.
2. Use the TextBox tool to add four text boxes to the form.
3. Use the Button tool to add two buttons to the form.
4. Use the chart shown in Figure 11.3 to set the properties of each control.
5. Position the controls as shown in Figure 11.2.
6. Lock the controls in place on the form.
7. Use Figure 11.4 to set the appropriate tab order.
8. Save the solution.

Now that the interface is complete, you can begin coding the application. First, you will define a class named Check that contains four Private variables and Property procedures. The Private variables and Property procedures will store the check information entered by the user. The class also will contain two methods: the default constructor and a method that saves the check information to a sequential access file.

To define the Check class:

1. Click **Project** on the menu bar, and then click **Add Class**. The Add New Item – Cornwall Calendars Project dialog box opens with Class selected in the Templates list box.
2. Type **Check.vb** in the Name box, as shown in Figure 11.6.

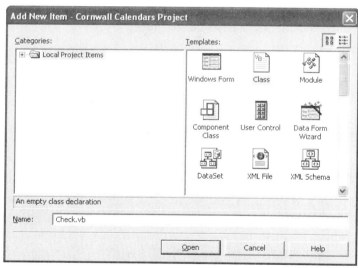

FIGURE 11.6 Add New Item – Cornwall Calendars Project dialog box

3. Click the **Open** button. The computer adds a file named Check.vb to the current project and also opens the file in the Code Editor window.
4. Temporarily display the Solution Explorer window. See Figure 11.7.

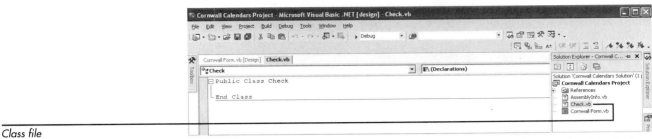

Class file

FIGURE 11.7   Check.vb file added to the project and opened in the Code Editor window

5. Insert a blank line above the `Public Class Check` clause.

6. Type '**Class name:** and press **Tab**, then type **Check** and press **Enter** twice.

7. Type **option explicit on** and press **Enter**, then type **option strict on** and press **Enter**.

First declare the class's Private variables. The class will use four Private variables to store the check number, check date, payee, and check amount.

8. Type the comment and additional lines of code shown in Figure 11.8, and then position the insertion point as shown in the figure.

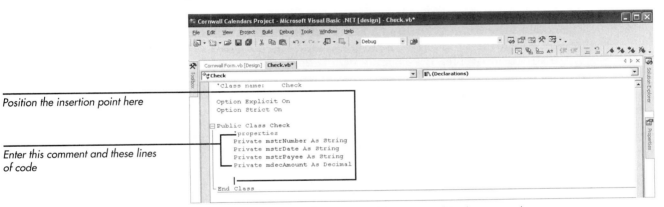

Position the insertion point here

Enter this comment and these lines of code

FIGURE 11.8   Private variables entered in the procedure

When an application needs to assign data to or retrieve data from a Private variable in a class, it must use a Public property to do so. In other words, an application cannot refer, directly, to a Private variable in a class. Rather, it must refer to the variable indirectly, through the use of a Public property. Recall that you create a Public property using a Property procedure.

9. Type **public property Number as string** and press **Enter**. The property procedure's template appears in the Code Editor window, as shown in Figure 11.9.

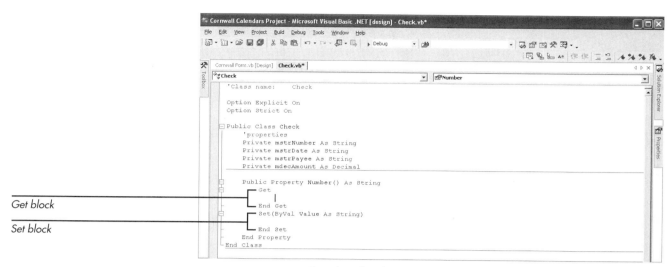

FIGURE 11.9 Template for the Number property procedure

TIP ••••: The data type of the Property procedure must be the same as the data type of the Private variable associated with the Property procedure.

The code in the Get block allows an application to retrieve the contents of the Private variable associated with the property. Most times, you will enter only one instruction in the Get block. The instruction—typically `Return` *privateVariable*—directs the computer to return the contents of the Private variable.

10. Type **return mstrnumber**.

The code in the Set block, on the other hand, allows the application to assign a value to the Private variable associated with the property.

11. Type the additional statement shown in Figure 11.10, and then position the insertion point as shown in the figure.

```
        Public Property Number() As String
            Get
                Return mstrNumber
            End Get
            Set(ByVal Value As String)
                mstrNumber = Value
            End Set
        End Property

    End Class
```

Enter this line of code

Position the insertion point here

FIGURE 11.10   Property procedure associated with the mstrNumber variable

TIP ••••: You can enter one or more instructions within the Set block. For example, you can enter the code to validate the value received from the application before assigning it to the Private variable. If the value is valid, the last instruction in the Set block should assign the content of the Value parameter to the Private variable. However, if the value received from the application is not valid, the last instruction in the Set block should assign a default value to the Private variable.

12. Create a Property procedure for the mstrDate variable. Name the property **CheckDate**. Complete the Get and Set blocks appropriately.

13. Create a Property procedure for the mstrPayee variable. Name the property **Payee**. Complete the Get and Set blocks appropriately.

14. Create a Property procedure for the mdecAmount variable. Name the property **Amount**.

Complete the Get and Set blocks appropriately.

15. Position the insertion point two lines below the last `End Property` clause, but above the `End Class` clause.

Every class should have at least one constructor. A constructor is a method whose instructions the computer processes, automatically, each time an object is created (instantiated) from the class. The sole purpose of a constructor is to initialize the class's variables. Each constructor included in a class has the same name (New), but its parameters (if any) must be different from any other constructor in the class. A constructor that has no parameters is called the default constructor. According to the pseudocode shown earlier in Figure 11.5, the Check class will use only one constructor: the default constructor. In this case, the default constructor will initialize the mstrNumber, mstrDate, and mstrPayee variables to the empty string, and initialize the mdecAmount variable to the number zero.

16. Type the comments and additional lines of code shown in Figure 11.11, and then position the insertion point as shown in the figure.

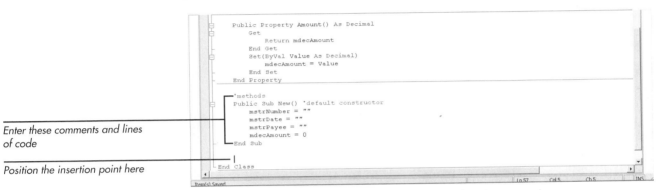

Enter these comments and lines of code

Position the insertion point here

FIGURE 11.11   Default constructor entered in the procedure

The Check class will also contain a method named SaveRecord that saves the contents of the Private variables to a sequential access file. The SaveRecord method will receive the name of the file from the procedure that invokes it.

17. Type **public sub SaveRecord(byval strFile as string)** and press **Enter**.

18. Type '**saves the contents of the Private variables to a sequential access file** and press **Enter** twice.

First, declare a StreamWriter variable that the method will use to store the address of a StreamWriter object.

19. Type '**declare variables** and press **Enter**.

20. Type **dim swrStreamWriter as io.streamwriter** and press **Enter** twice.

According to the pseudocode, the first step in the SaveRecord method is a Try/Catch block.

21. Type **try** and press **Enter**.

The first instruction in the Try section should open a sequential access file for append. The name of the file to be opened is passed to the SaveRecord method by the procedure that invokes the method. When the method receives the filename, it stores the name in the strFile variable.

22. Type '**open the file for append** and press **Enter**.

23. Type **swrstreamwriter = io.file.appendtext(strfile)** and press **Enter**.

The next instruction should write the contents of the Private variables to the sequential access file. You will write the contents of the variables in four columns.

24. Type '**write the contents of the Private variables** and press **Enter**.

25. Type **swrstreamwriter.writeline(mstrnumber.padright(10) & mstrdate.padright(15)** _ and press **Enter**.

26. Press **Tab**, then type **& mstrpayee.padright(25) & mdecamount.tostring("N2"). padleft(15))** and press **Enter**.

The last instruction in the SaveRecord method should close the sequential access file.

27. Type **'close the file** and press **Enter**.

28. Type **swrstreamwriter.close()** and press **Enter**.

You have finished coding the Try section. Next, you code the Catch section.

29. Enter the MessageBox.Show method shown in Figure 11.12.

```
Public Sub SaveRecord(ByVal strFile As String)
    'saves the contents of the Private variables to a sequential access file

    'declare variables
    Dim swrStreamWriter As IO.StreamWriter

    Try
        'open the file for append
        swrStreamWriter = IO.File.AppendText(strFile)
        'write the contents of the Private variables
        swrStreamWriter.WriteLine(mstrNumber.PadRight(10) & mstrDate.PadRight(15) _
            & mstrPayee.PadRight(25) & mdecAmount.ToString("N2").PadLeft(15))
        'close the file
        swrStreamWriter.Close()

    Catch ex As Exception
        MessageBox.Show(ex.Message, "File Error", _
            MessageBoxButtons.OK, MessageBoxIcon.Information, MessageBoxDefaultButton.Button1)
    End Try
End Sub
```

Enter these lines of code

FIGURE 11.12   Completed SaveRecord method

30. Click **File** on the menu bar, and then click **Save All** to save the solution.

Now that you have finished coding the Check class, you can code the procedures in the Cornwall Calendars application. First, you will enter the appropriate comments and Option statements.

To enter the appropriate comments and Option statements:

1. Click the **Cornwall Form.vb [Design]** tab.

2. Right-click the **form**, and then click **View Code** to open the Code Editor window.

3. Type the comments shown in Figure 11.13, replacing `<enter your name and date here>` with your name and the current date. Also type the Option statements shown in the figure.

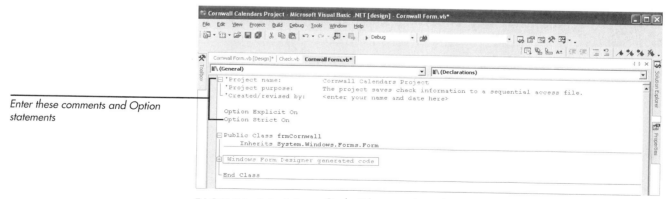

Enter these comments and Option statements

FIGURE 11.13   Code Editor window showing comments and Option statements

Next, you will code the btnSave Click event procedure.

To code the btnSave Click event procedure:

1. Click the **Class Name** list arrow, and then click **btnSave** in the list.

2. Click the **Method Name** list arrow, and then click **Click** in the list. The code template for the btnSave_Click procedure appears in the Code Editor window.

3. Type **'saves the check information to a sequential access file** and press **Enter** twice.

According to the pseudocode shown earlier in Figure 11.5, the first step in the btnSave_Click procedure is to create a Check object using the Check class. You can create an object from a class using the syntax **Dim** *objectVariable* **As New** *class*.

4. Type **'create Check object** and press **Enter**.

5. Type **dim objCheck as new check** and press **Enter** twice.

The next step in the pseudocode is a selection structure that determines whether the user entered the check information—in this case, the check number, date, payee, and amount. If the user neglected to enter one or more of the items, the selection structure's false path should display an appropriate message.

6. Type the comment and additional lines of code shown in Figure 11.14, and then position the insertion point as shown in the figure.

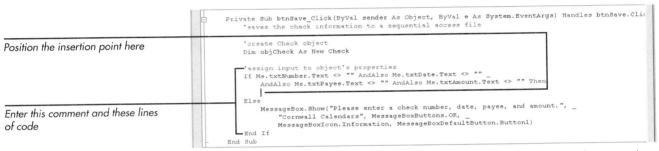

Position the insertion point here

Enter this comment and these lines of code

FIGURE 11.14 Comment and additional lines of code shown in the procedure

However, if the user entered all of the check information, the selection structure's true path should assign each item of information to a property of the Check object.

7. Type **objcheck.number = me.txtnumber.text** and press **Enter**. This statement assigns the check number to the Number property of the Check object.

8. Type the statement to assign the check date to the CheckDate property of the Check object, and then press **Enter**.

9. Type the statement to assign the payee to the Payee property of the Check object, and then press **Enter**.

10. Type the statement to convert the check amount to Decimal, assign the result to the Amount property of the Check object, and then press **Enter** twice.

After assigning the check information to the Check object's properties, the selection structure's true path should call the Check object's SaveRecord method to write the check information to a sequential access file named checks.txt.

11. Type **'call object's method to write information to the checks.txt sequential access file** and press **Enter**.

12. Type **objcheck.saverecord("checks.txt")**.

The last step in the pseudocode is to send the focus to the txtNumber control.

13. Position the insertion point two lines below the End If clause, but above the End Sub clause.

14. Type '**set the focus** and press **Enter**.

15. Type the statement to send the focus to the txtNumber control.

Next, you will code the Enter event procedures for the txtNumber, txtDate, txtPayee, and txtAmount controls. The procedures are responsible for selecting the text in their respective text box when the text box receives the focus.

To code the txtNumber, txtDate, txtPayee, and txtAmount Enter event procedures:

1. Display the code template for the txtNumber control's Enter event procedure.

2. Type '**selects the existing text** and press **Enter**.

3. Type **me.txtnumber.selectall()**.

4. On your own, code the txtDate control's Enter event procedure.

5. On your own, code the txtPayee control's Enter event procedure.

6. On your own, code the txtAmount control's Enter event procedure.

Now code the KeyPress event procedures for the txtAmount, txtNumber, and txtDate controls.

To code the KeyPress event procedures for the txtAmount, txtNumber, and txtDate controls:

1. Display the code template for the txtAmount control's KeyPress event procedure.

The txtAmount_KeyPress procedure should allow the text box to accept only numbers, the period, and the Backspace key.

2. Type the comment and additional lines of code shown in Figure 11.15.

Enter this comment and these lines of code

```
Private Sub txtAmount_KeyPress(ByVal sender As Object, ByVal e As System.Windows.Forms.KeyPressEvei
    'allows the text box to accept only numbers, the period, and the Backspace key
    If (e.KeyChar < "0" OrElse e.KeyChar > "9") AndAlso e.KeyChar <> "." _
        AndAlso e.KeyChar <> ControlChars.Back Then
        e.Handled = True
    End If
End Sub
```

FIGURE 11.15 Completed txtAmount_KeyPress procedure

3. On your own, code the KeyPress event procedure for the txtNumber control. The procedure should allow the text box to accept only numbers and the Backspace key.

4. On your own, code the KeyPress event procedure for the txtDate control. The procedure should allow the text box to accept only numbers, the slash (/), and the Backspace key.

The last procedure you need to code is the btnExit control's Click event procedure, which is responsible for ending the application.

To code the btnExit control's Click event procedure:

1. Display the code template for the btnExit control's Click event procedure.

2. Type '**ends the application** and press **Enter**.

3. Type the statement to close the application.

Now that you have finished coding the application, you can test the application to verify that the code is working correctly.

To test the application:

1. Save the solution.

2. Start the application by clicking **Debug** on the menu bar, and then clicking **Start**.

First, observe what happens when you click the Save button without entering the check information.

3. Click the **Save** button. The message box shown in Figure 11.16 appears on the screen.

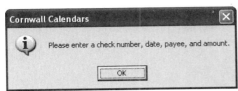

FIGURE 11.16   Message box that appears when the user does not enter all of the check information

4. Click the **OK** button to close the message box.

5. On your own, verify that the message box shown in Figure 11.16 appears when you enter one item, two items, or three items of check information.

Next, you will enter all of the required check information.

6. Enter **104** in the Check number box, **10/25/2005** in the Check date box, **Tri-County Electric** in the Payable to box, and **125.67** in the Check amount box. Click the **Save** button. The btnSave_Click procedure uses the properties and methods of the Check object to save the check information to the checks.txt file. It then sends the focus to the txtNumber control, as shown in Figure 11.17.

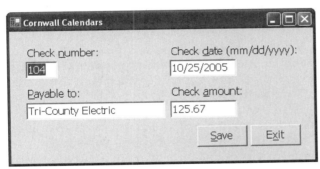

FIGURE 11.17   Cornwall Calendars application

7. Use the application to save the information for the following two checks:

Check number:	**105**
Check date:	**10/30/2005**
Payable to:	**Henson Grocery**
Check amount:	**45.89**

Check number:	**106**
Check date:	**11/01/2005**
Payable to:	**Jacob Hardware**
Check amount:	**6.78**

8. Click the **Exit** button to end the application.

Now open the checks.txt file to verify its contents.

9. Click **File** on the menu bar. Point to **Open**, and then click **File**. The Open File dialog box opens.

10. Open the bin folder contained in the VbDotNetLab\Chap11\Cornwall Calendars Solution\Cornwall Calendars Project folder. The checks.txt filename should be selected in the list of filenames.

11. Click the **Open** button to open the checks.txt file. Figure 11.18 shows the contents of the file.

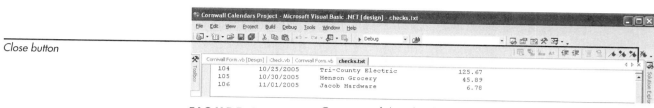

104	10/25/2005	Tri-County Electric	125.67
105	10/30/2005	Henson Grocery	45.89
106	11/01/2005	Jacob Hardware	6.78

FIGURE 11.18   Contents of the checks.txt file

12. Close the checks.txt window by clicking its **Close** button.

13. Close the Output window, and then close the Cornwall Form.vb window and the Check.vb window.

You are finished with the solution, so you can close it.

14. Click **File** on the menu bar, and then click **Close Solution**.

LAB 11.2 MAYFLOWER COLLEGE

Scenario Mariah Jacobsen, a professor at Mayflower College, wants an application that allows her to enter each student's name and three test scores. The application should calculate and display each student's average test score.

Solution Discussion The Mayflower College application will provide text boxes for entering the student's name and three test scores, and a text box for displaying each student's name and average text score. As you learned in Lab 5.4 in Chapter 5, rather than using a label control to display information that you don't want the user to modify, you also can use a text box whose ReadOnly and Multiline properties are set to True. The advantage of using a text box in this case is that, unlike a label control, a text box has a ScrollBars property that allows you to display a vertical scroll bar, a horizontal scroll bar, both horizontal and vertical scroll bars, or no scroll bars. Because you do not know how many student names and average test scores the application will need to display at any one time, a text box with a vertical scroll bar is a better choice than a label control for displaying the information. The vertical scroll bar will allow the user to scroll the text box to view all of the student information.

The application will use the KeyPress event to prevent the user from entering a test score that contains an inappropriate character. The application also will use a button control that allows the user to calculate and display each student's name and average test score, and a button control for exiting the application.

In this lab, you will create a class named Student that contains four properties and two methods. The application will use the Student class to create a Student object. It will store the user input in the object's properties, and use the object's methods to initialize the Private variables and calculate and return the average test score.

TOE Chart

Task	Object	Event
Get and display the student name	txtName	None
Select the existing text		Enter
Get and display the three test scores	txtTest1, txtTest2, txtTest3	None
Select the existing text		Enter
Allow the text box to accept numbers, the period, and the Backspace key		KeyPress
1. Calculate the average test score 2. Display the student name and average test score in txtAverages	btnCalc	Click
End the application	btnExit	Click
Display the student names and average test scores (from btnCalc)	txtAverages	None

FIGURE 11.19

User Interface

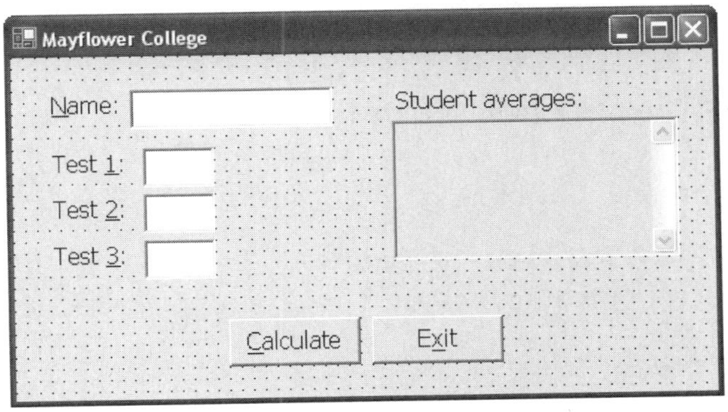

FIGURE 11.20

Pseudocode

New method (default constructor) – Student class
1. initialize the mstrName variable to the empty string
2. initialize the mdecTest1, mdecTest2, and mdecTest3 variables to zero

CalculateAverage method – Student class
1. calculate the average test score by adding together the three test scores and then dividing the sum by 3
2. return the average test score

btnCalc Click event procedure
1. use the Student class to create a Student object
2. if the user entered a name and three test scores
    assign the student name to the Name property of the Student object
    assign the first test score to the Test1 property of the Student object
    assign the second test score to the Test2 property of the Student object
    assign the third test score to the Test3 property of the Student object
    call the Student object's CalculateAverage method to calculate the average test score
    display the student name and average test score in the txtAverages control
    else
    display an appropriate message in a message box
    end if
3. send the focus to the txtName control

txtTest1, txtTest2, txtTest3 KeyPress event procedures
1. allow the text box to accept only numbers, the period, and the Backspace key

btnExit Click event procedure
1. close the application

txtName, txtTest1, txtTest2, txtTest3 Enter event procedures
1. select the existing text

F I G U R E   1 1 . 2 1

Activity

1. If necessary, start Visual Studio .NET.
2. Open the Mayflower Solution (Mayflower Solution.sln) file, which is contained in the VbDotNetLab\Chap11\Mayflower Solution folder. The interface shown in Figure 11.20 appears on the screen.
3. Open the Code Editor window. Notice that the btnExit_Click, txtName_Enter, txtTest1_Enter, txtTest2_Enter, and txtTest3_Enter procedures have been coded for you.
4. Replace the <enter your name and date here> text with your name and the current date.
5. Save the solution.

First, you will define a class named Student that contains four Private variables and Property procedures. The Private variables and Property procedures will store the name and test scores entered by the user. The class also will contain two methods: the default constructor and a method that calculates and returns the average test score.

To define the Student class:

1. Click **Project** on the menu bar, and then click **Add Class**. The Add New Item – Mayflower Project dialog box opens with Class selected in the Templates list box.

2. Type **Student.vb** in the Name box, and then click the **Open** button. The computer adds a file named Student.vb to the current project and also opens the file in the Code Editor window.

3. Insert a blank line above the `Public Class Student` clause.

4. Type '**Class name:** and press **Tab**, then type **Student** and press **Enter** twice.

5. Type **option explicit on** and press **Enter**, then type **option strict on** and press **Enter**.

First, declare four Private variables that the procedure can use to store the student name and test scores.

6. Position the insertion point in the blank line below the `Public Class Student` clause. Type '**properties** and press **Enter**.

7. Type the statement to declare a String variable named **mstrName**, and then press **Enter**.

8. Type the statement to declare a Decimal variable named **mdecTest1**, and then press **Enter**.

9. Type the statement to declare a Decimal variable named **mdecTest2**, and then press **Enter**.

10. Type the statement to declare a Decimal variable named **mdecTest3**, and then press **Enter** twice.

11. Create a Property procedure for the mstrName variable. Name the property **Name**. Complete the Get and Set blocks appropriately.

12. Create a Property procedure for the mdecTest1 variable. Name the property **Test1**. Complete the Get and Set blocks appropriately.

13. Create a Property procedure for the mdecTest2 variable. Name the property **Test2**. Complete the Get and Set blocks appropriately.

14. Create a Property procedure for the mdecTest3 variable. Name the property **Test3**. Complete the Get and Set blocks appropriately.

15. Position the insertion point two lines below the last `End Property` clause, but above the `End Class` clause.

According to the pseudocode shown earlier in Figure 11.21, the Student class will contain two methods: the default constructor and a method named CalculateAverage. The default constructor should initialize the Private variables in the class. The CalculateAverage method should calculate and return the average test score.

16. Type '**methods** and press **Enter**.

17. Create a default constructor that initializes the mstrName variable to the empty string, and initializes the mdecTest1, mdecTest2, and mdecTest3 variables to the number zero.

18. Position the insertion point two lines below the default constructor's `End Sub` clause, but before the `End Class` clause.

19. Type **public function CalculateAverage() as decimal** and press **Enter**.

20. Type '**calculates and returns the average of three test scores** and press **Enter** twice.

21. Use the pseudocode shown in Figure 11.21 to finish coding the CalculateAverage method, which should calculate the average test score and then return the result to the procedure that invoked the method.

You are finished defining the Student class, so you can save the solution and close the Student.vb window.

22. Click **File** on the menu bar, and then click **Save All** to save the solution.

23. Close the Student.vb window by clicking its **Close** button.

Next, use the pseudocode shown in Figure 11.21 to code the btnCalc control's Click event procedure.

To code the btnCalc control's Click event procedure:

1. Display the code template for the btnCalc control's Click event procedure.

2. Type '**calculates and displays a student's average score** and press **Enter** twice.

First, declare a Decimal variable that the procedure can use to store the average test score.

3. Type '**declare variable** and press **Enter**.

4. Type the statement to declare a Decimal variable named **decAverage**, and then press **Enter**.

The first step in the pseudocode is to create a Student object. The procedure will use the object to store the user input.

5. Type '**create Student object** and press **Enter**

6. Type the statement to create a Student object named **objStudent**, and then press **Enter** twice.

The next step in the pseudocode is a selection structure that determines whether the user entered the student name and three test scores. If the user neglected to enter one or more of the items, the selection structure's false path should display an appropriate message.

7. Type the additional lines of code shown in Figure 11.22, and then position the insertion point as shown in the figure.

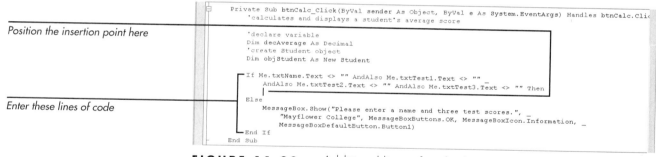

```
         Private Sub btnCalc_Click(ByVal sender As Object, ByVal e As System.EventArgs) Handles btnCalc.Clic
              'calculates and displays a student's average score

Position the insertion point here     'declare variable
                 Dim decAverage As Decimal
                 'create Student object
                 Dim objStudent As New Student

                 If Me.txtName.Text <> "" AndAlso Me.txtTest1.Text <> "" _
                     AndAlso Me.txtTest2.Text <> "" AndAlso Me.txtTest3.Text <> "" Then

Enter these lines of code    Else
                     MessageBox.Show("Please enter a name and three test scores.", _
                          "Mayflower College", MessageBoxButtons.OK, MessageBoxIcon.Information, _
                          MessageBoxDefaultButton.Button1)
                 End If
             End Sub
```

FIGURE 11.22   Additional lines of code shown in the procedure

However, if the user entered the student name and three test scores, the selection structure's true path should assign each item to a property of the Student object.

8. Type '**assign input to the properties of the Student object** and press **Enter**.

9. Type the statement to assign the student name to the Name property of the Student object, and then press **Enter**.

10. Type the statement to assign the first test score to the Test1 property of the Student object, and then press **Enter**.

11. Type the statement to assign the second test score to the Test2 property of the Student object, and then press **Enter**.

12. Type the statement to assign the third test score to the Test3 property of the Student object, and then press **Enter** twice.

After assigning the user input to the Student object's properties, the selection structure's true path should call the Student object's CalculateAverage method to calculate and return the average test score.

13. Type '**call the Student object's method to calculate the average** and press **Enter**.

14. Type the statement that calls the Student object's CalculateAverage method and then assigns the return value to the decAverage variable, and then press **Enter** twice.

The next instruction in the selection structure's true path should display the student name and average test score in the txtAverages control.

15. Type '**display name and average** and press **Enter**.

16. Type **me.txtaverages.text = me.txtaverages.text & objstudent.name.padright(10)** _ and press **Enter**.

17. Press **Tab**, and then type **& decaverage.tostring("N2").padleft(6) & controlchars.newline**.

The last step in the pseudocode is to send the focus to the txtName control.

18. Position the insertion point two lines below the End If clause, but above the End Sub clause.

19. Type '**set the focus** and press **Enter**.

20. Type the statement to send the focus to the txtName control, and then press **Enter**.

21. Save the solution.

Next, you will code the KeyPress event procedures for the txtTest1, txtTest2, and txtTest3 controls. The procedures are responsible for preventing their respective text box from accepting characters other than numbers, the period, and the Backspace key. Because the code for each event procedure will be identical, you will enter the code in an independent Sub procedure named CheckCharacters, and then use the Handles clause to associate the CheckCharacters procedure with the three event procedures.

To code the txtTest1, txtTest2, and txtTest3 KeyPress event procedures:

1. Display the code template for the txtTest1 control's KeyPress event procedure.

2. Change txtTest1_KeyPress in the procedure header to **CheckCharacters**.

3. Modify the Handles clause in the procedure header as shown in Figure 11.23, and then position the insertion point as shown in the figure.

Modify the Handles clause

```
Private Sub CheckCharacters(ByVal sender As Object, ByVal e As System.Windows.Forms.KeyPressEventA
    Handles txtTest1.KeyPress, txtTest2.KeyPress, txtTest3.KeyPress

End Sub
```

Position the insertion point here

FIGURE 11.23 Modified CheckCharacters procedure header

4. Type '**allows the text box to accept only numbers, the period, and the Backspace key** and press **Enter** twice.

5. Complete the CheckCharacters procedure by entering the code that allows the text box to accept only numbers, the period, and the Backspace key.

Now test the application to verify that it is working correctly.

To test the application:

1. Save the solution, then start the application. The blinking insertion point indicates that the txtName control has the focus.

First, observe what happens when you click the Calculate button without entering all of the student information.

2. Click the **Calculate** button. The message box shown in Figure 11.24 appears on the screen.

Mayflower College

Please enter a name and three test scores.

OK

FIGURE 11.24   Message box that appears when the user does not enter all of the student information

3. Click the **OK** button to close the message box.

4. On your own, verify that the message box shown in Figure 11.24 appears when you enter one item, two items, or three items of student information.

Next, you will enter all of the required student information.

5. Type **Sam Chen** in the Name box, and then type **90** in the Test 1 box. Type **85** in the Test 2 box, and then type **75** in the Test 3 box.

6. Click the **Calculate** button. The student name (Sam Chen) and average test score (83.33) appear in the txtAverages control, as shown in Figure 11.25.

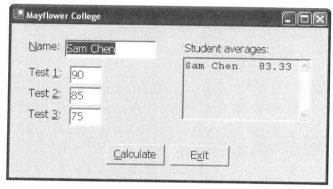

FIGURE 11.25   Mayflower College application

7. Type **Mary Smith** in the Name box, and then type **100** in the Test 1 box. Type **90** in the Test 2 box, and then type **95** in the Test 3 box.

8. Click the **Calculate** button. The student name (Mary Smith) and average test score (95.00) appear below Sam Chen's information in the txtAverages control.

9. Test the application several more times to verify that it is working correctly.

10. Click the **Exit** button to end the application.

11. Close the Output window, then close the Code Editor window.

You are finished with the solution, so you can close it.

12. Close the solution. Temporarily display the Solution Explorer window to verify that the solution is closed.

LAB 11.3 MODIFIED MAYFLOWER COLLEGE

Scenario In this lab, you modify the Student class and Mayflower College application you created in Lab 11.2.

Solution Discussion The modified Student class will include an additional method named ValidateScores. The ValidateScores method will verify that each test score is greater than or equal to a minimum value, but less than or equal to a maximum value. The minimum and maximum values will be passed to the method by the procedure that invokes the method.

You also will modify the btnCalc_Click procedure in the application. The modified procedure will invoke the ValidateScores method, passing it the minimum and maximum values for a test score. In this case, the minimum value will be zero and the maximum value will be 100.

Modified pseudocode

ValidateScores method – Student class

1. if each of the three test scores is greater than or equal to the minimum value, but less than or equal to the maximum value

      assign True to blnDataInRange

    else

      assign False to blnDataInRange

    end if

2. return contents of blnDataInRange

btnCalc Click event procedure (changes made to the original pseudocode are shaded in the figure)

1. use the Student class to create a Student object

2. if the user entered a name and three test scores

      assign the student name to the Name property of the Student object

      assign the first test score to the Test1 property of the Student object

      assign the second test score to the Test2 property of the Student object

      assign the third test score to the Test3 property of the Student object

      call the Student object's ValidateScores method to verify that each test score is from 0 through 100

      if each test score is from 0 through 100

            call the Student object's CalculateAverage method to calculate the average test score

            display the student name and average test score in the txtAverages control

      else

            display "Each test score must be from 0 through 100." message in a message box

      end if

    else

      display an appropriate message in a message box

    end if

3. send the focus to the txtName control

FIGURE 11.26

Activity

1. Use Windows to make a copy of the Mayflower Solution folder, which is contained in the VbDotNetLab\Chap11 folder. Rename the copy Modified Mayflower Solution.
2. If necessary, start Visual Studio .NET.
3. Open the Mayflower Solution (Mayflower Solution.sln) file contained in the VbDotNetLab\ Chap11\Modified Mayflower Solution folder.
4. Right-click **Mayflower Form.vb** in the Solution Explorer window, and then click **View Designer**. The user interface shown in Figure 11.20 in Lab 11.2 appears on the screen.

First you will modify the Student class.

To modify the Student class:

1. Right-click **Student.vb** in the Solution Explorer window, and then click **View Code**.
2. If necessary, insert two blank lines above the `End Class` clause.

Now add the ValidateScores method to the class. The method will receive two Decimal numbers, which will be passed *by value*. The first number represents the minimum value for a test score; the second number represents the maximum value. The ValidateScores method will return a Boolean value that indicates whether the test scores are within the minimum and maximum values.

3. Type the comment and additional lines of code shown in Figure 11.27, and then position the insertion point as shown in the figure.

Position the insertion point here

Enter this comment and these lines of code

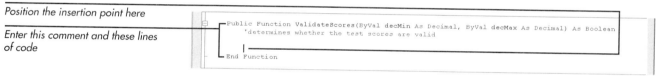

```
Public Function ValidateScores(ByVal decMin As Decimal, ByVal decMax As Decimal) As Boolean
    'determines whether the test scores are valid

    |

End Function
```

FIGURE 11.27   Comment and additional lines of code shown in the class

4. Type **'declare variable** and press **Enter**.
5. Type **dim blnDataInRange as boolean** and press **Enter** twice.
6. Type **'determine whether the test scores are within the minimum and maximum values** and press **Enter**.
7. Enter a selection structure that determines whether each of the test scores is greater than or equal to the minimum value, but less than or equal to the maximum value. The selection structure's true path should assign the Boolean value True to the blnDataInRange variable. Its false path should assign the Boolean value False to the blnDataInRange variable.
8. Type the statement to return the contents of the blnDataInRange variable, and then press **Enter**.
9. Save the solution, and then close the Student.vb window.

Next, you will modify the btnCalc_Click procedure.

To modify the btnCalc_Click procedure:

1. Right-click the **form**, and then click **View Code** to open the Code Editor window.
2. Locate the btnCalc_Click procedure in the Code Editor window.
3. Insert a blank line above the `'create Student object` comment.
4. In the blank line, type the statement to declare a Boolean variable named **blnGoodData**, and then press **Enter**.

5. Use the pseudocode shown earlier in Figure 11.26 to modify the btnCalc_Click procedure's code. Include meaningful comments in the procedure.

Now that you have finished modifying the Student class and btnCalc_Click procedure, you can test the application to verify that the code is working correctly.

To test the application:

1. Save the solution, then start the application.

First, observe what happens when you click the Calculate button without entering all of the student information.

2. Click the **Calculate** button. The message box shown earlier in Figure 11.24 in Lab 11.2 appears on the screen.

3. Close the message box.

4. On your own, verify that the message box shown in Figure 11.24 appears when you enter one item, two items, or three items of student information.

Next, you will enter all of the required student information; however, you will enter an invalid score for the third test.

5. Type **Sam Chen** in the Name box, and then type **90** in the Test 1 box. Type **85** in the Test 2 box, and then type **106** in the Test 3 box.

6. Click the **Calculate** button. The message box shown in Figure 11.28 appears on the screen.

FIGURE 11.28   Message box that appears when a test score is invalid

7. Close the message box.

8. On your own, verify that the message box shown in Figure 11.28 appears when you enter an invalid score for the first test.

9. On your own, verify that the message box shown in Figure 11.28 appears when you enter an invalid score for the second test.

Now enter a name and three valid test scores.

10. Type your name in the Name box, and then type three valid test scores in the remaining boxes. Click the **Calculate** button. Your name and average test score appear in the txtAverages control.

11. Click the **Exit** button to end the application.

12. Close the Output window, then close the Code Editor window.

You are finished with the solution, so you can close it.

13. Close the solution. Temporarily display the Solution Explorer window to verify that the solution is closed.

BEYOND THE TEXT

LAB 11.4 MODIFIED CORNWALL CALENDARS

Scenario   In this lab, you learn how to use the With statement.

Solution Discussion   The With statement provides a convenient way of accessing the properties and methods of an object. Figure 11.29 shows the syntax and an example of the With statement. In the syntax, *object* is the name of the object whose properties or methods you want to access. You enter the appropriate instructions—for example, instructions that assign values to the object's properties or invoke its methods—between the With and End With clauses. The example in Figure 11.29 shows how you can access two of the properties of an object named objCheck. Notice that you do not need to preface the object's properties (Number and CheckDate) with the object's name (objCheck); the With statement handles that for you. However, it is necessary to place a period before the object's properties and methods within the With statement—for example, .Number and .CheckDate.

```
Syntax
With object
    [statements]
End With


Example
With objCheck
      .Number = Me.txtNumber.Text
      .CheckDate = Me.txtDate.Text
End With
```

FIGURE 11.29   Syntax and example of the With statement

Activity

1. Use Windows to make a copy of the Cornwall Calendars Solution folder, which is contained in the VbDotNetLab\Chap11 folder. Rename the copy Modified Cornwall Calendars Solution.

2. If necessary, start Visual Studio .NET.

3. Open the Cornwall Calendars Solution (Cornwall Calendars Solution.sln) file contained in the VbDotNetLab\Chap11\Modified Cornwall Calendars Solution folder.

4. Right-click **Cornwall Form.vb** in the Solution Explorer window, and then click **View Designer**. The user interface shown in Figure 11.2 in Lab 11.1 appears on the screen.

5. Open the Code Editor window.

6. Locate the btnSave_Click procedure in the Code Editor window. Use the With statement to code the selection structure's true path.

7. Save the solution, then start the application.

8. Use the application to save the information for the following check:

Check number:	**207**
Check date:	**01/20/2006**
Payable to:	**Acme Insurance**
Check amount:	**200**

9. Click the **Exit** button to end the application.

Now open the checks.txt file to verify its contents.

10. Click **File** on the menu bar. Point to **Open**, and then click **File**. Open the bin folder contained in the VbDotNetLab\Chap11\Modified Cornwall Calendars Solution\Cornwall Calendars Project folder. The checks.txt filename should be selected in the list of filenames.

11. Click the **Open** button to open the checks.txt file. The information for check number 207 appears as the last line in the file.

12. Close the checks.txt window by clicking its **Close** button.

13. Close the Output window, and then close the Code Editor window.

14. Close the solution, and then exit Visual Studio .NET.

12 Using ADO.NET

Labs included in this chapter:

LAB 12.1 CREDIT CARDS

Scenario   In this lab, you create an application that displays the contents of a Microsoft Access database named Credit.mdb. The database has one table, which is named tblCreditCards; the table contains three fields and five records. The Card and Number fields store the names and numbers of credit cards. The Phone field stores the phone numbers that should be called when the credit card is either lost or stolen.

Solution Discussion   The Credit Cards application will display the contents of the Credit.mdb database in a DataGrid control. The application will provide a button control for exiting the application.

TOE Chart

Task	Object	Event
Fill the dataset with data	frmCredit	Load
Display the data contained in the dataset	dgdCards	None
Access the data contained in the Credit.mdb database	oledb_adapCards, oledb_conCards, DstCards1	None
End the application	btnExit	Click

FIGURE 12.1

User Interface

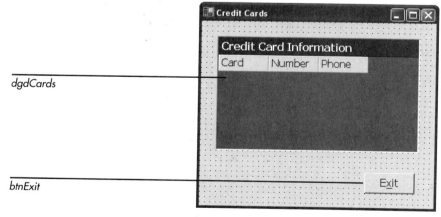

dgdCards

btnExit

FIGURE 12.2

Objects, Properties, and Settings

Object	Property	Setting
DataGrid1	Name	dgdCards
	CaptionText	Credit Card Information
	PreferredColumnWidth	100
	ReadOnly	True
	RowHeadersVisible	False
	Size	304, 176
	TabIndex	1
Button1	Name	btnExit
	TabIndex	0
	Text	E&xit

FIGURE 12.3

Pseudocode

frmCredit Load event procedure
1. fill the dataset with data

btnExit Click event procedure
1. close the application

FIGURE 12.4

Activity

1. Start Visual Studio .NET.
2. Click **File** on the Visual Studio .NET menu bar, point to **New**, and then click **Project**. The New Project dialog box opens.
3. If necessary, click **Visual Basic Projects** in the Project Types list box, and click **Windows Application** in the Templates list box.
4. Type **Credit Cards Project** in the Name text box.
5. Use the **Browse** button to open the **VbDotNetLab\Chap12** folder.
6. If necessary, click the **More** button.
7. If necessary, select the **Create directory for Solution** check box.
8. Type **Credit Cards Solution** in the New Solution Name text box.
9. Click the **OK** button to close the New Project dialog box.

Now set the appropriate properties of the form file object and form object.

To set the appropriate properties of the form file object and form object:

1. Right-click **Form1.vb** in the Solution Explorer window, then click **Rename**. Change the form file object's name from Form1.vb to **Credit Cards Form.vb**.
2. Click the **form**, then click **(Name)** in the Properties window. Change the form object's name from Form1 to **frmCredit**.

3. Right-click **Credit Cards Project** in the Solution Explorer window, then click **Properties**. Click the **Startup object** list arrow, and then click **frmCredit** in the list. Click the **OK** button.

4. Click the **form**, then change the values assigned to the following properties:

Font	**Tahoma, 12 pt**
StartPosition	**CenterScreen**
Text	**Credit Cards**

5. Save the solution by clicking **File** on the menu bar, and then clicking **Save All**.

Recall that you use three ADO.NET objects (DataAdapter, Connection, and DataSet) and a provider to access a database from a Visual Basic .NET application.

To access the Credits.mdb database:

1. Click the **Data** tab on the Toolbox window.

2. Click the **OleDbDataAdapter tool** in the toolbox, and then drag an OleDbDataAdapter control to the form. When you release the mouse button, the control appears in the component tray, and the Welcome screen shown in Figure 12.5 appears on the screen.

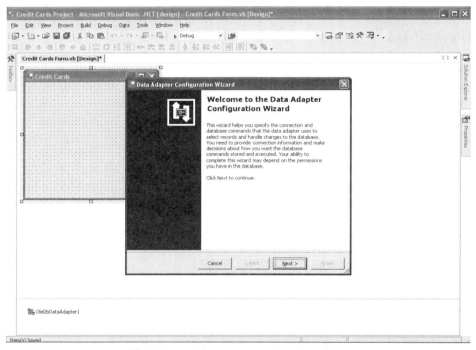

FIGURE 12.5   OleDbDataAdapter control and Welcome screen

3. Click the **Next >** button to display the Choose Your Data Connection screen.

4. Click the **New Connection** button on the Choose Your Data Connection screen. The Data Link Properties dialog box opens.

5. Click the **Provider** tab on the Data Link Properties dialog box, then click **Microsoft Jet 4.0 OLE DB Provider** in the OLE DB Provider(s) list box.

6. Click the **Connection** tab on the Data Link Properties dialog box, then click the ... (ellipsis) button that appears next to the "Select or enter a database name" text box. The Select Access Database dialog box opens.

7. Open the VbDotNetLab\Chap12\Databases folder. If necessary, click **Credit.mdb** in the list of filenames.

8. Click the **Open** button, and then click the **Test Connection** button. The "Test connection succeeded." message appears in the Microsoft Data Link dialog box, as shown in Figure 12.6.

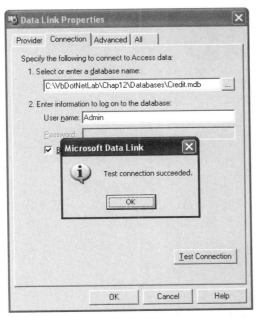

FIGURE 12.6   Microsoft Data Link dialog box

9. Click the **OK** button to close the Microsoft Data Link dialog box.

10. Click the **OK** button to close the Data Link Properties dialog box. The Choose Your Data Connection screen appears, as shown in Figure 12.7.

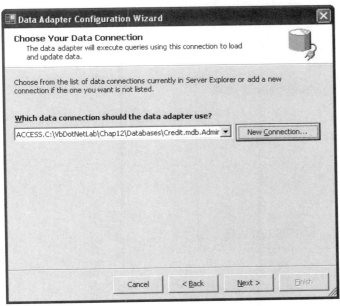

FIGURE 12.7   Choose Your Data Connection screen

11. Click the **Next >** button to display the Choose a Query Type screen.

12. Verify that the Use SQL statements radio button is selected on the Choose a Query Type screen, and then click the **Next** > button. The Generate the SQL statements screen appears, as shown in Figure 12.8.

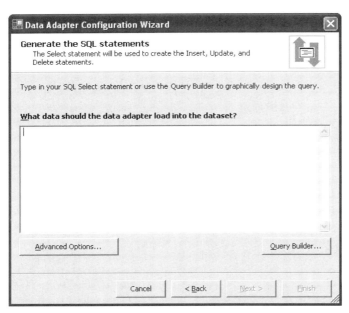

FIGURE 12.8   Generate the SQL statements screen

13. Click the **Query Builder** button to display the Query Builder and Add Table dialog boxes shown in Figure 12.9.

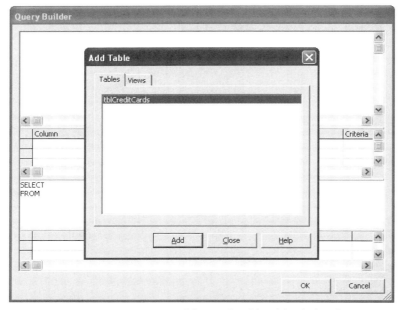

FIGURE 12.9   Query Builder and Add Table dialog boxes

14. Click the **Add** button to add the tblCreditCards table to the Query Builder dialog box.

15. Click the **Close** button to close the Add Table dialog box. The names of the fields contained in the tblCreditCards table appear in the Query Builder dialog box.

16. Click the **Card** check box to select it.

You will display the credit card names in ascending alphabetical order.

17. Click the **empty box** below the Sort Type column heading. Click the **list arrow**, and then click **Ascending**.

18. Click the **Number** check box to select it.

19. Click the **Phone** check box to select it. Figure 12.10 shows the completed Query Builder dialog box.

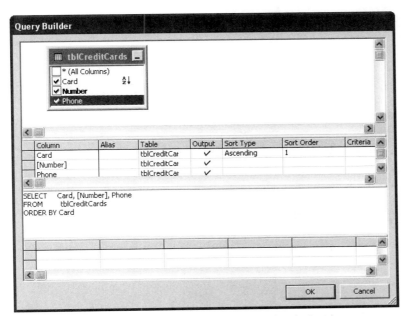

FIGURE 12.10   Completed Query Builder dialog box

20. Click the **OK** button to close the Query Builder dialog box. The Generate the SQL statements screen appears, as shown in Figure 12.11.

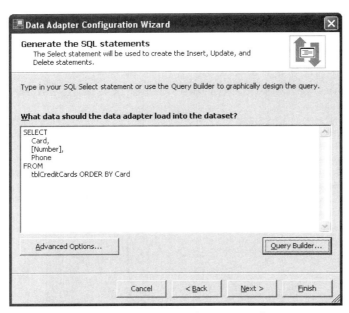

FIGURE 12.11   Completed Generate the SQL statements screen

21. Click the **Next >** button to display the View Wizard Results screen shown in Figure 12.12.

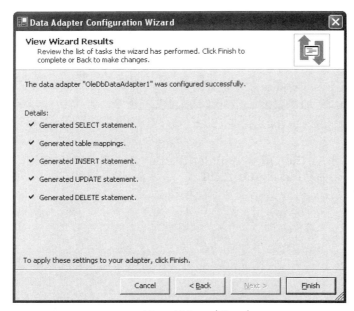

FIGURE 12.12   View Wizard Results screen

22. Click the **Finish** button. If the "Do you want to include the password in the connection string?" dialog box opens, click the **Don't include password** button. Visual Basic .NET adds an OleDbConnection object to the component tray, as shown in Figure 12.13.

FIGURE 12.13 OleDbConnection object added to the component tray

23. Change the OleDbDataAdapter object's name to **oledb_adapCards**.
24. Change the OleDbConnection object's name to **oledb_conCards**.

Now you can generate the dataset.

25. Right-click the **oledb_adapCards** object in the component tray, then click **Generate Dataset**. The Generate Dataset dialog box opens.
26. Verify that the New radio button is selected in the Generate Dataset dialog box. Also verify that the tblCreditCards (oledb_adapCards) and Add this dataset to the designer check boxes are selected.
27. In the text box that appears to the right of the New radio button, replace DataSet1 with **dstCards**. Figure 12.14 shows the completed Generate Dataset dialog box.

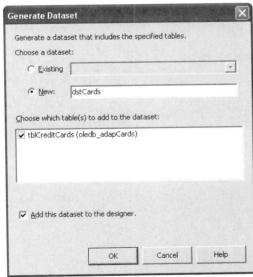

FIGURE 12.14 Completed Generate Dataset dialog box

28. Click the **OK** button to close the Generate Dataset dialog box. Visual Basic .NET adds a DataSet object to the component tray and adds an XML schema definition file to the Solution Explorer window.
29. Temporarily display the Solution Explorer window. See Figure 12.15.

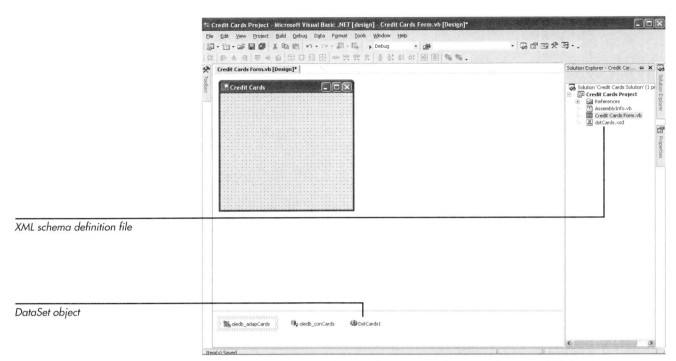

XML schema definition file

DataSet object

FIGURE 12.15 Screen showing the DataSet object and XML schema definition file

Now preview the contents of the dataset.

30. Right-click the **oledb_adapCards** object in the component tray, and then click **Preview Data**. The Data Adapter Preview dialog box opens.

31. Click the **Fill Dataset** button in the Data Adapter Preview dialog box. The contents of the Credit.mdb database file appears in the dialog box, as shown in Figure 12.16. Notice that the records appear in ascending alphabetical order by the card names.

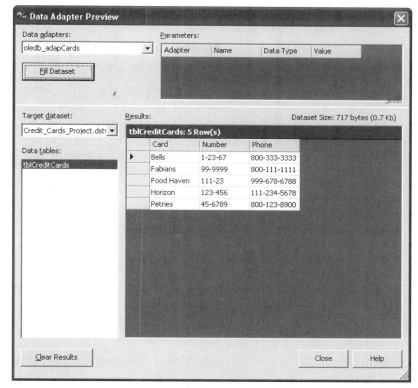

FIGURE 12.16   Data Adapter Preview dialog box

32. Click the **Close** button to close the Data Adapter Preview dialog box.

Next, add the appropriate controls to the interface, and then set the values of some of their properties.

To add the appropriate controls, then set the values of some of their properties:

1. Click the Windows Forms tab on the Toolbox window.
2. Use the DataGrid tool to add a data grid control to the form.
3. Use the Button tool to add a button to the form.
4. Set the form's Size property to **360, 320**.
5. Use the chart shown in Figure 12.3 to set the properties of each control.

Now use the DataGrid control's DataSource and DataMember properties to bind the control to the DataSet object.

6. Set the dgdCards control's DataSource property to **DstCards1**.
7. Set the dgdCards control's DataMember property to **tblCreditCards**.
8. Position the controls as shown in Figure 12.2.
9. Lock the controls in place on the form.
10. Save the solution.

Now that the interface is complete, you can code the application.

To code the application:

1. Right-click the **form**, and then click **View Code** to open the Code Editor window.
2. Type the comments shown in Figure 12.17, replacing <enter your name and date here> with your name and the current date. Also type the Option statements shown in the figure.

Enter these comments and Option statements

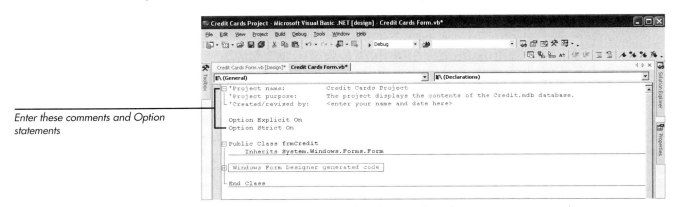

FIGURE 12.17   Code Editor window showing comments and Option statements

First you will code the form's Load event procedure, which is responsible for filling the dataset with data.

3. Click the **Class Name** list arrow, and then click **(frmCredit Events)** in the list.
4. Click the **Method Name** list arrow, and then click **Load** in the list. The code template for the frmCredit_Load procedure appears in the Code Editor window.
5. Type **'fills the dataset with data** and press **Enter**.

Recall that you use the DataAdapter object's Fill method to fill a dataset with data while an application is running. The SELECT statement you entered when configuring the DataAdapter object determines the appropriate data. The syntax of the Fill method is *dataAdapter*.**Fill**(*dataSet*), where *dataAdapter* is the name of a DataAdapter object and *dataSet* is the name of a DataSet object.

6. Type **me.oledb_adapcards.fill(me.dstcards1)** and press **Enter**.

Next, you will code the btnExit control's Click event procedure, which is responsible for ending the application.

7. Display the code template for the btnExit control's Click event procedure.
8. Type **'ends the application** and press **Enter**.
9. Type the statement to close the application.

Now that you have finished coding the application, you can test the application to verify that the code is working correctly.

To test the application:

1. Save the solution.
2. Start the application by clicking **Debug** on the menu bar, and then clicking **Start**. The form's Load event procedure fills the dataset with data. The data is displayed in the DataGrid control, as shown in Figure 12.18.

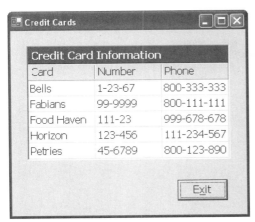

FIGURE 12.18 Credit Cards application

3. Click the **Exit** button to end the application.

4. Close the Output window, and then close the Code Editor window.

You are finished with the solution, so you can close it.

5. Click **File** on the menu bar, and then click **Close Solution**.

LAB 12.2 CREDIT CARDS LIST BOX

Scenario In this lab, you modify the application you created in Lab 12.1. The modified application will allow the user to select a credit card name from a list box. Selecting the name will display (in label controls) the corresponding credit card number and phone number.

Solution Discussion You will delete the DataGrid control from the interface you created in Lab 12.1 and replace it with a list box and two label controls. The list box will display the credit card names stored in the Credit.mdb database. The label controls will display the credit card number and phone number corresponding to the name selected in the list box.

TOE Chart

Task	Object	Event
Fill the dataset with data	frmCredit	Load
Display the credit card names contained in the dataset	lstCards	None
Display the credit card number	lblCardNumber	None
Display the phone number	lblPhone	None
Access the data contained in the Credit.mdb database	oledb_adapCards, oledb_conCards, DstCards1	None
End the application	btnExit	Click

FIGURE 12.19

User Interface

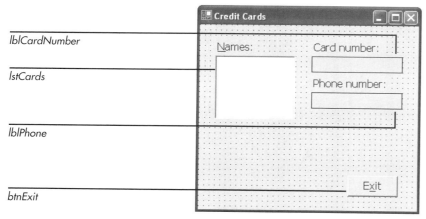

lblCardNumber

lstCards

lblPhone

btnExit

FIGURE 12.20

Objects, Properties, and Settings

Object	Property	Setting
Label1	AutoSize Text	True &Names:
Label2	AutoSize Text	True Card number:
Label3	AutoSize Text	True Phone number:
Label4	Name BorderStyle Size Text	lblCardNumber FixedSingle 136, 25 (empty)
Label5	Name BorderStyle Size Text	lblPhone FixedSingle 136, 25 (empty)
ListBox1	Name Size	lstCards 120, 99
btnExit	Location	224, 232

FIGURE 12.21

Tab Order

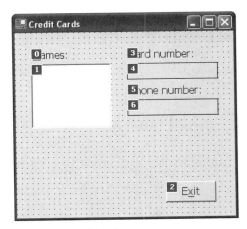

FIGURE 12.22

Activity

1. Use Windows to make a copy of the Credit Cards Solution folder, which is contained in the VbDotNetLab\Chap12 folder. Rename the copy Credit Cards List Box Solution.

2. If necessary, start Visual Studio .NET.

3. Open the Credit Cards Solution (Credit Cards Solution.sln) file contained in the VbDotNetLab\Chap12\Credit Cards List Box Solution folder.

4. Right-click **Credit Cards Form.vb** in the Solution Explorer window, and then click **View Designer**.

5. Unlock the controls on the form.

6. Delete the DataGrid control from the interface.

7. Use the ListBox tool to add a list box control to the form.

8. Use the Label tool to add five label controls to the form.

9. Use the chart shown in Figure 12.21 to set the properties of each control.

10. Position the controls as shown in Figure 12.20.

11. Use Figure 12.22 to set the appropriate tab order.

12. Lock the controls in place on the form.

Now use the list box control's DataSource and DisplayMember properties to bind the control to the DataSet object. The control should display the credit card names.

13. Click the **lstCards** control on the form to select the control. Set the lstCards control's DataSource property to **DstCards1**.

14. Click **DisplayMember** in the Properties list, then click the **list arrow** in the Settings box.

15. Click the **plus box** that appears to the left of tblCreditCards, then click **Card** in the list of field names.

Next, use the lblCardNumber control's DataBindings property to bind the control to the DataSet object. The lblCardNumber control should display the credit card number.

16. Click the **lblCardNumber** control on the form to select the control. Click **(DataBindings)** in the Properties list, and then click the **plus box** that appears to the left of (DataBindings).

TIP ••••••   The DataBindings property is listed first in the Properties list.

17. Click **Text** in the Properties list.
18. Click the **list arrow** in the Settings box, and then click the **plus box** that appears to the left of DstCards1 in the list.
19. Click the **plus box** that appears to the left of tblCreditCards, and then click **Number** in the list of field names.
20. On your own, bind the lblPhone control to the DataSet object. The lblPhone control should display the phone number.
21. Save the solution.

Now test the application to verify that it is working correctly.

To test the application:

1. Save the solution, then start the application. The form's Load event procedure fills the dataset with data. The application displays the credit card names in the list box, as shown in Figure 12.23. The card number and phone number corresponding to the name selected in the list box appear in label controls, as shown in the figure.

FIGURE 12.23   Credit Cards list box application

2. On your own, click each of the remaining card names, one at a time. After clicking a card name, use Figure 12.18 (shown earlier in Lab 12.1) to verify that the card number and phone number that appear in the label controls are correct.
3. Click the **Exit** button to end the application.
4. Close the Output window.

You are finished with the solution, so you can close it.

5. Close the solution. Temporarily display the Solution Explorer window to verify that the solution is closed.

LAB 12.3 CREDIT CARDS LABELS

Scenario In this lab, you modify the application you created in Lab 12.1. The modified application will allow the user to display (in label controls) each record contained in the dataset, one record at a time.

Solution Discussion You will delete the DataGrid control from the interface you created in Lab 12.1 and replace it with three label controls. The label controls will display the credit card name, credit card number, and phone number. You also will include a button control for viewing the next record in the dataset, and a button control for viewing the previous record.

TOE Chart

Task	Object	Event
Fill the dataset with data	frmCredit	Load
Display the credit card name	lblName	None
Display the credit card number	lblCardNumber	None
Display the phone number	lblPhone	None
Access the data contained in the Credit.mdb database	oledb_adapCards, oledb_conCards, DstCards1	None
Display the next record	btnNext	Click
Display the previous record	btnPrevious	Click
End the application	btnExit	Click

FIGURE 12.24

User Interface

btnPrevious

lblName

lblCardNumber

btnNext

lblPhone

btnExit

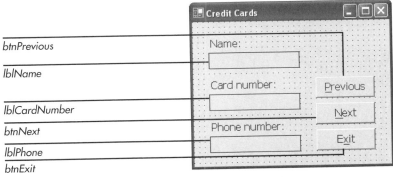

FIGURE 12.25

Objects, Properties, and Settings

Object	Property	Setting
Label1	AutoSize	True
	Text	Name:
Label2	AutoSize	True
	Text	Card number:
Label3	AutoSize	True
	Text	Phone number:
Label4	Name	lblName
	BorderStyle	FixedSingle
	Size	136, 25
	Text	(empty)
Label5	Name	lblCardNumber
	BorderStyle	FixedSingle
	Size	136, 25
	Text	(empty)
Label6	Name	lblPhone
	BorderStyle	FixedSingle
	Size	136, 25
	Text	(empty)
Button1	Name	btnPrevious
	Text	&Previous
Button2	Name	btnNext
	Text	&Next
btnExit	Location	184, 168
	Size	88, 32

FIGURE 12.26

Tab Order

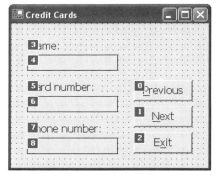

FIGURE 12.27

Activity

1. Use Windows to make a copy of the Credit Cards Solution folder, which is contained in the VbDotNetLab\Chap12 folder. Rename the copy Credit Cards Labels Solution.

2. If necessary, start Visual Studio .NET.

3. Open the Credit Cards Solution (Credit Cards Solution.sln) file contained in the VbDotNetLab\Chap12\Credit Cards Labels Solution folder.

4. Right-click **Credit Cards Form.vb** in the Solution Explorer window, and then click **View Designer**.

5. Unlock the controls on the form.

6. Delete the DataGrid control from the interface.

7. Use the Label tool to add six label controls to the form.

8. Use the Button tool to add two buttons to the form.

9. Use the chart shown in Figure 12.26 to set the properties of each control.

10. Position the controls as shown in Figure 12.25.

11. Use Figure 12.27 to set the appropriate tab order.

12. Lock the controls in place on the form.

13. Bind the lblName control to the DataSet object. The control should display the credit card name.

14. Bind the lblCardNumber control to the DataSet object. The control should display the credit card number.

15. Bind the lblPhone control to the DataSet object. The control should display the phone number.

16. Save the solution.

Now that the interface is complete, you can code the btnPrevious_Click and btnNext_Click procedures.

To code the btnPrevious_Click and btnNext_Click procedures:

1. Open the Code Editor window.

2. Display the code template for the btnPrevious control's Click event procedure.

3. Type '**moves the record pointer to the previous record in the dataset** and press **Enter** twice.

First declare an Integer variable to store the current position of the record pointer.

4. Type '**declare variable** and press **Enter**.

5. Type **dim intCurrentPosition as integer** and press **Enter** twice.

Next, assign the current position of the record pointer to the variable. You can access the current position using the BindingContext.Position property in the following syntax: **Me.BindingContext(***datasetObject***,** *tablename***).Position**. In the syntax, *datasetObject* is the name of the DataSet object associated with the dataset, and *tablename* (which must be enclosed in quotation marks) is the name of the table within the dataset.

6. Type '**assign current position** and press **Enter**.

7. Type **intcurrentposition = me.bindingcontext(me.dstcards1, "tblCreditCards").position** and press **Enter** twice.

Now you will move the record pointer to the previous record by subtracting the number one from the current position, and then assigning the result to the BindingContext.Position property.

8. Type **'move record pointer** and press **Enter**.

9. Type **me.bindingcontext(me.dstcards1, "tblCreditCards").position = intcurrentposition - 1** and press **Enter**.

Next, you will code the btnNext_Click procedure.

10. Display the code template for the btnNext control's Click event procedure.

11. On your own, code the procedure so that it moves the record pointer to the next record in the dataset. Include meaningful comments in the procedure.

Now test the application to verify that it is working correctly.

To test the application:

1. Save the solution, then start the application. The form's Load event procedure fills the dataset with data. The application displays the first record in the label controls, as shown in Figure 12.28.

FIGURE 12.28   Credit Cards Labels application

2. Click the **Next** button four times to view each of the remaining records in the dataset.

3. Click the **Previous** button four times to view the first record in the dataset.

4. Click the **Exit** button to end the application.

5. Close the Output window, then close the Code Editor window.

You are finished with the solution, so you can close it.

6. Close the solution. Temporarily display the Solution Explorer window to verify that the solution is closed.

BEYOND THE TEXT

LAB 12.4 FAVORITE SONGS

Scenario In this lab, you create an application that allows the user to display the song titles associated with the artist whose name is selected in a list box. The artist names and song titles are stored in a Microsoft Access database named Songs.mdb. Figure 12.29 shows the database opened in Microsoft Access.

tblSongs : Table	
Title	**Artist**
Colors	Midnight Blue
Country	Dolly Draton
Happy Home	Cynthia Jones
Heavens	Midnight Blue
Lovely Nights	Midnight Blue
Near to You	James Gleason
Night on the Road	Dolly Draton
Old Red	Jack Kingsley
Old Times	Dolly Draton
Sarah's Song	James Gleason

FIGURE 12.29 Songs.mdb database opened in Microsoft Access

Solution Discussion The Favorite Songs application will display the artist names in a list box. It will display the song titles in a DataGrid control. The application also will use a button control that allows the user to display the song titles and a button control for exiting the application. Additionally, the application will use a Connection object to connect to the Songs.mdb database. It also will use two DataAdapter objects. The first DataAdapter object will create a DataSet object named DstArtists1 that contains the unique artist names from the database. You will use the following SELECT statement to create the DstArtists1 object: SELECT DISTINCT Artist FROM tblSongs. In this case, the DISTINCT keyword tells the SELECT statement to select only the unique artist names from the database.

The second DataAdapter object will create a DataSet object named DstTitles1; the DstTitles1 object will contain the song titles corresponding to the artist name selected in the list box. You will use the following SELECT statement to create the DstTitles1 object: SELECT Title FROM tblSongs WHERE (Artist = ?). Notice that the SELECT statement contains a WHERE clause, which allows you to limit the records that will be selected. However, in this application, the song titles to select cannot be determined until the application is running and the user chooses the artist name in the list box. When the records to select cannot be determined until the application is running, you use a question mark in the WHERE clause; the question mark is a placeholder for the missing data—in this case, the artist's name. A SELECT statement that contains a question mark in the WHERE clause is called a parameterized query.

User Interface

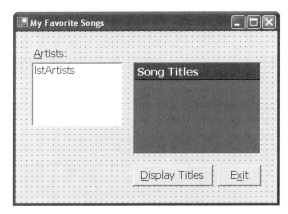

FIGURE 12.30

Activity

1. If necessary, start Visual Studio .NET.
2. Open the Favorite Songs Solution (Favorite Songs Solution.sln) file, which is contained in the VbDotNetLab\Chap12\Favorite Songs Solution folder. The user interface shown in Figure 12.30 appears on the screen.

First, create a dataset that contains the unique artist names from the Songs.mdb database, which is shown in Figure 12.29.

To create a dataset that contains the unique artist names from the Songs.mdb database:

1. Click the **Data** tab on the Toolbox window.
2. Click the **OleDbDataAdapter tool** in the toolbox, and then drag an OleDbDataAdapter control to the form. When you release the mouse button, the control appears in the component tray, and a Welcome screen appears on the screen.
3. Click the **Next >** button to display the Choose Your Data Connection screen.
4. Click the **New Connection** button on the Choose Your Data Connection screen. The Data Link Properties dialog box opens.
5. Click the **Provider** tab on the Data Link Properties dialog box, then click **Microsoft Jet 4.0 OLE DB Provider** in the OLE DB Provider(s) list box.
6. Click the **Connection** tab on the Data Link Properties dialog box, then click the ... (ellipsis) button that appears next to the "Select or enter a database name" text box. The Select Access Database dialog box opens.
7. Open the VbDotNetLab\Chap12\Databases folder. Click **Songs.mdb** in the list of filenames.
8. Click the **Open** button, and then click the **Test Connection** button. The "Test connection succeeded." message appears in the Microsoft Data Link dialog box.
9. Click the **OK** button to close the Microsoft Data Link dialog box.
10. Click the **OK** button to close the Data Link Properties dialog box. The Choose Your Data Connection screen appears.
11. Click the **Next >** button to display the Choose a Query Type screen.
12. Verify that the Use SQL statements radio button is selected on the Choose a Query Type screen, and then click the **Next >** button. The Generate the SQL statements screen appears.

13. Click the **Query Builder** button to display the Query Builder and Add Table dialog boxes.

14. Click the **Add** button to add the tblSongs table to the Query Builder dialog box.

15. Click the **Close** button to close the Add Table dialog box. The names of the fields contained in the tblSongs table appear in the Query Builder dialog box.

16. Click the **Artist** check box to select it.

The Songs.mdb database contains duplicate artist names. To include only unique artist names in the dataset, you enter the SQL keyword DISTINCT after the keyword SELECT.

17. Type **DISTINCT** after the keyword SELECT, as shown in Figure 12.31.

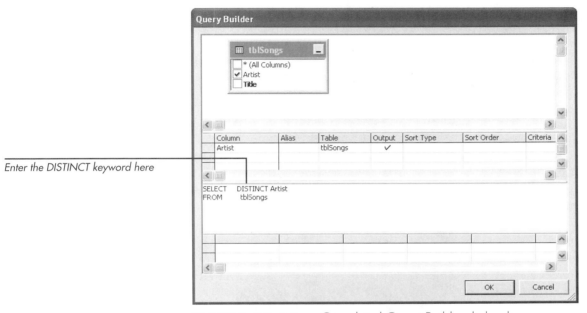

FIGURE 12.31   Completed Query Builder dialog box

18. Click the **OK** button to close the Query Builder dialog box. The Generate the SQL statements screen appears.

19. Click the **Next >** button, then click the **No** button in the Primary Key Columns Missing dialog box. The View Wizard Results screen appears and indicates that the INSERT, UPDATE, and DELETE statements could not be generated.

20. Click the **Finish** button. If the "Do you want to include the password in the connection string?" dialog box opens, click the **Don't include password** button. Visual Basic .NET adds an OleDbConnection object to the component tray.

21. Change the OleDbDataAdapter object's name to **oledb_adapArtists**.

22. Change the OleDbConnection object's name to **oledb_conArtists**.

Now you can generate the dataset.

23. Right-click the **oledb_adapArtists** object in the component tray, then click **Generate Dataset**. The Generate Dataset dialog box opens.

24. Verify that the New radio button is selected in the Generate Dataset dialog box. Also verify that the tblSongs (oledb_adapArtists) and Add this dataset to the designer check boxes are selected.

25. In the text box that appears to the right of the New radio button, replace DataSet1 with **dstArtists**.

26. Click the **OK** button to close the Generate Dataset dialog box. Visual Basic .NET adds a DataSet object to the component tray and adds an XML schema definition file to the Solution Explorer window.

Now preview the contents of the dataset.

27. Right-click the **oledb_adapArtists** object in the component tray, and then click **Preview Data**. The Data Adapter Preview dialog box opens.

28. Click the **Fill Dataset** button in the Data Adapter Preview dialog box. The unique artist names from the Songs.mdb database file appear in the dialog box, as shown in Figure 12.32. Notice that the names appear in ascending alphabetical order.

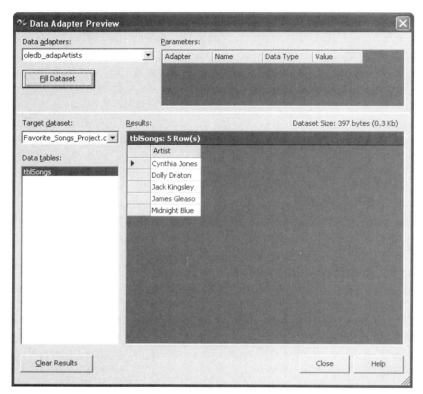

FIGURE 12.32   Unique artist names shown in the Data Adapter Preview dialog box

29. Click the **Close** button to close the Data Adapter Preview dialog box.

Next, create a dataset that contains the song titles associated with the artist name selected in the list box.

To create a dataset that contains the appropriate song titles:

1. Drag another OleDbDataAdapter object to the component tray.

2. Click the **Next >** button to display the Choose Your Data Connection screen.

3. If necessary, click the **down arrow** in the "Which data connection should the data adapter use?" list box, and then click the data connection associated with the Songs.mdb database.

4. Click the **Next >** button to display the Choose a Query Type screen.

5. Verify that the Use SQL statements radio button is selected, and then click the **Next** > button. The Generate the SQL statements screen appears.

6. Click the **Query Builder** button to display the Query Builder and Add Table dialog boxes.

7. Click the **Add** button to add the tblSongs table to the Query Builder dialog box.

8. Click the **Close** button to close the Add Table dialog box. The names of the fields contained in the tblSongs table appear in the Query Builder dialog box.

9. Click the **Title** check box to select it.

You need to display the song titles associated with a specific artist. However, you will not know the artist's name until the application is running and the user clicks the name in the list box. You can use a parameterized query to display the appropriate song titles. As mentioned earlier, a parameterized query is a SELECT statement that contains a question mark in the WHERE clause. The question mark is a placeholder for the missing data—in this case, the artist name.

10. Click the **empty box** below the Criteria column heading. In the empty box, type **artist=?**, as shown in Figure 12.33.

Enter this criteria

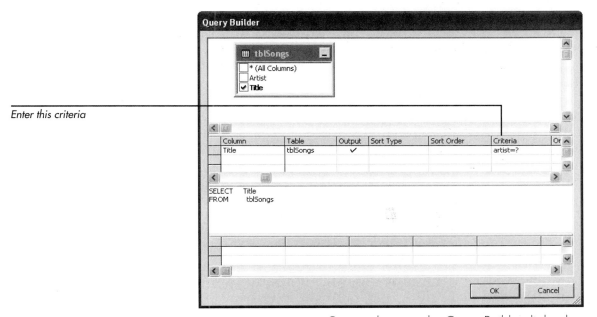

FIGURE 12.33   Criteria shown in the Query Builder dialog box

11. Click the **OK** button to close the Query Builder dialog box. The Generate the SQL statements screen appears, as shown in Figure 12.34.

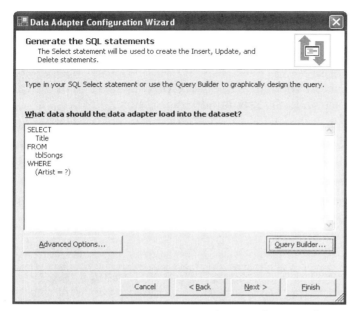

FIGURE 12.34   Parameterized query shown in the Generate the SQL statements screen

12. Click the **Next >** button to display the View Wizard Results screen, and then click the **Finish** button.

13. Change the OleDbDataAdapter object's name to **oledb_adapTitles**.

Now generate the dataset.

14. Right-click the **oledb_adapTitles** object in the component tray, then click **Generate Dataset**. The Generate Dataset dialog box opens.

15. Click the **New** radio button.

16. Verify that the tblSongs (oledb_adapTitles) and Add this dataset to the designer check boxes are selected.

17. In the text box that appears to the right of the New radio button, replace DataSet1 with **dstTitles**.

18. Click the **OK** button to close the Generate Dataset dialog box. Visual Basic .NET adds another DataSet object to the component tray and adds another XML schema definition file to the Solution Explorer window.

Now bind the DstTitles1 object to the DataGrid control.

19. Set the dgdTitles DataSource property to **DstTitles1**.

20. Set the dgdTitles DataMember property to **tblSongs**.

21. Save the solution.

Now that the interface is complete, you can code the application and then test it to verify that the code is working correctly.

To code the application and then test it:

1. Open the Code Editor window. Notice that the btnExit_Click procedure is already coded for you.

2. Replace the `<enter your name and date here>` text with your name and the current date.

3. Display the code template for the form's Load event procedure.

4. Type **'fills the DstArtists1 dataset with data, then uses the data to load the lstArtists control** and press **Enter** twice.

5. Type **'declare variable** and press **Enter**.

6. Type **dim intX as integer** and press **Enter** twice. The procedure will use the intX variable in a loop that fills the list box with data.

7. Type **'fill DstArtists1 dataset with data** and press **Enter**.

8. Type the statement to fill the DstArtists1 dataset with data and press **Enter** twice.

Now use a loop to fill the lstArtists control with the data contained in the DstArtists1 dataset.

9. Type **'load list box with artist names from the dataset** and press **Enter**.

10. Type **for intx = 0 to me.dstartists1.tblsongs.count - 1** and press **Enter**.

11. Type **me.lstartists.items.add(me.dstartists1.tblsongs.item(intx).artist)**.

12. Change the `Next` clause to **Next intX**.

Now select the first item in the list box.

13. Position the insertion point two lines below the `Next intX` clause, but above the `End Sub` clause.

14. Type **'select the first item in the list box** and press **Enter**.

15. Type the statement to select the first item in the lstArtists control, and then press **Enter**.

Next, code the btnDisplay_Click procedure.

16. Display the code template for the btnDisplay control's Click event procedure.

17. Type **'clear the DstArtists1 dataset, then select the song titles corresponding** and press **Enter**.

18. Type **'to the artist name selected in the list box, and then fill the DstTitles1 dataset with data** and press **Enter** twice.

19. Type **me.dsttitles1.clear()** and press **Enter**. This statement clears the contents of the DstArtists1 dataset.

20. Type **me.oledb_adaptitles.selectcommand.parameters("Artist").value = me.lstartists. selecteditem** and press **Enter**. This statement tells the oledb_adapTitles control to replace the question mark in the SELECT statement (shown earlier in Figure 12.34) with the item selected in the list box. The SELECT statement will select the song titles corresponding to the artist name selected in the list box.

21. Type **me.oledb_adaptitles.fill(me.dsttitles1)** and press **Enter**. This statement fills the DstTitles1 dataset with data.

Now test the application to verify that the code is working correctly.

22. Save the solution, then start the application.

23. Click **Dolly Draton** in the Artists list box, and then click the **Display Titles** button. The song titles associated with Dolly Draton appear in the DataGrid control, as shown in Figure 12.35.

FIGURE 12.35 Favorite Songs application

24. Click each of the other artist names, one at a time. After clicking a name, click the **Display Titles** button, and then use Figure 12.29 to verify that the correct song titles appear in the DataGrid control.

25. Click the **Exit** button to end the application.

26. Close the Output window, and then close the Code Editor window.

27. Close the solution, and then exit Visual Studio .NET.

13

Creating Web Applications Using ASP.NET

Labs included in this chapter:

LAB 13.1 LOTTERY

Scenario In Lab 9.3 in Chapter 9, you created a Windows application that selected six unique lottery numbers in the range of 1 through 54. In this lab, you change the Windows application to a Web application.

Solution Discussion The Lottery application will use the Visual Studio .NET random number generator to generate random numbers from 1 through 54. Each lottery number will need to be unique; to accomplish this, you will use a one-dimensional array to store only the first six unique numbers produced by the generator. The application will use a label control to display the six lottery numbers. It also will use a button control that allows the user to display the lottery numbers.

TOE Chart

Task	Object	Event
1. Generate six unique random numbers	btnDisplay	Click
2. Display random numbers in lblNumbers		
Display six unique random numbers (from btnDisplay)	lblNumbers	None

FIGURE 13.1

User Interface

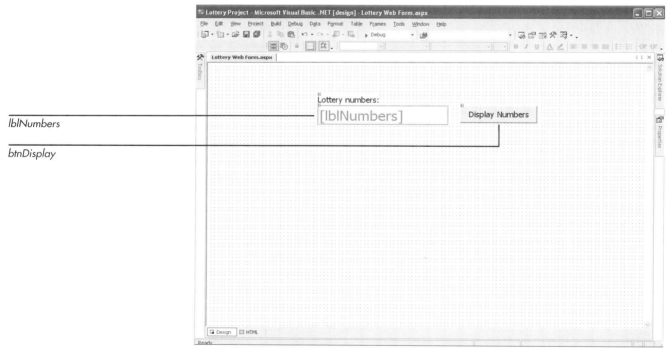

FIGURE 13.2

Pseudocode

---

btnDisplay Click event procedure

1. generate first random number, assign to first position in intNumbers array
2. fill remaining array elements with random numbers as follows:

   assign 1 to intSubscript

   repeat until intSubscript is greater than the highest subscript in the array

   > generate another random number

   > search the array to determine whether it contains the random number, as follows:

   >> assign 0 to intSearchSubscript to begin the search with the first element

   >> assign False to blnNumberFound

   >> repeat until there are no more elements to search or the random number is found

   >>> if the value in the current array element is equal to the random number

   >>>> assign True to blnNumberFound

   >>> else

   >>>> add 1 to intSearchSubscript to continue the search in the next element

   >>> end if

   >> end repeat

   >> if the random number was not found in the array

   >>> assign the random number to the current array element

   >>> add 1 to intSubscript to continue filling array elements

   >> end if

   > end repeat

3. display the contents of the intNumbers array in lblNumbers

---

FIGURE 13.3

Activity

1. Start Visual Studio .NET.

First, create a new, blank solution.

2. Click **File** on the menu bar, point to **New**, and then click **Blank Solution**. The New Project dialog box opens with Visual Studio Solutions selected in the Project Types box, and Blank Solution selected in the Templates box.

3. Type **Lottery Solution** in the Name box.

4. In the Location box, type the path to the folder that stores your Web applications. In Figure 13.4, the path is C:\Inetpub\wwwroot\Chap13Lab.

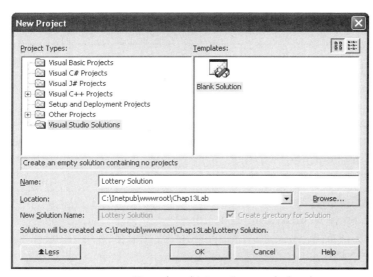

FIGURE 13.4 Completed New Project dialog box

5. Click the **OK** button to close the New Project dialog box.

Now add a Web project to the solution.

6. Click **File** on the menu bar, point to **Add Project**, and then click **New Project**. The Add New Project dialog box opens.

7. Verify that Visual Basic Projects is selected in the Project Types box, then click **ASP.NET Web Application** in the Templates box.

8. In the Location box, type the URL of the Web server and folder where you want to create your project, followed by the project name. In Figure 13.5, the URL and project name are http://localhost/Chap13Lab/Lottery Solution/Lottery Project.

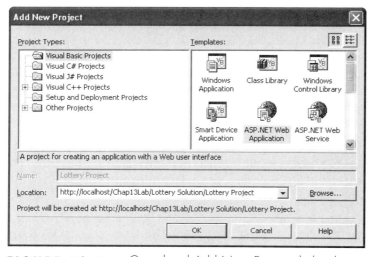

FIGURE 13.5 Completed Add New Project dialog box

9. Click the **OK** button to close the Add New Project dialog box. The Create New Web message box appears momentarily, and then a new Web application appears on the screen.

10. Permanently display the Solution Explorer and Properties windows, as shown in Figure 13.6. Notice that the default name for the Web form file in the application is WebForm1.aspx.

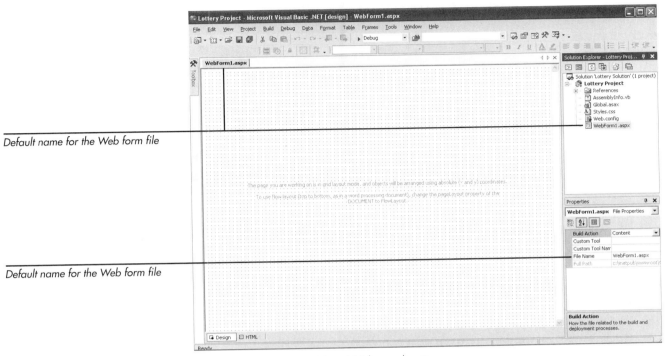

Default name for the Web form file

Default name for the Web form file

FIGURE 13.6   New Web application

Next, assign a more meaningful name to the Web form file.

11. Right-click **WebForm1.aspx** in the Solution Explorer window, and then click **Rename**. Type **Lottery Web Form.aspx** and press **Enter**.

Now assign a more meaningful value to the title property of the DOCUMENT object, which is the Web form itself. When the Web form is displayed in a browser, the contents of its title property appears in the browser's title bar.

12. Click the **Lottery Web Form.aspx * tab** in the Web Form Designer window, then click **title** in the Properties list. Type **Lottery Numbers** and press **Enter**. Figure 13.7 shows the changes made to the form file's name and the DOCUMENT object's title property.

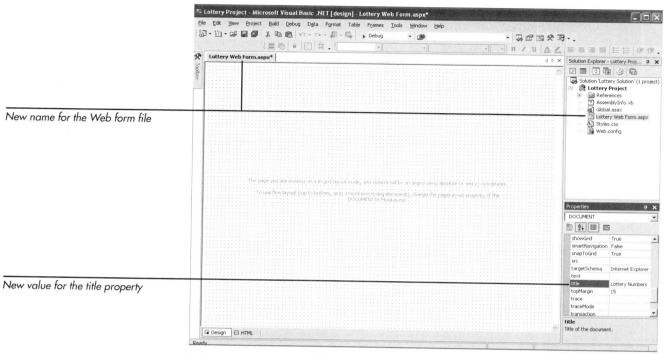

New name for the Web form file

New value for the title property

FIGURE 13.7   Changes made to the Web application

In the next set of steps, you add the appropriate controls to the interface, and then set the values of some of their properties.

To add the appropriate controls, then set the values of some of their properties:

1. Use the Label tool to add two label controls to the Web form.
2. Use the Button tool to add a button to the Web form.

Now change the Label1 control's Font property to Tahoma, Medium. Also change its Text property to Lottery numbers:.

3. Click the **Label1** control on the Web form to select the control.
4. Click the **plus box** that appears to the left of the Font property in the Properties window. Click **Name** in the Properties list, and then click the **down arrow** in the Settings box.
5. Scroll the list of font names until you see Tahoma, and then click **Tahoma** in the list.
6. Click **Size** in the Properties list, click the **down arrow** in the Settings box, and then click **Medium** in the list.
7. Click **Text** in the Properties list. Type **Lottery numbers:** and press **Enter**.

Now change some of the properties of the Label2 control.

8. Click the **Label2** control on the Web form to select the control.
9. Change the following properties of the Label2 control:

(ID)	**lblNumbers**
BorderStyle	**Groove**
Font	**Tahoma, X-Large**
ForeColor	**Red** (choose the Red square on the Web tab)
Height	**40px**
Text	(empty)
Width	**288px**

TIP ••••⋮ Recall that Web controls have an ID property rather than a Name property.

Next, change some of the properties of the Button1 control.

10. Click the **Button1** control on the Web form to select the control.

11. Change the following properties of the Button1 control:

(ID)	**btnDisplay**
Font	**Tahoma, Medium**
Height	**40px**
Text	**Display Numbers**
Width	**168px**

12. Auto-hide the Solution Explorer and Properties windows.

13. Position the controls as shown in Figure 13.2.

14. Click **File** on the menu bar, and then click **Save All** to save the solution.

Now that the interface is complete, you can code the application.

To begin coding the application:

1. Right-click the **Web form**, and then click **View Code** to open the Code Editor window.

2. Type the comments shown in Figure 13.8, replacing `<enter your name and date here>` with your name and the current date. Also type the Option statements shown in the figure, and change the name of the class from WebForm1 to **LotteryNumbers**.

Enter these comments and Option statements

Change the class name to LotteryNumbers

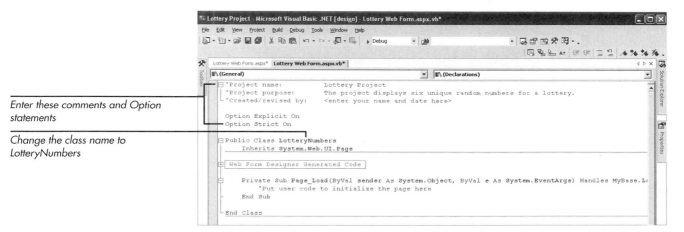

FIGURE 13.8 Code Editor window showing comments, Option statements, and new class name

According to the pseudocode shown earlier in Figure 13.3, only the btnDisplay control's Click event procedure needs to be coded.

To code the btnDisplay control's Click event procedure:

1. Click the **Class Name** list arrow, and then click **btnDisplay** in the list.

2. Click the **Method Name** list arrow, and then click **Click** in the list. The code template for the btnDisplay_Click procedure appears in the Code Editor window.

3. Type '**displays six unique random lottery numbers from 1 through 54** and press **Enter** twice.

First, declare a Random object to represent the random number generator.

4. Type '**declare Random object to represent the random number generator** and press **Enter**.

5. Type **dim rndGenerator as new random** and press **Enter** twice.

Next, declare four variables for the procedure to use.

6. Type '**declare variables** and press **Enter**.

7. Type **dim intRandomNumber as integer** and press **Enter**. This variable will store a number generated by the random number generator.

8. Type **dim intSubscript as integer** and press **Tab** three times, then type '**used to fill and display the array** and press **Enter**. The intSubscript variable will keep track of the array subscript while the array is being filled and also while it is being displayed.

9. Type **dim intSearchSubscript as integer** and press **Tab**, then type '**used to search the array** and press **Enter**. The intSearchSubscript variable will keep track of the array subscript while the array is being searched.

10. Type **dim blnNumberFound as boolean** and press **Enter** twice. This variable will keep track of whether the current random number is already in the array.

Now declare a one-dimensional array to store the six unique random numbers.

11. Type '**declare six-element one-dimensional array** and press **Enter**.

12. Type the statement to declare a six-element one-dimensional Integer array named intNumbers, and then press **Enter** twice.

The first step in the pseudocode for this procedure is to generate the first random number and assign it to the first position in the intNumbers array.

13. Type '**generate first random number and store it in the first array element** and press **Enter**.

14. Type **intnumbers(0) = rndgenerator.next(1, 55)** and press **Enter** twice.

The second step is to fill the remaining array elements—in this case, the elements with subscripts from one through five. You begin by assigning the number one to the intSubscript variable.

15. Type '**fill remaining array elements with unique random numbers** and press **Enter**.

16. Type the statement to assign the number one to the intSubscript variable, and then press **Enter**.

Next, you need to enter a loop that repeats its instructions until the value in the intSubscript variable is greater than the highest subscript in the array. The highest subscript is always one number less than the number of elements in the array. The number of elements is stored in the array's Length property.

17. Type **do until intsubscript > intnumbers.length – 1** and press **Enter**.

According to the pseudocode, the first instruction in the loop should generate another random number.

18. Type '**generate another random number** and press **Enter**.

19. Type the statement to generate the next random number and assign the number to the intRandomNumber variable, and then press **Enter** twice.

Next, the loop instructions should search the intNumbers array to determine whether it contains the random number. You begin by assigning the number zero to the intSearchSubscript variable to ensure that the search begins with the first array element. You also assign the Boolean value False to the blnNumberFound variable because, before the search begins, the loop should assume that the number is not in the array.

20. Type '**search the array to determine whether it contains the random number** and press **Enter**.

21. Type '**stop the search when there are no more array elements or when** and press **Enter**.

22. Type '**the random number is found in the array** and press **Enter**.

23. Type **intsearchsubscript = 0** and press **Enter**.

24. Type **blnnumberfound = false** and press **Enter**.

Now enter a nested loop that repeats its instructions either until there are no more elements to search or until the random number is found in the array. There are no more elements to search when the value in the intSearchSubscript variable is greater than the value in the intSubscript variable.

25. Type **do until intsearchsubscript > intsubscript orelse blnnumberfound** and press **Enter**.

The nested loop contains a selection structure that determines whether the value in the current array element is equal to the random number. If both numbers are the same, the selection structure's true path should assign the Boolean value True to the blnNumberFound variable to indicate that the random number is a duplicate. If both numbers are not the same, however, the selection structure's false path should add the number one to the intSearchSubscript variable; this allows the nested loop to continue the search in the next array element.

26. Type **'if the random number is in the array, assign True to blnNumberFound** and press **Enter**.

27. Type **'otherwise, search the next element in the array** and press **Enter**.

28. Type the appropriate selection structure, including the instructions in the true and false paths.

After the nested loop completes its processing, the next instruction in the outer loop is a selection structure that determines whether the random number was found in the array. If the random number was not found in the array, the selection structure's true path should assign the random number to the current array element. It then should add the number one to the intSubscript variable to allow the procedure to fill the next array element.

29. Position the insertion point two lines below the first `Loop` clause, but above the second `Loop` clause.

30. Type **'if the array does not contain the random number** and press **Enter**.

31. Type **'assign the random number to the array, then move to the next array element** and press **Enter**.

32. Type the appropriate selection structure, including the instructions in the true path.

The last step in the btnDisplay Click event procedure is to display the contents of the intNumbers array in the lblNumbers control.

33. Position the insertion point two lines below the second `Loop` clause, but above the `End Sub` clause.

34. Type **'display the contents of the array in lblNumbers** and press **Enter**.

First, clear the contents of the lblNumbers control.

35. Type the statement to clear the contents of the lblNumbers control, and then press **Enter**.

36. Enter the code to display the contents of the intNumbers array in the lblNumbers control. Use the For...Next statement. Display the six numbers on the same line in the lblNumbers control, but use two space characters to separate each number from the next number.

Now that you have finished coding the application, you can test the application to verify that the code is working correctly.

To test the application:

1. Save the solution.

You can display the Web form in your default browser or in the internal Web browser built into Visual Studio .NET. First you will display the Web form in your default browser.

2. Click **Debug** on the menu bar, and then click **Start** to display the Web form in your default browser.

3. Click the **Display Numbers** button. The btnDisplay_Click procedure generates a series of random numbers, storing the first six unique numbers in the intNumbers array. The procedure then displays the contents of the intNumbers array in the lblNumbers control. If your default browser is Microsoft Internet Explorer, the screen appears similar to Figure 13.9. (Because the numbers generated by the procedure are random, the numbers appearing on your screen might be different from the ones shown in the figure.)

Close button

FIGURE 13.9   Lottery Numbers application in Microsoft Internet Explorer

4. Close the Lottery Numbers application by clicking its **Close** button.

5. Close the Output window.

Now display the Web form in the internal Web browser built into Visual Studio .NET.

6. Click **File** on the menu bar, and then click **View in Browser** to display the Web form in the Visual Studio .NET internal Web browser.

7. Click the **Display Numbers** button. Your screen appears similar to Figure 13.10.

Close button

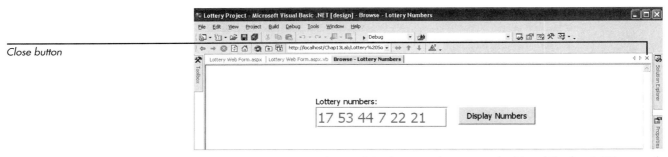

FIGURE 13.10   Lottery Numbers application in the Visual Studio .NET internal Web browser

8. Close the Browse – Lottery Numbers window by clicking its **Close** button.

9. Close the Code Editor window.

You are finished with the solution, so you can close it.

10. Click **File** on the menu bar, and then click **Close Solution**.

LAB 13.2 WESTERN VETERINARIANS

Scenario In Lab 4.2 in Chapter 4, you created a Windows application that allowed the user to display the doctor's fee for a specific medical procedure. In this lab, you change the Windows application to a Web application. The medical procedures and fees are as follows:

Procedure	Fee
Teeth Cleaning	$50
Rabies Vaccination	15
Other Shots	5
Heartworm Test	15
Fecal Check	5
Office Visit	15

Solution Discussion The Western Veterinarians application will display the medical procedures in a list box, and display the doctor's fee in a label control. The application will use a button control to allow the user to display the fee.

TOE Chart

Task	Object	Event
Get and display the medical procedures	lstProcedures	None
Display the doctor's fee in lblFee	btnDisplay	Click
Display the doctor's fee (from btnDisplay)	lblFee	None
Fill lstProcedures with data and select first item	Page	Load

FIGURE 13.11

User Interface

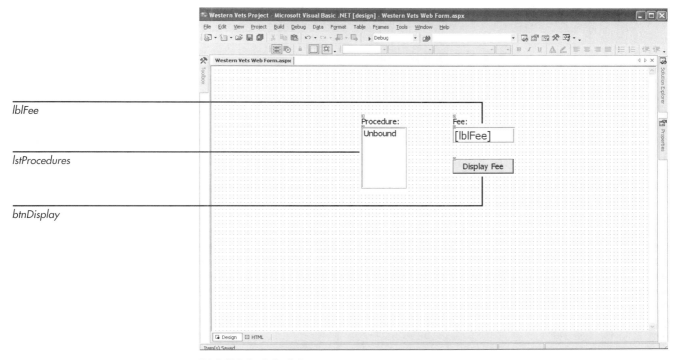

FIGURE 13.12

Objects, Properties, and Settings

Object	Property	Setting
Label1	Font/Name Font/Size Text	Tahoma Medium Procedure:
Label2	Font/Name Font/Size Text	Tahoma Medium Fee:
Label3	ID BorderStyle Font/Name Font/Size Text Width	lblFee Groove Tahoma Large (empty) 136px
ListBox1	ID Font/Name Font/Size Height Rows	lstProcedures Tahoma Medium 150px 6
Button1	ID Font/Name Font/Size Text	btnDisplay Tahoma Medium Display Fee

FIGURE 13.13

Pseudocode

Page Load event procedure
1. if it's the first time the Web form is displayed
        fill the lstProcedures control with data
        select the first item in the lstProcedures control
   end if

btnDisplay Click event procedure
1. assign to a variable the procedure selected in lstProcedures
2. assign the doctor's fee to a variable, as follows:
   selected procedure:
   Teeth Cleaning   assign 50
   Rabies Vaccination, Heartworm Test, Office Visit   assign 15
   Other Shots, Fecal Check   assign 5
3. display the doctor's fee in the lblFee control

FIGURE 13.14

Activity

1. Start Visual Studio .NET.

First, create a new, blank solution.

2. Click **File** on the menu bar, point to **New**, and then click **Blank Solution**. The New Project dialog box opens with Visual Studio Solutions selected in the Project Types box, and Blank Solution selected in the Templates box.

3. Type **Western Vets Solution** in the Name box.

4. In the Location box, type the path to the folder that stores your Web applications. (For example, type C:\Inetpub\wwwroot\Chap13Lab.)

5. Click the **OK** button to close the New Project dialog box.

Now add a Web project to the solution.

6. Click **File** on the menu bar, point to **Add Project**, and then click **New Project**. The Add New Project dialog box opens.

7. Verify that Visual Basic Projects is selected in the Project Types box, then click **ASP.NET Web Application** in the Templates box.

8. In the Location box, type the URL of the Web server and folder where you want to create your project, followed by the project name. (For example, type http://localhost/Chap13Lab/ Western Vets Solution/Western Vets Project.)

9. Click the **OK** button to close the Add New Project dialog box. The Create New Web message box appears momentarily, and then a new Web application appears on the screen.

Next, assign a more meaningful name to the Web form file.

10. Right-click **WebForm1.aspx** in the Solution Explorer window, and then click **Rename**. Type **Western Vets Web Form.aspx** and press **Enter**.

Now assign a more meaningful value to the title property of the DOCUMENT object, which is the Web form itself.

11. Click the **Western Vets Web Form.aspx*** tab in the Web Form Designer window, then click **title** in the Properties list. Type **Western Veterinarians** and press **Enter**.

In the next set of steps, you add the appropriate controls to the interface, and then set the values of some of their properties.

To add the appropriate controls, then set the values of some of their properties:

1. Use the Label tool to add three label controls to the Web form.

2. Use the ListBox tool to add a list box to the Web form.

3. Use the Button tool to add a button to the Web form.

4. Use the chart shown in Figure 13.13 to set the properties of each control.

5. Position the controls as shown in Figure 13.12.

6. Save the solution.

Now that the interface is complete, you can code the application.

To begin coding the application:

1. Right-click the **Web form**, and then click **View Code** to open the Code Editor window.

2. Type the comments shown in Figure 13.15, replacing <enter your name and date here> with your name and the current date. Also type the Option statements shown in the figure, and change the name of the class from WebForm1 to **WesternVets**.

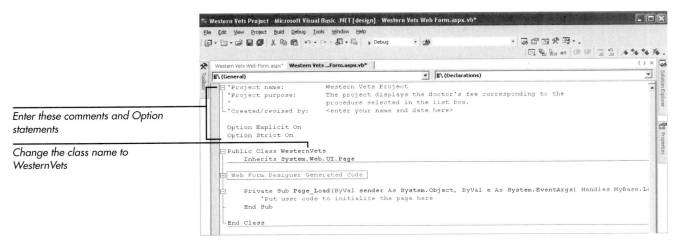

Enter these comments and Option statements

Change the class name to WesternVets

FIGURE 13.15   Code Editor window showing comments, Option statements, and new class name

According to the pseudocode shown earlier in Figure 13.14, only the Page Load event procedure and the btnDisplay Click event procedure need to be coded. First, code the Page Load event procedure, which is responsible for filling the list box with data and also selecting the first item in the list.

To code the Page Load event procedure:

1. Locate the Page_Load procedure in the Code Editor window.

2. Insert a blank line below the 'Put user code to initialize the page here comment.

3. Type **'fills the list box with data, and selects the first item** and press **Enter** twice.

The Page Load event occurs the first time the Web form appears. It also occurs each time the user clicks the Display Fee button. This is because those actions cause a postback to occur. Recall that a postback refers to the client requesting data from the server, and the server responding. Each time a postback occurs, the instructions contained in the Page_Load procedure are processed. In this case, you want the Page_Load procedure to load the list box and select the first item only when the Web form appears the first time, and to ignore the instructions when it is a postback. Recall that you can use the Web form's IsPostBack property to determine whether the Web form is appearing for the first time or as a result of a postback. The property contains the Boolean value False the first time the form appears; otherwise, it contains the Boolean value True.

4. Type **if not me.ispostback then** and press **Enter**.

Now add the procedure names to the lstProcedures control.

5. Type **me.lstprocedures.items.add("Teeth Cleaning")** and press **Enter**.

6. Enter the instructions to add the Rabies Vaccination, Other Shots, Heartworm Test, Fecal Check, and Office Visit procedures to the lstProcedures control, and then press **Enter** twice.

Now select the first item in the lstProcedures control.

7. Type **'select the first item in the list** and press **Enter**.

8. Type the instruction to select the first item in the lstProcedures control.

9. Save the solution.

Next, you will code the btnDisplay control's Click event procedure.

To code the btnDisplay control's Click event procedure:

1. Click the **Class Name** list arrow, and then click **btnDisplay** in the list.

2. Click the **Method Name** list arrow, and then click **Click** in the list. The code template for the btnDisplay_Click procedure appears in the Code Editor window.

3. Type '**displays the doctor's fee** and press **Enter** twice.

First, declare two variables for the procedure to use.

4. Type '**declare variables** and press **Enter**.

5. Type **dim strProcedure as string** and press **Enter**. This variable will store the value selected in the lstProcedures control.

6. Type **dim intFee as integer** and press **Enter** twice. This variable will store the doctor's fee.

According to Figure 13.14, the first step in the pseudocode for this procedure is to assign to a variable the procedure selected in the lstProcedures control. The selected procedure is stored in the lstProcedures control's SelectedValue property.

7. Type '**assign input to variable** and press **Enter**.

8. Type the instruction to assign the SelectedValue property to the strProcedure variable, and then press **Enter** twice.

The second step is to assign the doctor's fee to a variable. The doctor's fee is based on the procedure whose name is contained in the strProcedure variable.

9. Type '**assign fee to variable** and press **Enter**.

10. Type the code to assign the appropriate fee to the intFee variable. Use the Select Case statement. After typing the code, press **Enter** twice.

The last step in the pseudocode is to display the doctor's fee in the lblFee control.

11. Type '**display fee** and press **Enter**.

12. Type the statement to display the doctor's fee in the lblFee control. Display the fee with a dollar sign and zero decimal places.

Now that you have finished coding the application, you can test the application to verify that the code is working correctly.

To test the application:

1. Save the solution.

2. Click **Debug** on the menu bar, and then click **Start** to display the Web form in your default browser (typically Microsoft Internet Explorer). The Page_Load procedure fills the list box with the procedure names and selects the first name (Teeth Cleaning) in the list.

3. Click **Other Shots** in the list box, and then click the **Display Fee** button. The btnDisplay_Click procedure displays the appropriate fee, as shown in Figure 13.16.

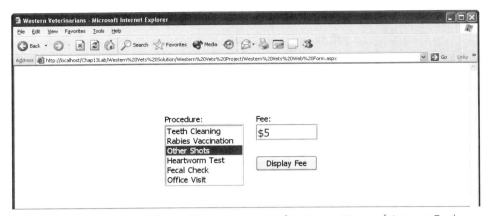

FIGURE 13.16   Western Veterinarians application in Microsoft Internet Explorer

4. Close the Western Veterinarians application by clicking its **Close** button.

5. Close the Output window.

6. Click **File** on the menu bar, and then click **View in Browser** to display the Web form in the Visual Studio .NET internal Web browser.

7. Click the **Display Fee** button. Your screen appears similar to Figure 13.17.

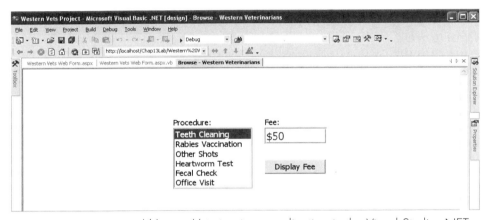

FIGURE 13.17   Western Veterinarians application in the Visual Studio .NET internal Web browser

8 Close the Browse – Western Veterinarians window by clicking its **Close** button.

9. Close the Code Editor window.

You are finished with the solution, so you can close it.

10. Close the solution. Temporarily display the Solution Explorer window to verify that the solution is closed.

LAB 13.3 AREA CODES

Scenario In this lab, you create a Web application that allows the user to enter an area code and then display the name of the corresponding state. The area codes and state names are stored in a sequential access file named area.txt. Figure 13.18 shows the contents of the area.txt file, which is contained in the VbDotNetLab/Chap13 folder.

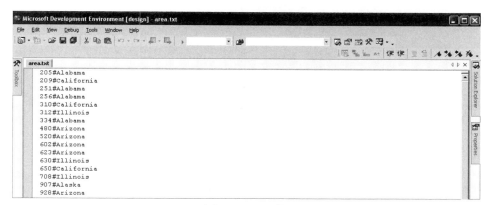

FIGURE 13.18 Contents of the area.txt file

Solution Discussion The Area Codes application will use a list box to display the area codes stored in the area.txt file, and use a label control to display the state name. The application will use a button control to allow the user to display the state name.

TOE Chart

Task	Object	Event
Get and display the area codes	lstCodes	None
Display the state name in lblState	btnDisplay	Click
Display the state name (from btnDisplay)	lblState	None
Fill lstCodes with data and select first item	Page	Load

FIGURE 13.19

User Interface

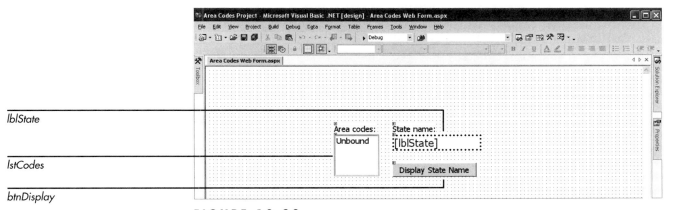

FIGURE 13.20

Objects, Properties, and Settings

Objects	Properties	Settings
Label1	Font/Name Font/Size Text	Tahoma Medium Area codes:
Label2	Font/Name Font/Size Text	Tahoma Medium State name:
Label3	ID BorderStyle Font/Name Font/Size Text Width	lblState Dotted Tahoma Large (empty) 195px
ListBox1	ID Font/Name Font/Size	lstCodes Tahoma Medium
Button1	ID Font/Name Font/Size Height Text Width	btnDisplay Tahoma Medium 32px Display State Name 184px

FIGURE 13.21

Pseudocode

Page Load event procedure
1. if it's the first time the Web form is displayed
        open the area.txt file for input
        repeat while it is not the end of the file
            read a record
            assign to a variable the area code from the record
            add the area code to the lstCodes control
        end repeat
        select the first item in the lstCodes control
    end if

btnDisplay Click event procedure
1. open the area.txt file for input
2. repeat for index 0 through the index of the item selected in the list box
        read a record
    end repeat
3. display the state name in the lblState control

FIGURE 13.22

Activity

1. Start Visual Studio .NET.
2. Create a blank solution named Area Codes Solution. Save the solution in the folder that stores your Web applications.

Now add a Web project to the solution.

3. Add an ASP.NET Web Application project to the solution. Be sure to type the URL of the Web server and folder where you want to create your project, followed by the project name. (For example, type http://localhost/Chap13Lab/Area Codes Solution/Area Codes Project.)
4. Change the name of the Web form file to **Area Codes Web Form.aspx**.
5. Change the DOCUMENT object's title property to **Area Code Locator**.
6. Use the Label tool to add three label controls to the Web form.
7. Use the ListBox tool to add a list box to the Web form.
8. Use the Button tool to add a button to the Web form.
9. Use the chart shown in Figure 13.21 to set the properties of each control.
10. Position the controls as shown in Figure 13.20.
11. Save the solution.

Now that the interface is complete, you can code the application.

To code the application:

1. Open the Code Editor window. Insert a blank line above the `Public Class WebForm1` statement.
2. Type the following comments, replacing *<enter your name and date here>* with your name and the current date. After typing the last comment, press **Enter** twice.

'Project name:	**Area Codes Project**
'Project purpose:	**The project displays the state name corresponding**
'	**to the area code selected in the list box.**
'Created/revised by:	*<enter your name and date here>*

3. Type **option explicit on** and press **Enter**, and then type **option strict on** and press **Enter** twice.
4. Change the class name from WebForm1 to **AreaCodes**.
5. Use the pseudocode shown in Figure 13.22 to code the Page_Load procedure. The area.txt file is located in the VbDotNetLab\Chap13 folder. Include meaningful comments in the procedure.
6. Display the code template for the btnDisplay control's Click event procedure.
7. Use the pseudocode shown in Figure 13.22 to code the btnDisplay_Click procedure. Include meaningful comments in the procedure.

Now that you have finished coding the application, you can test the application to verify that the code is working correctly.

To test the application:

1. Save the solution.
2. Click **File** on the menu bar, and then click **View in Browser** to display the Web form in the Visual Studio .NET internal Web browser. The Page_Load procedure fills the list box with the area codes and selects the first area code (205) in the list.

3. Click the **Display State Name** button. The btnDisplay_Click procedure displays the appropriate state name, as shown in Figure 13.23.

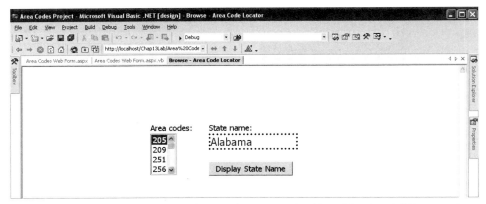

FIGURE 13.23   Area Codes application in the Visual Studio .NET internal Web browser

4. On your own, click each of the remaining area codes in the list box. Use Figure 13.18 to verify that the appropriate state name appears in the lblState control.

5. Close the Browse – Area Code Locator window by clicking its **Close** button.

6. Close the Code Editor window.

You are finished with the solution, so you can close it.

7. Close the solution. Temporarily display the Solution Explorer window to verify that the solution is closed.

Beyond the Text

LAB 13.4 PASSWORD

Scenario   In this lab, you create an application that determines whether two passwords entered by the user are the same. You also learn about the TextMode and Visible properties.

Solution Discussion   The Password application will provide two text boxes that allow the user to enter a password and also confirm the password. You will set the TextMode property of both text boxes to Password. When the TextMode property is set to Password, any character typed in the text box appears as a large dot; this prevents anyone from seeing the actual character. In addition, the application will use two RequiredFieldValidator controls to verify that the text boxes contain data.

The application will use a button control that displays a message indicating whether both passwords are the same; the message will appear in a label control. When the interface first appears on the screen, the label control will be invisible; this is accomplished by setting the control's Visible property to False in the Properties window. However, after the application has assigned the appropriate message to the label control, the control's Visible property will be set to True and the control will be visible on the screen.

TOE Chart

Task	Object	Event
Get and display the passwords	txtPassword, txtConfirmPassword	None
Verify that the two text boxes contain data	RequiredFieldValidator1, RequiredFieldValidator2	None
Display appropriate message in lblMessage	btnSubmit	Click
Display message (from btnSubmit)	lblMessage	None

FIGURE 13.24

User Interface

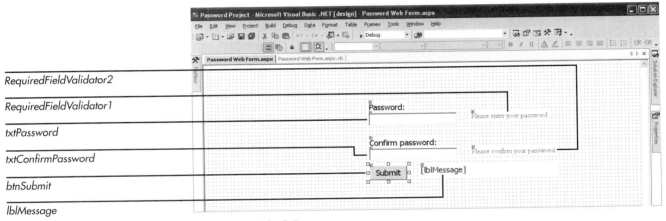

RequiredFieldValidator2

RequiredFieldValidator1

txtPassword

txtConfirmPassword

btnSubmit

lblMessage

FIGURE 13.25

Objects, Properties, and Settings

Objects	Properties	Settings
Label1	Font/Name Font/Size Text	Tahoma Medium Password:
Label2	Font/Name Font/Size Text	Tahoma Medium Confirm password:
Label3	ID Font/Name Font/Size ForeColor Height Text Visible Width	lblMessage Tahoma Medium Green (select the Green square on the Web tab) 32px (empty) False 296px
TextBox1	ID Font/Name Font/Size TextMode	txtPassword Tahoma Medium Password
TextBox2	ID Font/Name Font/Size TextMode	txtConfirmPassword Tahoma Medium Password
Button1	ID Font/Name Font/Size Text	btnSubmit Tahoma Medium Submit
RequiredFieldValidator1	ControlToValidate ErrorMessage	txtPassword Please enter your password.
RequiredFieldValidator2	ControlToValidate ErrorMessage	txtConfirmPassword Please confirm your password.

FIGURE 13.26

Pseudocode

btnSubmit Click event procedure
1. if, ignoring case, the contents of both text boxes are equal
      assign "The passwords are the same." message to lblMessage
   else
      assign "The passwords are not the same." message to lblMessage
   end if
2. assign True to the lblMessage control's Visible property

FIGURE 13.27

Activity

1. Start Visual Studio .NET.
2. Create a blank solution named Password Solution. Save the solution in the folder that stores your Web applications.

Now add a Web project to the solution.

3. Add an ASP.NET Web Application project to the solution. Be sure to type the URL of the Web server and folder where you want to create your project, followed by the project name. (For example, type http://localhost/Chap13Lab/Password Solution/Password Project.)
4. Change the name of the Web form file to **Password Web Form.aspx**.
5. Change the DOCUMENT object's title property to **Password**.
6. Use the Label tool to add three label controls to the Web form.
7. Use the TextBox tool to add two text boxes to the Web form.
8. Use the Button tool to add a button to the Web form.
9. Use the RequiredFieldValidator tool to add two RequiredFieldValidator controls to the Web form.
10. Use the chart shown in Figure 13.26 to set the properties of each control.
11. Position the controls as shown in Figure 13.25.
12. Save the solution.

Now that the interface is complete, you can code the application.

To code the application:

1. Open the Code Editor window. Insert a blank line above the `Public Class WebForm1` statement.
2. Type the following comments, replacing *<enter your name and date here>* with your name and the current date. After typing the last comment, press **Enter** twice.

'Project name:	**Password Project**
'Project purpose:	**The project displays a message indicating whether**
'	**the passwords entered by the user are the same.**
'Created/revised by:	*<enter your name and date here>*

3. Type **option explicit on** and press **Enter**, and then type **option strict on** and press **Enter** twice.
4. Change the class name from WebForm1 to **Password**.
5. Display the code template for the btnSubmit control's Click event procedure.
6. Use the pseudocode shown in Figure 13.27 to code the btnSubmit_Click procedure. Include meaningful comments in the procedure.

Now that you have finished coding the application, you can test the application to verify that the code is working correctly.

To test the application:

1. Save the solution.
2. Click **File** on the menu bar, and then click **View in Browser** to display the Web form in the Visual Studio .NET internal Web browser.

First observe what happens when you click the Submit button without entering any data.

3. Click the **Submit** button. The two RequiredFieldValidator controls display the messages shown in Figure 13.28.

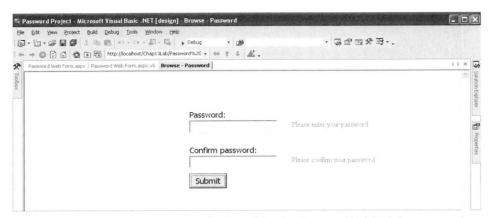

FIGURE 13.28   Messages displayed by the RequiredFieldValidator controls

Now enter two passwords that are not the same.

4. Type **abc45** in the Password box. Notice that each character in the box appears as a large dot.

5. Type **xyz66** in the Confirm password box. Notice that each character in the box appears as a large dot.

6. Click the **Submit** button. The btnSubmit_Click procedure assigns the appropriate message to the lblMessage control and also sets the control's Visible property to True, as shown in Figure 13.29.

FIGURE 13.29   Message that displays when the passwords are not the same

Now enter two passwords that are the same.

7. Type **hello** in the Password box, then type **hello** in the Confirm password box.

8. Click the **Submit** button. The message "The passwords are the same" appears in the lblMessage control.

9. Close the Browse – Password window by clicking its **Close** button.

10. Close the Code Editor window.

You are finished with the solution, so you can close it.

11. Close the solution, and then exit Visual Studio .NET.